Networks of sound, style and subversion

MANCHEStER
1824

Manchester University Press

Music and Society

Series editors Peter J. Martin and Tia DeNora

Music and Society aims to bridge the gap between music scholarship and the human sciences. A deliberately eclectic series, its authors are nevertheless united by the contention that music is a social product, social resource and social practice. As such it is not autonomous but is created and performed by real people in particular times and places; in doing so they reveal much about themselves and their societies.

In contrast to the established academic discourse, *Music and Society* is concerned with all forms of music, and seeks to encourage the scholarly analysis of both 'popular' styles and those which have for too long been marginalised by that discourse – folk and ethnic traditions, music by and for women, jazz, rock, rap, reggae, muzak and so on. These sounds are vital ingredients in the contemporary cultural mix, and their neglect by serious scholars itself tells us much about the social and cultural stratification of our society.

The time is right to take a fresh look at music and its effects, as today's music resonates with the consequences of cultural globalisation and the transformations wrought by new electronic media, and as past styles are reinvented in the light of present concerns. There is, too, a tremendous upsurge of interest in cultural analysis. *Music and Society* does not promote a particular school of thought, but aims to provide a forum for debate; in doing so, the titles in the series bring music back into the heart of socio-cultural analysis.

Nick Crossley

Networks of sound, style and subversion

The punk and post-punk worlds of Manchester,
London, Liverpool and Sheffield, 1975–80

Manchester University Press

The right of Nick Crossley to be identified as the author of this work has been asserted by him in accordance with the Copyright, Designs and Patents Act 1988.

Published by Manchester University Press
Altrincham Street, Manchester M1 7JA, UK
www.manchesteruniversitypress.co.uk

British Library Cataloguing-in-Publication Data
A catalogue record for this book is available from the British Library

Library of Congress Cataloging-in-Publication Data applied for

ISBN   978 0 7190 8864 3   hardback

ISBN   978 0 7190 8865 0   paperback

First published 2015

The publisher has no responsibility for the persistence or accuracy of URLs for any external or third-party internet websites referred to in this book, and does not guarantee that any content on such websites is, or will remain, accurate or appropriate.

Typeset in Sabon by
Servis Filmsetting Ltd, Stockport, Cheshire
Printed in Great Britain
by Bell & Bain Ltd, Glasgow

This book is dedicated to my wife, Michele, who not only has to put up with the music but also now with me writing about it, and to my son, Jake, whose first gig (aged 9) was a cover version of Frank Turner's Eulogy at an open mic session at the Levellers' Beautiful Days Festival, 2013

Contents

Figures and tables

Figures

Tables

Acknowledgements

The ideas expressed in this book have been brewing for some time and I have benefited from discussions with many people. Parts of chapters were presented at the universities of Manchester, Sheffield, Edinburgh, York, Oxford, Southampton, Huddersfield, Leicester and Warwick, and also at conferences organised both by the Mitchell Centre for Social Network Analysis (Manchester) and the Centre for Research on Social and Cultural Change (CRESC), co-hosted by Manchester University and the Open University. Thank you to all participants at these presentations. Your interest in both punk and networks was a major spur and your questions and criticisms invaluable.

I would also like to thank the many colleagues that I have discussed my ideas with. The main culprits, in alphabetical order, are: Elisa Bellotti, Wendy Bottero, Ashley Brown, Gemma Edwards, Rachel Emms, Martin Everett, Fay Hield, Joseph Ibrahim, Johan Koskinen, Siobhan McAndrew, Susan O'Shea, James Rhodes, Lindsay Richards, Rachel Stevenson, Mark Tranmer, Paul Widdop, Kath Woolf and Luke Yates.

Special thanks go to my wife, Michele, who read and reviewed the manuscript. The arguments are tighter due to her, and many of my more irritating linguistic habits have been corrected. Thanks also to my son, Jake. He has been my gig buddy for a few years now and his enthusiasm for music is great. As gig histories constitute important cultural capital I should say, for the record, that his first, as an audience member, was the Levellers at Manchester Academy in March 2011 (aged 6). You can't live their lives for them but it is important to give them a good start.

The love of music is a shared pursuit and my excitement and enthusiasm over the years have been helped along by many friends, too many to mention. I should probably mention Carl McKenzie, however. His intervention and attempt to put me right during one of my many John

Travolta impersonations at primary school is the true origin of this book, and his big brother's record collection provided an invaluable education. Having to swear lifelong allegiance to the Clash was a small price to pay for that privilege (and, as it happens, I stuck to my word). I would also like to thank Rob Lloyd. He died far too young but not before we gave the post-punk world of the early 1980s a good go.

1

Introduction

When I was 10 years old I was introduced to a 'music world' (on 'worlds' see below and Chapter 2) which had a huge impact upon me. The excitement I experienced in relation to punk gave me a lifelong passion for music. It established music as a key element in my identity and relationships, wedding me to practices of record-buying, gig-going and rudimentary music-making which I still participate in with passion today. Moreover, beyond music, punk aroused my interest in politics, the society I lived in and various fascinating political and aesthetic undercurrents of that society, perhaps even spurring me in the professional direction I eventually took as a sociologist. It changed the way in which I thought about myself and oriented to the world.

Year zero, in my case, was 1978, by which time most of punk's pioneers were declaring it dead and a new, more heterogeneous beast was beginning to take shape. 'Post-punk', interrupted by the occasional return to punk, would occupy me throughout my teenage years, generating much the same excitement as punk had and at a time when I was becoming old enough to more fully engage with what was going on. I spent a few years enjoying the final years of the first wave of punk before I switched to post-punk, however; long enough to make it my first musical love.

For the pioneers and early risers punk and post-punk demystified music. Their rallying cry was 'do-it-yourself' (DIY) and many did, enjoying the sense of empowerment that engendered. For me and my friends, however, perhaps because we were younger, perhaps because we were playing 'catch up' during our early years of involvement and perhaps also because we lived in a small town, a good distance from either of the two closest big cities where things were really happening (Liverpool and Manchester), punk and post-punk were clouded in mystery – and were all the more exciting for that. Grotty bars that we read about in the music press assumed the status of sacred spaces in our shared imaginings, and Johnny Rotten, Siouxsie, Kirk Brandon and the Ians, Curtis and McCulloch, to name only a fraction of the main cast, seemed every bit as exotic as the stars overthrown in the punk revolution. They were so far removed from anybody we ever met in our daily lives that they may as well have fallen to earth from another planet, like David Bowie. Where did these fabulous and exotic beings, their styles and ideas come from? Why not our town? How did it happen that the Sex Pistols, the Clash, the Damned, the Banshees and others all appeared around the same time, doing very similar things? How did the punks hear about punk? And why in London? Why were all the exciting clubs we heard about in Liverpool or Manchester? How did all of this come about?

The naivety of youth is apparent in some of this puzzlement but it does raise genuine sociological questions. *Why and how did punk and then post-punk emerge, when, where, in the way and involving the people they did?* These are some of the questions that drive this book. Specifically, I analyse:

1 The formation of the punk 'world' in London between January 1975 and December 1976.
2 The process whereby this world expanded to encompass Manchester in the latter half of 1976 and much of the rest of the UK at the close of the year.
3 The transformation of punk into various forms of post-punk in Manchester, Liverpool and Sheffield between 1977 and 1980 – again focusing primarily upon the structure and dynamics of emergent music worlds.

The book is not only an attempt to satisfy the curiosity of my adolescent self, however. Punk and post-punk were important episodes in British post-war cultural and especially musical history. They had a significant impact, not least upon national and regional identities. Punk in particular, as Hesmondhalgh (1998: 255) notes, enjoys a 'widely accepted status as a watershed in British music-making'.

That punk and the Sex Pistols were featured in the opening ceremony of Britain's 2012 Olympic Games illustrates some of this significance, as do the numerous television retrospectives devoted to punk and its aftermath. Punk has become a symbol of Britain. Likewise, living and working in Manchester I am struck by the role which its musical history, particularly the post-punk music of Joy Division, the Smiths and the Fall, play within its identity. Overseas students and colleagues know the city in a way they do not know other British cities (apart from

Liverpool) and want to know more because of this heritage. The identity of the city is its history, as known both from within and without, and punk and post-punk are central to that history.

Punk and post-punk occupy this place, both nationally and locally, because they made a difference to popular music and popular culture more widely. Punk was genuinely provocative; exciting many, terrifying others. It incited young people to rebel and authority figures to condemn it and defend their position. It could not be ignored by the powers that be in the way that popular music currents so often are. Whatever the motivations of individual pioneers, which were varied, punk generated debate about moral, political and aesthetic ideas, challenging the apparent preference of many powerful players in the music industry to limit their role to entertainment (though punk was certainly entertaining too), and doing so in a direct and democratic manner which challenged the pretentions and elitism of the rock aristocracy. Punk made music matter and that is why it is important and valued. Moreover, it inspired many of those who followed in its wake, many post-punks, to treat music similarly, according it an importance and a role which many would like to deny it.

Punk was a catalyst, battering a hole in the walls of the popular music world, creating opportunities and encouraging widespread participation. It persuaded people who would never have believed they could form a band to do so, and others to promote gigs, write fanzines and form independent record labels. It gave rise to an alternative music world on the margins, unconstrained or at least less constrained by the commercial imperatives of the mainstream. And in the context of post-punk in particular, this facilitated a flourishing of new, sometimes experimental and often exciting ways of making, performing and appreciating music: new forms of what Christopher Small (1998) calls 'musicking'. Punk and post-punk may not have changed the world but they did cultivate a desire to do so, and they changed the music world, at least for a while, establishing a high-profile and provocative protest camp at its perimeter. Moreover, they changed their participants – some of whom now run the institutions they once rebelled against – in enduring ways, giving rise to a musical and political 'generation' whose decisions in some ways still betray their punk origins.

Even if punk and post-punk were not significant topics in their own right, however, the dynamics of their emergence and diffusion would be. If we abstract from their concrete content, the punk and post-punk worlds and their emergence manifest processes and mechanisms of collective action and mobilisation which are common across a range of social worlds and movements, from political insurgencies and social movements through criminal underworlds to the conspiratorial circles of what Mills (1956) used to call 'the power elite'. Each of these types of collective activity has its own unique elements and dynamics of course, and individual cases will vary too. The story of the emergence and rise of punk is not identical to that of Motown or rock 'n' roll, let alone of feminism or an international drug-trafficking ring. However, in so far as each entails the formation of networks, whose members act collectively and generate, by way of their interaction, a distinctive culture, it is reasonable to assume that there will be some overlap in the mechanisms and processes involved. And these mechanisms and processes are sociologically significant.

In seeking to explain punk and post-punk, therefore, I am exploring processes and mechanisms which might help to explain much else in social life, contributing to the general project of sociology. Punk and post-punk are important case studies of collective action, as well as fascinating and important phenomena in their own right. But what do we mean by 'punk' and 'post-punk'?

Defining punk and post-punk: from styles to worlds

Punk and post-punk are sometimes defined as musical and visual 'styles' (e.g. Hebdige 1988), a concept which implies stylistic 'conventions'; that is, shared ways of doing things which distinguish certain artists, works and performances from others, giving them an identity (Meyer 1989, 2000). In traditional Western musicology such conventions are conceived in terms of harmonic, melodic and rhythmic structures, alongside the more elusive quality of timbre. Ethnomusicologists, who study non-Western and folk musical forms, however, have argued that these variables reflect the preoccupations of Western art-music and have called for a much broader approach to the mapping of styles, incorporating such things as the time and place of performance, the ways in which musical competence is acquired and the typical relations between audience and performers, where they are distinguished (Lomax 1959). Even this more encompassing approach is insufficient for purposes of defining punk and post-punk, as I explain below. However, it is useful and it would be instructive to spell out some of the key stylistic conventions of punk, both sonic and visual, at this point.

Punk music was raw and basic, a characteristic amplified by a DIY ethos which encouraged everyone to have a go, irrespective of their (lack of) musical experience and training. It was (electric) guitar-based and akin to rock but inflected with an aggressive and confrontational attitude uncommon in much rock, such that lyrics, whose content was often provocative, were spat out or shouted rather than sung, to musical accompaniment which had a harsh timbre and often a jagged, choppy rhythm. And this aggression was matched in audiences, whose dancing often involved them jumping up and down, shaking their heads and banging into one another (the pogo), and who often showed their appreciation for bands by spitting at them.

These characteristics were often pitted in opposition to the mellow approach of the hippies and this opposition was evident in relation to clothing also. Although the DIY ethic was evident here too, generating some diversity, hair was often cut short and made spiky, in direct opposition to the long hair of the hippies. Likewise trousers: in contrast to hippy flares they were either straight-legged or tight. There was also an emphasis upon using old clothing, bought from jumble sales, which were then modified with paint and household items, most notably the safety pin, which was used both to hold (sometimes deliberately) ripped clothing together and as an item of jewellery (e.g. an earring). Moreover, under the influence of Malcolm McLaren and Vivienne Westwood, the trappings of sexual fetishism (bondage, bumflaps, leathers, etc.) were often incorporated into the punk look, as were confrontational symbols such as the swastika, the inverted crucifix and the circled letter 'A' of anarchism.

In addition, particular artistic and graphical techniques, including provocative and subversive montages and the cut-out newspaper lettering popularly associated with ransom notes, became common, initially on shop-bought T-shirts and record sleeves but then spreading to home-made designs too. The record sleeves and promotional posters which Jamie Reid designed for the Sex Pistols are key examples. His promotional poster for the Pistols' 'God Save the Queen' single had a picture of the monarch with a safety pin through her lip, while his cover for 'Pretty Vacant' involved two buses whose destinations were identified as 'Nowhere' and 'Boredom' respectively.

This description of stylistic conventions is useful for giving us a feel of what punk was like. However, it is indicative rather than definitive. Not every punk subscribed to every convention and some of the conventions are not specific to punk. Moreover, conventions evolve over time, even within a style, and may vary between clusters of works. They are certainly important to the identity of a style but more in the manner of what Wittgenstein (1953) calls 'family resemblance', each work within the style having something in common with certain of the others but without any one stylistic convention being both sufficiently widely shared and sufficiently exclusive to serve a demarcation function.

If it is difficult to pin punk down to a style, however, it is even more so for post-punk. There were many distinctive styles within the post-punk camp, from the synthesiser-based 'futurism' of Cabaret Voltaire, John Foxx, Orchestral Manoeuvres in the Dark and the Human League, through the retro-inflected, guitar-based psychobilly of the Cramps, the Meteors and the Inca Babies, to the reappropriation of traditional instruments and song structures in the largely acoustic folk-punk of the Pogues, the Men They Couldn't Hang and the Violent Femmes. From the neo-psychedelic sound of the Fall, Echo and the Bunnymen, Wah! and the Teardrop Explodes, through goth and ska to the neo-funk of the Pop Group and Gang of Four. From the dark, angst-ridden mini-malism of Joy Division, Theatre of Hate and their many copyists to the self-consciously superficial glamour of the new romantics. In many respects these styles couldn't be more different and yet they are all, by common agreement, strands of 'post-punk' (Reynolds 2005), and 'post-punk' designates something meaningful; a coherent musical phenom-enon and not simply a catch-all category for everything that happened after punk (*ibid.*).

Genre classification as a social process

Punk and post-punk are difficult to pin down to definitive stylistic con-ventions because they are not academic categories, rooted in the analytic concerns and based on the variables of the musicologist or sociologist and imposed from outside. Like many genre labels they were devised in the heat of the action, by participants, on the basis of practical interests. And we must work with them as such.

A useful source for these purposes is Paul DiMaggio (1987). He suggests that genres and schools are typically defined (acquiring sym-bolic existence) through one or more of four basic processes (see also DiMaggio 2011):

1 *Administrative classification.* This is classification by agencies of the state, national or local. States may wish to classify art for the purposes of funding or censorship and their criteria will reflect these interests.
2 *Commercial classification.* In the case of popular music this is clas-sification by record labels, shops and journalists. It is motivated by their desire to sell records or magazines and, in the case of journal-ists, establish reputations. A music journalist who 'discovers' a new genre will make their name and this creates an incentive for them to seek out clusters of artists who they can present and label as such. Likewise record labels and companies may revive flagging markets by relabelling tired genres or 'discovering' new ones.

3 *Professional classification.* Artists too may seek to give a name to what they are doing, sometimes for similar commercial reasons to those above, sometimes in an effort to capture what they believe is distinctive about their work and other times either to associate or dissociate themselves with/from other artists.

4 *Ritual classification.* This involves audiences. They may explicitly label new musical forms but also, less explicitly, classify artists and works through the structure of their preferences. Artists are grouped together because they share an audience:

> Just as populations of persons can be partitioned into groups on the basis of the works of art they like, so populations of art works can be partitioned into groups, or genres, on the basis of the persons who choose them. (DiMaggio 1987: 445)

What united the Sex Pistols and the Clash in a single genre, for example, was the fact that the same people liked them, buying their records and attending their gigs. Of course artists often share an audience because they have certain aesthetic and stylistic qualities in common but audience preferences are not based on consistent application of classificatory principles and may select or reject different artists on different bases, mobilising ad hoc considerations to allow exceptions. Furthermore, DiMaggio envisages this occurring, in some cases, within a process of collective identity formation among an emerging social group, with those involved seizing upon certain objects (including but not exclusively artists and works) as totems of their group. The unifying element in ritual classification is the group which attaches itself to the classified objects. Although DiMaggio associates this process with audiences, artists and journalists may be involved too (the roles are not mutually exclusive), blurring the boundaries between the forms of classification which he distinguishes.

We can find elements of each of these processes of classification in relation to punk and elements of at least two in relation to post-punk. I expand upon this in a moment. First, however, I want to add a further consideration.

In a paper which complements DiMaggio's, Samuel Gilmore (1988) warns against genre classifications which lack 'sociological reality'. Some genre categories, he suggests, are convenient labels which allow critics, journalists and academics to organise their surveys, reflections and reviews (in DiMaggio's terms they are 'professional classifications') but which draw together artists who, whatever their superficial stylistic similarities, have no concrete connection; no social tie or interdependence. For sociological purposes, he argues, individual artists must enjoy some sort of demonstrable connection in order to be deemed members of a common genre or school. There must be evidence of influence between them, however diffuse. This is what merits our treating them as a collective entity and it helps to explain observed stylistic similarities (i.e. by reference to mutual influence between them), lending those similarities the status of genuine conventions rather than mere contingent similarities.

Gilmore's position is developed out of a more general conception of 'art worlds' first posited by Howard Becker (1974, 1982). Becker's concept of art worlds seeks to capture interactions within and between the sets of artists, audiences and 'support personnel' (e.g. managers, promoters, producers, engineers, journalists) who collectively make particular forms of art happen and shape those forms. Art of any kind is 'collective action', for Becker, and the sociological study of art is the study of this collective action.

Becker's concept of art worlds is pivotal to this book. It is a central argument of the book that punk and post-punk, whatever their respective internal stylistic heterogeneity, enjoyed 'sociological reality' in Gilmore's and Becker's sense. And it is a central aim of the book to explore and analyse that sociological reality. However, Gilmore is wrong to dismiss all classifications which do not map onto underlying networks. The very act of classification, as DiMaggio observes, is a sociological fact which merits investigation. When a genre is named it acquires a social–symbolic reality which both artists and audiences may orient to, in various ways, however arbitrary or opportunistic the act of definition may have been. Furthermore, even where we can identify an underlying network behind a classification, as in the cases of punk and post-punk, it is important to explore the process of classification. Music worlds involve both networks and classifications or categories. They are, to borrow a term from Harrison White (2008), 'catnets', and we must explore both the 'cat' and the 'net'.

Naming punk and post-punk

With this said it would be useful to return briefly to DiMaggio's four forms of classification to consider whether and to what extent each may have impacted upon punk and post-punk respectively. I begin with administrative classification.

Post-punk was never administratively classified as far as I am aware. However, early controversies, discussed in Chapter 6, led to 'punks' and the Sex Pistols in particular being banned from live performance by many local authorities and venue owners. This is an example of administrative classification and it had impact; decimating the Sex Pistols first national tour and limiting the pool of venues which would accept them and other punk bands for gigs throughout the late 1970s. The authorities who stamped down on punk did not invent the label, however. It was already in circulation in the music and wider media. They merely appropriated it.

The administrative classification of punk did contribute to the formulation of a further category, however. Responding to the combination of excitement and horror inspired by punk, certain record labels and artists who wanted to cash in on its popularity but avoid the constraints and sanctions which its reputation attracted coined a further genre label, 'new wave', to designate acts who were said to be exciting and rebellious, like punk, but not troublemakers. In so far as this was a record company initiative it is an example of commercial classification. In so far as bands themselves were actively involved it is an example of professional classification; artists devising genre labels as a means of positioning themselves in a bid for audiences.

If we count journalists as belonging to the commercial sector, then 'punk' and 'post-punk' themselves might be deemed examples of commercial classification. Though not the first journalist to use the term 'punk' in relation to the bands who would later be known as such, Caroline Coon (1982) is often credited with christening 'punk' in a *Melody Maker* article of August 1976, triggering more widespread use of the term by insiders and outsiders alike, including Sex Pistols' manager, Malcolm McLaren, who organised a 'punk festival' in September of that same year. And the term 'post-punk' is often credited to music journalist, Paul Morley (2008), who coined and popularised it in various articles in the music press in the late 1970s and early 1980s.

Coon, Morley and other journalists were very influential and played a role in shaping what they were describing. However, what they named, in each case, existed and had coherence before their intervention. The grass-roots networks which DiMaggio identifies with ritual classification, and Becker and Gilmore with 'worlds', were already taking shape, giving those involved a sense that something was taking shape. Coon and Morley 'merely' named that something. Furthermore, they were enthusiastic participants in these networks as well as journalists looking for a story. Indeed Morley became a journalist through his participation in punk, initially by starting a fanzine.[1] In other words, the official naming of punk and post-punk in the music press was based upon prior, ritual classification within a network of insiders who knew that they were doing something new and exciting, even if they hadn't settled upon a name for it.

It is these grass-roots networks and activities that constitute my primary interest in this book. The book is about punk and post-punk as social worlds or 'music worlds'. I am interested in networks of bands, audiences, venues, managers, promoters and others. It was their interactions, both competitive and cooperative, imitative and self-distinguishing, I submit, which generated what we think of as punk and post-punk music, and those interactions are my focus.

Narrowing the field

This is a potentially very big topic which needs to be narrowed down if it is to be made researchable. In order to stay focused upon concrete relations and interactions I have elected to focus upon four local worlds. In relation to punk I look at its UK origin in London, between 1975 and 1976, and its subsequent spread to and development within Manchester in the latter half of 1976. A large number of punk bands were involved in the local punk worlds of these two cities within the specified period and I attempt to capture as many of them as possible in my account. For purposes of orienting the reader currently, however, the main innovators were: the Sex Pistols, the Clash, the Damned, Buzzcocks, Subway Sect, Siouxsie and the Banshees, the Slits, Chelsea, Generation X, the Stranglers and Slaughter and the Dogs.

The question of the emergence of UK punk, as I approach it in this book, is about the origin of these two punk worlds. How did it happen that a punk world took shape in London between 1975 and 1976, involving the people that it did, and how and why did that world spread, taking root and flourishing in Manchester? I also give some attention to the further diffusion of punk across the UK, however, not least to Liverpool and Sheffield which, along with Manchester, constitute the geographical focus of my analysis of post-punk.

As with the London punk world I have sought to identify the pioneers in these worlds, beginning with a focus upon key bands. I will not name all of the bands here as each list is potentially quite long. For purposes of orientation, however, the best known of the Manchester bands, excluding the punks (e.g. Buzzcocks and Slaughter and the Dogs) were Magazine, Joy Division, the Fall, Durruti Column and A Certain Ratio. In Liverpool, the main punk bands were the Spitfire Boys and the Accelerators. The main post-punk bands were Big in Japan, Echo and the Bunnymen, Teardrop Explodes, Wah!, Orchestral Manoeuvres in the Dark, Dead or Alive and Lori and the Chameleons. In Sheffield, the best known names were the Human League, Cabaret Voltaire, Clock DVA, Artery, Vice Versa, I'm So Hollow, Graph and They Must Be Russians.

I have already alluded to the way in which post-punk emerged out of punk, partly inspired by it, partly reacting against it or what it was becoming, and drawing upon its networks and resources to do something different. My analysis of post-punk in the book elaborates upon this claim and explores how the various networks that facilitated this transformation took shape. In addition, in the final chapter of the book, before the conclusion, I explore the larger national network that linked these city-based worlds together, with others, in a national post-punk world.

Time and space

Focusing upon just four UK cities constrains my ability to fully convey and explore the geographical spread of punk and post-punk. What happened in London, as I explain in Chapter 3, was influenced by what was happening in New York, among other places, and its own impact was felt well beyond Liverpool, Manchester and Sheffield, both within and beyond the UK. Furthermore, post-punk assumed a wider range of forms than my four city focus captures. I have nothing to say in this book about the emergence of the two-tone ska revival in Coventry, for example, or the funk and jazz inflected forms of post-punk which emerged around Bristol. I need to focus upon specific cities, however, because the different camps and strands that can be identified in post-punk were very often city-based (Reynolds 2005), as my references to Coventry and Bristol suggest. Music, as a thread within the fabric of social life, is a product of human interaction; collective action. As such it always happens somewhere, in a particular time–space nexus which becomes part of its structure and which the sociologist must endeavour to capture (Abbott 1997, 2001; Giddens 1979, 1984; Hägerstrand 1975). Technological developments, from the train to the internet, have expanded the size of such nexus and I give consideration to this fact when I explore both the diffusion of punk (Chapter 7) and the inter-connection of geographically dispersed sites of post-punk interactivity (Chapter 10). This is always diffusion from somewhere (e.g. London) to somewhere (e.g. Manchester), however, and, to reiterate, much punk and post-punk interactivity was concentrated within particular geographical sites, mostly cities, whose interconnection contributed to the national and international structure of this always-evolving 'musical world'. A proper sociological analysis and explanation of punk and post-punk requires a detailed and concrete focus upon the networks of interactivity which gave rise to it; networks which were inevitably localised in time and space. And my resources are such that I can only focus on a handful of these temporally–spatially embedded networks.

My choice of cities reflects my own biographical time–space trajectory[2] to some extent but more importantly, London, Manchester, Liverpool and Sheffield are identified in many accounts as key sites of early and successful punk and post-punk developments. This makes them important to the story of punk and post-punk and made it easier for me to find sufficient amounts of data to conduct a thorough analysis.

I focus on the period 1975–80 because this allows me to follow UK punk from its inception, through its first wave and into the first, most obviously punk-influenced wave of post-punk. Post-punk extended beyond 1980 and is arguably still with us, as is punk. 1980 was a year of turning points in the cities I am investigating, however. To give a few examples: 1980 was the year in which Joy Division singer, Ian Curtis, died, leading Joy Division to became New Order and certain of Manchester's movers and shakers to take the first tentative steps away from post-punk, towards what would become the 'Madchester' dance world. 1980 was also the year that Manchester's seminal post-punk venue, the Factory, closed its doors. Likewise in Sheffield: 1980 was the year in which the original, more experimental line up of the Human League split, with both halves moving in a more self-consciously poppy direction (one half as the Human League, the other as Heaven 17). And it was the year when Vice Versa, until then a synth-based post-punk outfit, donned glitzy outfits, changed their name to ABC and set sail for mainstream pop success. Cabaret Voltaire held the fort a little longer but lost Chris Watson in 1981 and made a similar, if less commercially successful shift two years after that. Furthermore, local music journalist, Martin Lilleker, who has documented the many Sheffield bands of the punk and post-punk era, identifies the glory days as 1978–80, citing others who do likewise:

> Sheffield's music scene had peaked ... from the start of the Now Society at Sheffield University in 1978, through to the Blitz club at the George IV pub on Infirmary Road in early 1980 'after which it rapidly lost its sense of excitement and adventure and disintegrated', wrote Sheffield fanzine NMX in 1982. (2005: 7)

In many respects Liverpool was reaching the zenith of its post-punk influence in 1980, with Echo and the Bunnymen, the Teardrop Explodes and Wah! each assuming cult status, and Orchestral Manoeuvres in the Dark still producing the moody and more experimental music that saw them compared to the likes of Joy Division and Cabaret Voltaire. However, 1980 was the year when Eric's, the focal point of the city's punk and post-punk world, closed. And it was the year when both Frankie Goes to Hollywood and Dead or Alive were formed. Both were still much closer to post-punk than to the 'new pop' (Reynolds 1990) for which they would become famous at this point. Dead or Alive, in particular, were cultivating a gothic sound and style more redolent of Bauhaus and the Banshees than their later dance floor fillers. They were the start of something new, something post- post-punk, however, and with Eric's gone the ground was shifting.

I am not suggesting that there was a sudden volte-face in 1980 or denying that many significant post-punk innovations came later. My own post-punk favourites, Spear of Destiny, didn't form until 1983, and their equally exciting predecessors, Theatre of Hate, only formed in 1980. However, I have to stop somewhere and the seeds of change which first become visible in 1980 mark it out as a suitable point.

My approach: relational sociology and networks

Punk and, to a lesser extent, post-punk have been analysed before. There are a number of good academic accounts and some of the journalism in the area is excellent. I have drawn and learned from these accounts. My approach is different to the others that I have come across, however, even the other sociological accounts (some of which I review in Chapters 2–3). I look at punk from a different angle, asking different questions with respect to it.

My angle is 'relational sociology' (see Crossley 2011, 2013, 2014; Depelteau and Powell 2013a, 2013b; Emirbayer 1997; Mische 2003, 2011; Tilly 2006). Put briefly, this approach claims that social interactions, relations and networks are the most basic elements in social life; the generative force and building blocks from which all else emerges. And it recommends that we focus upon these elements in social analysis, not to the exclusion of other elements, such as 'resources', 'norms', 'conventions', 'power', etc., but always recognising the way in which these other elements either emerge or at least assume the qualities we commonly associate with them in the context of interactions, relations and networks.

Human agency or at least inter-agency, and also the agency of such corporate entities as governments, trade unions and economic firms, assume a key role in this form of sociology. Social interaction is, after all, driven by the desires and intelligence of those party to it. However, relational sociology maintains that actors are constrained by their relations with others and their position in wider social networks. Networks form a social structure which generates opportunities and constraints for its members, a structure which those members may manoeuvre and jostle for position within but which they cannot extricate themselves from. Human life is collective life; action is interaction; and social actors are always-already enmeshed in relations with others.

Furthermore, human organisms only become social actors, as commonly conceived, through formative social interaction, particularly but not exclusively in early life. Setting aside basic biological dependence, social interaction is the means through which human organisms acquire: language and the related capacity for reflective thought; a sense of self, other and identity, and a capacity for self-control (Mead 1967); the 'body techniques' necessary to everyday functioning (Mauss 1979); basic moral sense (Mead 1967); tastes (Becker 1996; Mark 1998) and much besides. This is not a matter of passive absorption. Even the newly born actively engages in and shapes the learning experience (Crossley 1996). But they learn and become who and what they are through interaction (Crossley 1996, 2011).

Analysing networks

Of the various relational concepts referred to above, 'social network' has particular importance in this book. In my earlier discussion of the definition of punk and post-punk I claimed that I would analyse them as 'music worlds', and I claimed that music worlds are, among other things, social networks. Furthermore, in the course of the book I will be arguing that the existence of a network is an essential precondition for the emergence of a music world. The formation of a music world, I will argue, involves collective action by a critical mass of individuals with the necessary interests, commitments and resources to make it happen but this can only happen if members of this mass are connected to one another in a network. Moreover, I will suggest that collective action is much more likely where this network manifests certain key properties. Differently structured networks can generate different opportunities and constraints (both individual and collective) for those involved in them, making different courses of action (again both individual or collective) more or less likely.

'Social network' has a specific, technical meaning here, drawn from 'social network analysis' (SNA) (see Borgatti *et al.* 2012; Scott 2000; Wasserman and Faust 1994). Some key concepts of SNA and not least the network–analytic definition of 'network' need to be briefly elaborated if the arguments and analyses of subsequent chapters, which draw upon the method, are to be fully understood.

In its most basic form a network involves a set of nodes and a set of ties (some networks involve more than one set of ties and may also involve a set of node attributes, such as gender, ethnicity, income, etc.).

It can be visualised in the form of a 'graph', where nodes are represented by coloured shapes ('vertices') and ties between nodes by lines ('edges') connecting these shapes (see Figure 1.1).

In this study my nodes are key participants in each of the four music worlds under consideration. They are divided into four sets (and thus four networks) according to the world in which they participated. I have a node set for Liverpool, a node set for London, etc. My decision about who was a key player in each world was based upon the secondary and archival resources referred to below. I included in my node sets all participants who were identified across a number of sources as being active in a particular local world and who I could gather sufficient data about – in effect I was able to get sufficient information about all of those participants who appeared to be 'key'.

Ties between nodes were deemed to exist where I found evidence either of a longstanding friendship between them which pre-dated punk or of direct collaboration between them on a musical project. Often this would mean playing in a band together but it was not restricted to that and might include co-founders of record labels or other such activities. In the case of London, for which most information was available, I was able to survey ties across six different time points between January 1975 and December 1976, allowing me to chart the evolution of the network, and I was able to survey how new ties were formed, allowing me to explore the mechanisms involved in that process of evolution. No comparable information was available for the other three cities. In each case I have a single snapshot of the network, capturing ties which were active at any point between 1976 and 1980. In the case of Manchester, however, I was able to compare ties between a smaller subset of the nodes at two time points: June 1976, immediately prior to the Sex Pistols' first visit to Manchester, and April 1980, immediately prior to Ian Curtis's death.

This was useful because it allowed me both to confirm that the rise of a punk and post-punk world in Manchester, as in London, involved a process of network formation between that world's key participants, and because it allowed me to compare networks in London and Manchester at an early stage in punk's development and thereby to test (and in the event support) my claim, discussed in Chapter 4, that punk emerged in London before Manchester because a critical mass of appropriately oriented and resourced 'proto-punks' had begun to converge and form a network in the capital at a time when the equivalent individuals in Manchester were still largely unknown to one another.

Graphs such as that in Figure 1.1, which visualises the network of London's key punk protagonists as it was in June 1975, a very early stage

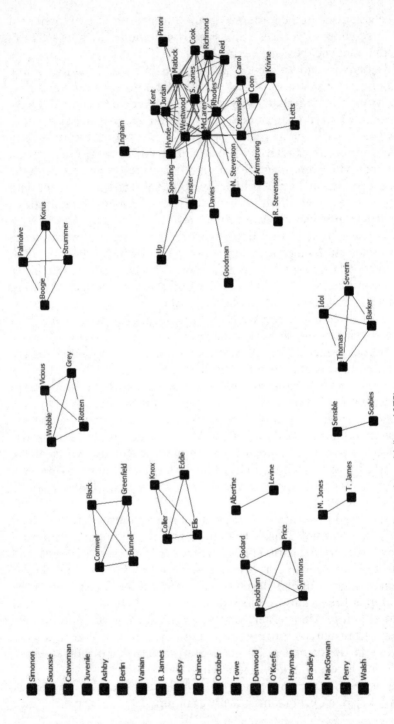

Figure 1.1 The network of the London punk world (June 1975)

in its evolution, prior to any significant punk developments, provide a useful first step for analysing networks. More significant, however, are the above-mentioned network properties which SNA allows us to measure. These properties may be defined at three basic levels: (1) the whole network; (2) subsets of nodes; (3) the individual 'node'.

Examples of whole network measures include:

- *Density*: a measure of the number of ties in the network, expressed as a proportion of the total number of ties that are possible. There are 112 ties in Figure 1.1, for example, out of a potential 2,775, giving a density of $224/2,775 = 0.004$.
- *Number of components*: a component is a subset of nodes each of which is at least indirectly connected to each of the others by a *path* (see below) of other nodes and ties. There are 29 components in Figure 1.1. They comprise: 19 nodes which have no connections at all (isolates), 3 components with two members, 6 components with four members and one big component (to the right of the plot, in the middle) with 26 members.
- *Paths and path lengths*: A path is a chain of connections which links two nodes. Path lengths are measured by the number of ties (referred to as 'degrees') they involve: e.g. (Ari) Up, who is sticking out at top left of the big component in Figure 1.1 is at a distance of one degree to her mum, Norah Forster. Up does not have a direct tie to Malcolm McLaren but her mum does so Up is linked to McLaren by a path of two degrees.
- *Average path length*: if we add up the path lengths separating every possible pair of actors in the network and divide by the number of pairs we get the average path length, which gives us a good idea of how far information and new ideas typically have to travel in the network before everyone has access to them. In the network in Figure 1.1 many path lengths are 'undefined' because there is no path between particular nodes: e.g. at this point in time there is no path between Mick Jones (linked to Tony James at the bottom left of the plot) and Joe Strummer (linked to Boogie, Kate Korus and Palmolive at the top right). Average path lengths only make sense where all nodes are connected by a path (i.e. where the network of interest forms a single component).

A network which forms a single component and has both a high density and a short average path length would be deemed more conducive to collective action for reasons discussed in Chapter 4.

Subsets of nodes are typically distinguished in one of two ways:

- *Endogenously*, by reference to distinctive patterns of connection: e.g. they all connect directly to one another or to another common set of alters, because they collectively form a component or because they are all isolates and have no connections.
- *Exogenously*, by reference to attributes such as gender or ethnicity.

Endogenously defined subgroups are often of interest because their existence may tell us about conflicts and power structures in a network, or because we might expect different subgroups to behave differently, either because their members are subject to different influences or because their position in the network enables/constrains them in different ways and to different degrees. Exogenously defined subgroups are often interesting because shared attributes or identities often increase the likelihood of connection (homophily) and we may want to test if this is so in a particular case. Furthermore, different exogenously defined groups may enjoy more or less advantaged positions in the network, which again we can test for.

The key examples of node-level properties are the various types of centrality. There are many ways of measuring a node's centrality within a network but the three main ones are:

1 *Degree*: the number of ties the node has. The mean degree (a whole network measure) for the network in Figure 1.1 is 2.99, with a standard deviation of 3.45, but some nodes score much higher. Sex Pistols' manager, Malcolm McLaren, has the highest degree, at 19. He is the most degree central node.

2 *Closeness*: the sum of the path lengths connecting the node to every other node in the network, normalised and inverted so that higher scores indicate shorter distances. Like average path length this measure only fully makes sense in relation to components, and as with degree (and betweenness) we are usually interested in rank orderings, particularly the highest and lowest scoring nodes.

3 *Betweenness*: a measure of how often the node falls along the shortest path connecting two other nodes, such that they might 'broker' between these parties. Again McLaren has a much higher score for this measure than anybody else in the network represented in Figure 1.1.

A high centrality in any of these forms can equate to a high level of constraint by the network and may drain a node's resources – having a lot of friends can be hard work, for example – but it may also bestow considerable advantage and opportunity. Central nodes are usually in a better position to mobilise the network to their advantage.

This brief description barely scratches at the surface of SNA. I hope, however, it does enough to illustrate what is meant by claiming that networks have properties and to hint both at how they might be measured and why they might make a difference, generating opportunities and constraints for both individual and collective action. Much of the analysis in the book is network analysis and I will elaborate upon these and other measures as I go. In all cases I have used the Ucinet software program for this analysis and its affiliated Netdraw program for network visualisation (Borgatti *et al.* 2002).

My analysis is not all about maths and measures, however. There has been a big push to integrate qualitative considerations more fully and systematically into SNA in recent years and I strongly endorse this (Crossley 2010a, 2010b; Edwards 2009; Edwards and Crossley 2009, Emirbayer and Goodwin 1994; Mische 2003, 2011). While much of the analysis in the book is formal SNA, therefore, I couple this with qualitative, historical–sociological analysis. My network data are drawn from rich textual sources (see below) and I use these sources both to flesh out the skeletal network representations generated in SNA and to further explore the content and dynamics of the relations/interactions involved, reaching beyond networks, narrowly defined, to music worlds.

Data

I have gathered data on the four worlds analysed in the book from both archived and secondary sources (listed in the Bibliography). A huge number of accounts of punk have emerged in recent years, often biographical or first hand. Using these data I have been able both to reconstruct the networks involved and to conduct the wider, historical–qualitative analysis just referred to.

Some social scientists might hesitate to call the published (auto)biographies and first-hand accounts that I have used 'data', preferring me to have conducted my own interviews. This would have been impossible because several of the key players are now dead and those remaining are widely geographically dispersed. More importantly, however, it was unnecessary because they have told their stories many times before, in interviews, (auto)biographies and memoirs, and there is no reason to suppose that they would tell those stories any differently to me.

In some cases the interviews upon which other studies are based are directly available and I have used them extensively. Jon Savage (2009) has published the fifty-eight interviews that he drew upon for his classic book on punk, *England's Dreaming* (Savage 1991), for example, and Simon Reynolds (2009) has published the thirty-two interviews that informed his celebrated reflection on post-punk, *Rip It Up* (Reynolds 2005). In addition, extensive oral history material on both punk and its trajectory in 'the north' has been published by John Robb (2006, 2009). Furthermore, I have consulted the archives of the music press, of local music worlds and private on-line collections. Alongside the first-hand histories and auto/biographical accounts referred to above, this makes for rich, extensive and high-quality data.

Of course writers selectively edit their memoirs, trying to persuade readers of their side of the story and 'bigging up' their role. But that is no less true of sociological interviews and can be dealt with where multiple accounts exist (as in this case), by cross-checking. Moreover, musicians writing and being interviewed for books know that what they say will be cross-checked against others' accounts and disputed if it is found to conflict with them, dissuading too much 'creative accounting'.

The structure of the book

In Chapter 2 I elaborate further upon the concept of 'music worlds' introduced in this chapter, contrasting it with alternatives from the sociological literature. In particular I contrast it with the concepts 'subculture', 'scene' and 'field'.

In Chapter 3 I review the most often cited explanations of punk in both the sociological and wider literature, identifying strengths, flaws and gaps in these explanations. Each has some value, in my view, but all talk in very abstract terms about the frustrations, inspirations and opportunities of mid 1970s Britain, failing to reflect either upon the specificities of the initially very small, geographically concentrated population of individuals who 'invented' punk or the process whereby it was invented. A proper explanation of punk, I argue, must engage with the details of its emergence.

In Chapter 4 I sketch out my own explanation, outlining a number of concepts which, I believe, allow us to explore the localised process in which punk took shape in a sociologically rigorous manner. In particular I discuss the concepts of 'critical mass' and 'social networks'.

In Chapter 5 I apply these concepts to the London punk world of 1976 and test my explanation. I then build upon this in Chapter 6, further analysing the network structure of the London punk world. Chapter 6 charts and explains the evolution of London's proto-punk network between January 1975 and December 1976, before punk 'went national'.

In Chapter 7 I explore this process of 'going national' and the mechanisms involved. In particular I consider how talk about punk migrated from face-to-face networks to mass media networks and the effects of that shift and I reflect upon the 'moral panic' sparked by an early Sex Pistols interview and the way in which it amplified audiences for punk (while closing down opportunities for performance and recording in the short term). Finally, I consider the specific and to some extent unique case of what was to become punk's 'second city': Manchester.

Continuing the discussion of punk's diffusion and growth, in Chapter 8 I consider how punk worlds took shape in Liverpool, Manchester and Sheffield. In addition, however, the chapter observes that many of punk's 'early risers' in these northern cities (as elsewhere) soon became frustrated at what punk was becoming and began experimenting with a variety of alternatives which would be collectively labelled 'post-punk'.

The analysis in Chapter 8 is primarily qualitative. Returning to the key concepts introduced in Chapter 4, however, Chapter 9 offers a more technical analysis of the network structures of the post-punk worlds of the three cities. Furthermore, extending this analysis, and combining qualitative and quantitative forms of analysis, in Chapter 10 I consider how activities in different local post-punk worlds were themselves linked in a network, constituting a national post-punk world.

The central arguments of the book are all revisited in Chapter 11, where I also begin to reflect upon future directions for further developing the approach and themes which the book has introduced.

Notes

1 Entitled 'Girl Trouble'.
2 I was born in Southport, a seaside town close to both Liverpool and Manchester, and my experience of punk and post-punk was affected by what was going on in these cities, especially Liverpool. The celebrated Liverpool club, Eric's, had closed before I became involved but I spent many a Saturday in the early 1980s dodging between the city's record and punk clothes shops (particularly Probe, Xtremes and Backtracks). I saw most of my early gigs either in Manchester or (more often) Liverpool. I studied for my BA and Ph.D. at Sheffield – having been drawn to the city, in some part, by its post-punk musical heritage – and worked as a lecturer there for five years, before moving to Manchester, where I have worked for fifteen years. My familiarity with each of these cities and their music worlds aided and eased my analysis of them in many ways.

2

Music worlds

In the previous chapter I suggested that punk and post-punk are best conceived, for sociological purposes, as 'music worlds', a concept I adapt from Howard Becker's notion of 'art worlds' (1951, 1963, 1974, 1976, 1982, 1995, 2004, 2006a, 2006b; Faulkner and Becker 2009; see also Bottero and Crossley 2011; Finnegan 1989; Lopes 2002; Martin 1995, 2005, 2006a, 2006b). In this chapter I elaborate upon this concept. Before I do, however, I briefly review three alternative conceptions, explaining why I have chosen 'music worlds' over them. As much sociological work on punk conceptualises it as a subculture I begin with and devote most attention to that alternative.

Subculture

Both 'subculture' and 'world' were formulated in the work of the Chicago School sociologists, where they were used interchangeably to denote:

1 A sub-community of actors located within a wider community context.
2 Characterised by a shared attribute and/or interest and a homophilous[1] interaction pattern.
3 Whose in-group interactions generated a distinct set of conventions and shared habits regarding such things as speech, dress, status and lifestyle, and a collective identity.

The tendency to treat 'subculture' and 'world' as interchangeable has persisted in some cases. Claude Fischer (1975,1982, 1995), whose work I return to in Chapter 4, for example, though he develops a theory of subculture, often draws upon Chicago School discussions of social worlds in doing so and sometimes uses the term 'world' in place of 'subculture'. However, from the late 1970s onwards, in British sociology, the concept of subculture acquired a more specific meaning, following its appropriation in the work of Birmingham's Centre for Contemporary Culture Studies (CCCS).

Subcultures, as the CCCS define them, are networks of working-class youths characterised by: (1) the music they listen to; (2) styles of dress, argot and ritual; (3) distinctive activities; (4) territories which they claim as their own (Clark *et al.* 1993). Examples include teddy boys, mods, skinheads, hippies and punks.

Subcultures form, according to the CCCS, in response to the twofold alienation and domination of working-class youth. They are cultures of resistance. I explore the explanatory aspect of this claim in Chapter 3. In this chapter I focus upon the way in which resistance is said to manifest.

The concept of 'style' is crucial. In rejecting conventional dress codes and the music of the mainstream, and replacing them with their own alternatives, Clarke *et al.* (1993) argue, subcultural participants refuse to signal the loyalty to normal society ordinarily communicated in these ways and expected by the wider community. Subcultural styles communicate a refusal to belong. Furthermore, in challenging dominant style codes they tear at the fabric of taken-for-granted assumptions which structure everyday life, potentially provoking a wider questioning and unsettling the 'natural' feel of the status quo.

This effect is enhanced, according to Hebdige (1988), by the fact that subcultural styles are obviously artificial themselves. Like the drag artist whose overstatement makes the artifice of gender visible, subcultural participants expose the conventional nature of everyday practices through the artificiality of their own. This was particularly true of punk style, in Hebdige's view, because it celebrated artificiality: e.g. unnatural hair colours, plastic and PVC clothing, and the use of everyday objects such as safety pins, tampons and toilet chains as jewellery.

Finally, in developing their own style, subcultural pioneers break free, to some extent, from their dependence upon the music and fashion industries – and, by extension, capitalism. They refuse to be dictated to, preferring to exercise their own agency and creativity. In punk this was particularly strong and the punks are often credited, if not with inventing the do-it-yourself (DIY) ethos still evident in some radical movements today, then at least with shifting it to the centre of the subcultural agenda (McKay 1996, 1998). Early punk pioneers encouraged others to make their own clothes (and clothing styles), form their own bands, make their own records, organise their own gigs and write their own fanzines.

Subcultural styles do not emerge out of thin air. Each successive subculture builds upon and responds to its predecessors according to the CCCS. This was especially true of punk, according to Hebdige, for whom: 'punk style contained a distorted reflection of all the major post-war subcultures' (1988: 26). Punk drew upon all that went before it, constituting itself as a culmination of post-war youth resistance:

> Punk represents the most recent phase … alienation assumed an almost tangible quality. It could almost be grasped. It gave itself up to the cameras in 'blankness', the removal of expression … the refusal to speak and be positioned. This trajectory – the solipsism, the neurosis, the cosmetic rage – had its origin in rock. (*Ibid.*: 28)

And it did so knowingly. Punk was the subculture wherein subculture became reflexively aware of itself. Punks played with the idea of themselves as a subculture in ways not previously observed.

All subcultures draw upon a variety of cultural sources in constructing their style. The CCCS label this 'bricolage'; a practice in which previously unrelated elements are juxtaposed in a new way, subverting 'their original straight meanings' (*ibid.*: 104). For example, punks modified existing clothing, bought from jumble sales or army surplus stores, by ripping and painting on it; and following the lead of Malcom McLaren and Vivienne Westwood, who in turn borrowed from designer, John Sutcliffe,[2] they appropriated ideas from gay, fetish and sadomasochist subcultures (e.g. rape masks, bondage, chains, bumflaps, nipple-less bras), redefining these as items of everyday wear. And, most famously, they turned the everyday safety pin into a symbol of rebellion, using it as jewellery, and pinning their ripped clothes together with it.

There is coherence in such eclecticism according to the CCCS, which they theorise in terms of 'homology'. Homology is a controversial concept which different theorists, both within and outside of the CCCS, use in different ways (Middleton 1990: 147–54, 159–66). For Paul Willis (1978, 1990, 2000), who offers the most persuasive account of it in my view, 'homology' indicates *perceived consistency* across the various practices of a group, rooted in *fidelity to a specific orientation towards the world*. The way that a subculture dresses, the music that it listens to and its various other activities, Willis argues, each reflect, at least in the eyes of its members, the same underlying ethos.

Willis (1978) elaborates this idea in an early ethnographic comparison of 'bike boy' and 'hippy' subcultures. Music was central to both, he argues, but in ways which reflect their very different orientations to life. To give a few examples: the bike boys were always on the move and put a great emphasis upon physical prowess and mastery, an orientation reflected in their preference for music they could dance to. The hippies, by contrast, seemed to cultivate and celebrate physical awkwardness. They seldom danced and dance played no role in their musical preferences. Another revealing contrast concerns meaning. The bike boys were not interested in the meaning of songs and only noticed song lyrics where they deviated from rock 'n' roll conventions, in which case, especially where lyrics were ambiguous, they became hostile. The bike boys framed the world in 'black and white' terms, believing it to be identical with their perception of it, and expressed hostility towards anything which challenged that. The hippies, by contrast, *were* interested in meaning, especially where it was ambiguous or elusive, because this affirmed their belief in transcendent realms beyond their experience and comprehension. They discussed song lyrics at great length and took delight in their inability to reduce songs to single meanings and sounds to words.

These differences also played out in term of preferences for singles and LPs respectively. The hippies preferred LPs, especially concept albums in which themes were developed over several (often lengthy) tracks. The bike boys preferred short catchy singles, claiming that LPs were a waste of time because the best songs were always released as singles. Furthermore, while both liked the Beatles, the bike boys preferred the simplicity of their early singles, pre *Sergeant Pepper* (an LP which they found weird and unlistenable), while the hippies preferred the later psychedelic works, with their unusual sound effects, unconventional formats and promise of deeper meanings. The 'weirdness' of *Sergeant Pepper* was as threatening and offputting to the bike boys as it was stimulating and attractive to the hippies.

Willis draws out many further contrasts and not only in relation to music. As a final point, however, note that in both cases music was not merely selected on the basis of pre-given orientations and identities but seemed also to inform and reinforce those orientations and identities. The swagger of early rock 'n' roll informed and contributed to the physical confidence and comportment of the bike boys, who loved it, for example, while the distorted sounds and effects used in the experimental music beloved of the hippies encouraged their belief in the existence of dimensions of existence beyond the everyday world.

Some accounts of homology would push this further, suggesting that the bike boys' orientation reflected their working-class and the hippies their middle-class origins. Indeed, it is the link of culture to social structure that defines 'homology' in many accounts. Willis does not take this step, however. We cannot read class origins from culture, he maintains, because culture is a creative and imaginative response to social conditions. Different responses to ostensibly the same conditions are common, as the contrast between the teds, mods, skins, bikers and punks – all working-class youth subcultures according to the CCCS – demonstrates. Furthermore, in addition to economic hardships subcultural innovations address wider existential and sexual concerns, including the desire for fun and excitement. Of course subcultures may borrow from and reference the wider class cultures of their members but wider class cultures are similarly irreducible to material conditions, for the same reasons.

Hebdige explores the idea of homology in relation to punk, beginning his account by echoing Willis's observations on consistency:

> The subculture was nothing if not consistent. There was a homological relation between the trashy cut-up clothes and spiky hair, the pogo and amphetamines, the spitting, the vomiting, the format of the fanzines, the insurrectionary poses and the soulless, frantically driven music. The punks wore clothes which were the sartorial equivalent of swear words, and they swore as they dressed ... Clothed in chaos. (1988: 144)

There is a problem with the concept of homology for Hebdige, however. It implies core values and meanings which he cannot identify in punk. Furthermore, he maintains that homology entails a class identification which, as he sees it, is missing in punk. Where the teds and skins sought to rearticulate class identities punk 'disguises' its class origin:

> Though punk rituals, accents and objects were deliberately used to signify workingclassness, the exact origins of individual punks were disguised or symbolically disfigured by the make-up, masks and aliases which seem to have been used, like Breton's art, as ploys to escape the principle of identity.
> This workingclassness therefore tended to retain, *even in practice, even in its concretized forms*, the dimensions of an idea. It was abstract, disembodied, decontextualized. Bereft of the necessary details – a name, a hope, a history – it refused to make sense, to be grounded, 'read back' to its origins. (*Ibid.*: 121, emphasis in original)

This interpretation is problematic. Hebdige assumes the importance of working-class origins and identity, and when he fails to find strong and consistent evidence to support this assumption he suggests that the effect of class must be concealed or refused. Another interpretation, consistent with further criticisms of the CCCS which I discuss in Chapter 3, is that class simply doesn't have the importance that Hebdige assumes. Some punks were working class and some articulated a discourse of class resistance but only some and this was only one of several discourses articulated. Punk had different meanings for different participants and even for the same participants across time and in different contexts.

There is a huge critical literature on subcultures. The concept has been dissected from every conceivable angle and found wanting on many counts. I am not convinced by all of this criticism and believe that there is much of value in the CCCS approach. In particular Willis addresses 'structure and agency' wonderfully, simultaneously capturing the ingenuity, imagination and creativity of young people and the considerable constraints within which they are exercised. Furthermore, the claim that subcultures offer their participants a sense of identity, purpose and belonging in conditions where these are difficult to find is both important and persuasive. And the concepts of style, bricolage and homology, as developed by the CCCS, are at the very least suggestive and worthy of further consideration. Whatever alternative we find to 'subculture' must allow us to hold on to these positives. However, there are problems with 'subculture' which force us to seek an alternative.

I return to some of these problems in the next chapter. Here I focus upon two. First, as Laing (1985) observes, the subculture literature says almost nothing about processes and contexts of music making and, in fact, very little about music at all. The CCCS's chief concern is working-class youths' resistance to domination. Music is important to this when and to the extent that subcultures identify with specific musical genres. But this is musical consumption, not music making, and 'subculture' has little to contribute to our understanding of the latter. In many cases, moreover, the subcultures exist at some remove, temporal, spatial and social, from the music they consume: e.g. the British skinheads' appropriation of Jamaican ska and (US-based) Motown.

In fairness, both Willis (1978), in relation to the hippies, and Hebdige (1988), in a section on reggae, do briefly consider how subcultures might shape music making. And Willis challenges the idea that cultural production and consumption are distinct, anticipating Becker, who argues that listening, interpretation and consumption are part of the process whereby music is made (see also Dewey 2005; Shusterman 2000; Small 1998). They are only part of the process, however, and the subculture concept says nothing about the other parts. This is a significant weakness in relation to punk and post-punk because both centred upon music making and to understand them we need a conceptual framework which is sensitive to this.

The second and related problem is that the subculture concept does not as readily fit post-punk as it does punk. As noted in the previous chapter, 'post-punk' refers to a heterogeneous ensemble of styles. We might perhaps say that post-punk involved various subcultures, including goths, new romantics, rude boys, psychobillies, cow punks and futurists but it wasn't a single subculture in the CCCS sense. In addition, while some of these strands were politicised and rebellious, as the CCCS account implies, others were not (I revisit this claim in relation to punk in Chapter 3). Psychobillies, futurists, new romantics and goths, for example, had no obvious political agenda or leaning. We therefore need to move beyond subculture to an alternative conception.

Beyond subculture: scenes and fields

Among the potential alternatives to subculture that we might turn to 'music scene' seems an obvious choice. There is a growing body of literature on music scenes, much of it good (e.g. Bennett and Peterson 2004). The concept of scenes is problematic too, however. Repeatedly, in writing this book, I have found myself wanting to write 'scenes', not for any technical or theoretical reason but because it is a familiar term which trips off the tongue and is widely used in journalistic and lay discussions. This may be a strength but, as Hesmondhalgh (2005) notes, it can also be a disadvantage. The term is already loaded and has different meanings for different people, which make it difficult to pin down for academic purposes. As I have found in my reading of academic accounts which use it, I have my own 'feel' for it as a term and this does not always seem to agree with that of the authors I am reading, leading to misunderstandings. Indeed, Hesmondhalgh shows that the two seminal academic works which use the concept (Shank 1994; Straw 1991) define it in conflicting ways.

Another possibility is Pierre Bourdieu's currently popular conception of 'fields'. However, this concept carries a great deal of theoretical baggage, making it rigid and overly constraining the possibilities for empirical observation. It predefines action as a strategic and competitive pursuit of 'capital' and domination, for example, and only admits of observations which fit with this schema (Becker 2006a). In addition, as I have argued elsewhere, there are significant theoretical flaws in Bourdieu's approach (Crossley 2011, 2013; Bottero and Crossley 2011).

A more promising option is Howard Becker's concept of 'art worlds', which I will render as 'music worlds'. I begin my discussion of this concept by discussing some of its antecedents, starting with Herbert Blumer's (1986) discussion of social worlds.

Precursors

Blumer introduces 'worlds' in the context of a methodological argument in which he insists that sociologists should strive to understand the meaning which objects (including self, other, actions and abstract concepts) have for social actors. Actors act in accordance with those meanings, he claims, and to understand and explain their actions we must focus upon these meanings.

Objects and situations acquire meaning, on this account, within and by way of interaction. For Blumer this is principally a matter of talk but in the work of G. H. Mead (1967), whom he draws from, it is equally a matter of physical manipulation and use. The meaning of an object or milieu is assigned in and through the ways in which actors handle and use it. A cooking pan becomes a drum, for example, if an actor taps out a beat on it, and a yacht salesroom became Manchester's famous Haçienda nightclub when a group of local cultural entrepreneurs decided to put it to that use.

Meanings may vary between actors, but Blumer's chief interest is with collective meanings. Actors who are co-involved in particular milieus, he argues, tend to generate shared meanings in the course of their interactions, which become integral to further interaction in those milieus and which lend the milieu a sense of being a distinct 'world'. A world, thus defined, is a 'space', social and physical, of interaction and of the shared meanings, symbols, definitions, objects and practices generated, across time, by such interaction.

Upon first acquaintance with such worlds, outsiders unfamiliar with the layers of sedimented meaning that have accumulated through time and lacking a world-relevant identity will often feel estranged and unsure of how to act. Indeed, we often respond to such situations by noting that 'it's a different world'. Much of the sociology of the Chicago School, to which Blumer belonged, sought to make sense of a range of human behaviours which, from the outside, seemed strange, exotic or deviant, by locating them back within the worlds from which they originated and which lent them their meaning. Behaviour which was difficult to understand or explain when considered out of context was rendered intelligible and explicable when considered in its environing world. Becker's (1951, 1963) early work on jazz musicians is one example of this work.

Worlds are not defined exclusively by reference to shared meanings on this account. Meanings are the outcome of interaction which, in turn, is motivated by the concerns and interests of those involved. Worlds form when and because actors are brought together by a shared interest or circumstance. Or, rather, when they are repeatedly brought together in interaction situations such that shared meanings, habits and conventions begin to take shape. Furthermore, in the course of their interaction they may generate 'internal goods'; that is, objects or ends which have value within their world but not outside of it (Crossley and Bottero 2014).

In the case of the punk and post-punk worlds interaction was centred upon music. It involved: live performance and its organisation;

formation of bands and rehearsal; recording; and distribution of recordings. Furthermore, it included activities centred upon the collective identity and style of the world, as manifest in the music, in visual appearance
and in other visual media. This wasn't just a matter of musical production, narrowly conceived. Audiences and their activities, their ways of
dancing and other forms of musical appreciation and interpretation
were an important part of these worlds too. As I suggested in my discussion of Willis and discuss further below, the consumption of music is an
integral element in the process whereby it comes into being as music, an
element in its production.

It is important to note the role of imagination and play in this account.
Objects, behaviours and people take on certain meanings and statuses
because those involved take the imaginative step of acting 'as if' they
had those meanings and statuses. They invent rituals and games, albeit
sometimes unwittingly, wrapping new and inventive narratives around
their activities. It is for this reason that outsiders initially struggle to
make sense of what is going on. They experience objects, behaviours
and people but not through the lens generated and maintained by the
collective imagination of the group.

This account of 'worlds' resonates with another that Becker draws
upon: Arthur Danto's (1964) concept of 'art worlds'. Danto formulates
the notion of art worlds in response to the perennial question, 'but is it
art?', which was being asked of Andy Warhol's *Brillo Box*[3] installation
at his time of writing. What is it, critics asked, that makes Warhol's Brillo
boxes any different from those sold in supermarkets? Why do Warhol's
Brillo boxes qualify as 'art' while those in supermarkets do not?

Danto's answer hinges upon 'the art world', which he conceptualises
as a community defined by its members' shared familiarity with and
adherence to specific understandings of art and its history. Brillo boxes
become art, he maintains, in virtue of the meanings which this understanding bestows upon them and upon Warhol's act of putting them in
a gallery, meanings which Warhol anticipated and oriented to in making
his installation. His work draws upon and simultaneously advances and
challenges these understandings.

A musical equivalent of Warhol's boxes is John Cage's 4'33", whose
score instructs musicians to put down their instruments and do nothing
for three consecutive periods ('movements') whose overall length adds
up to 4 minutes and 33 seconds. To the untrained ear this is 4 minutes
and 33 seconds of silence or perhaps, for those more acquainted with
Cage, of ambient background sounds, but to those fully in the know
this is an experiment, with various precursors, in the aesthetic ideas of
automaticism and they 'hear' it accordingly. Their listening is framed by

an aesthetic understanding which they share as members of a relatively small world of avant-garde music; an art world.

This is relevant to punk and post-punk. Simon Humphrey, who engineered the Clash's first album, for example, recalls:

> Mick would play a solo, and shout through, 'What was that like?' We didn't know what to say, because it wasn't that polished. In punk terms, we didn't know whether it was a good solo or a bad one, we didn't have any reference points. (cited in Gilbert 2005: 145)

Compared to the rock that he was familiar with, Mick Jones's guitar parts sounded unpolished but even if this was a reflection of Jones's musicianship at this point in his career, Humphrey knew that was not really the point. As an outsider to the emerging punk world, he lacked the aesthetic understanding necessary to make a judgement.

Another example is Siouxsie and the Banshees' first ever gig, at the 100 Club punk festival in September 1976. Sid Vicious, who played drums, had never played before the band was put together, three weeks before the festival. Likewise bassist, Steve Severin (aka Steve Spunker). And the band only rehearsed on one occasion, for less than an hour. Furthermore, guitarist, Marco Pironi, was drafted in with only days to go when the band's original guitarist, Billy Idol, pulled out to concentrate upon his other band, Chelsea. The performance, which consisted of a 20-minute version of the Lord's Prayer, peppered with snatches of 'Twist and Shout' and 'Knocking on Heaven's Door', was described by one music journalist as follows:

> With only one continuous but deeply felt chord from the red-streaked hair guitarist ... and the hypnotically compelling drumbeat like that of a bored five year old ... the minimal art vocalising of the thin dark young chanteuse with a Charity jacket and the striking swastika armband ... this band is finally received with politeness ... and occasional spasms of pogo dancing. (Geoff Hill, *New Musical Express*, cited in Gimarc 2005: 39)

It seems fair to conclude that anybody listening from the perspective of the standard rock aesthetic of the time would have heard a terrible cacophony. The Banshees couldn't play in the conventional sense and by the standard of conventional rock aesthetics were dreadful. But some audience members were moved to 'pogo', and though there are several reasons for this, including the loyal support of their friends (see below), it was partly because audience members were listening with a different ear; informed by the newly emerging punk aesthetic. It didn't matter that the band couldn't play in the conventional sense because this wasn't conventional music. As insiders knew, it was a challenge to such music. Kenny Morris, who was previously unacquainted with the band and its members, was so 'thrilled' by what he heard that he asked to join the band, which he did, replacing Sid on drums (cited in Paytress 2003: 54).

There is a danger in this argument that we lose sight of aesthetic experience or reduce it to intellectual appreciation. Danto can seem to suggest that artistic appreciation is a matter of theoretical interpretation and thereby to forget the sensuous pleasure that can be derived from our engagement with music; a pleasure which Dewey (2005) explores in a discussion which also challenges the notion, implied by Danto, that aesthetic experience is restricted to the sanctioned spaces of 'the art world' (see also Shusterman 2000, 2002).

With some revision, however, Danto's position stands up. Punk and post-punk music certainly had visceral appeal but, as important work (discussed below) by Meyer (1956) and Huron (2007) suggests, the physical and emotional pleasure derived from listening to music presupposes an embodied, sensuous understanding on behalf of listeners, which is acquired through involvement in specific music worlds. As with watching football, we can only derive the excitement and pleasure we do to the extent that we grasp the constitutive conventions of an activity and understand what is going on, and this grasping is practical and embodied rather than intellectual. What allows the enthusiast to derive pleasure from a type of music while others are left cold is, in some part, the former's embodied and habitual grasp of what the music is about, as structured by its conventions. In this sense what Danto says of the art world holds true of music worlds centred upon sensuous pleasure. Pleasure presupposes understanding.

We can develop this argument by introducing some conceptual distinctions. As Leonard Meyer observes, some people verbalise and intellectualise their experiences of music more than others, and some music worlds encourage this more than others:

> Intellectual experience (the conscious awareness of one's own expectations or, objectively, of the tendencies of the music) ... is largely a product of the listener's own attitude towards his responses ... some listeners, whether because of training or natural psychological inclination, are disposed to rationalise their responses, to make experience self-conscious; others are not so disposed. (1956: 40)

Nothing I have said so far assumes that an individual must reflect upon music in order to understand or enjoy it but some people do and in their case reflection enhances enjoyment and understanding. This begs the question of what understanding music entails. On this point Richard Shusterman (2000) draws an important distinction between understanding and interpreting. The former refers to our basic perceptual capacity to spot patterns and follow threads. This may entail reflection and verbalisation but not necessarily. The dancer who pre-reflectively follows the beat of a song, anticipating changes in tempo and other dynamics understands the music by way of movement and embodied engagement. Interpretation builds upon understanding and goes beyond it, positing deeper meanings. The dancer who gestures aggressively while dancing is moving beyond the basic pattern, for example, and giving the music further meaning. They are interpreting as well as understanding.

This begs the question of what we mean by 'meaning' in relation to music. Focusing initially upon the instrumental aspect of music (i.e. excluding lyrics) we can distinguish between internal and external meanings. The internal meaning of music, for Meyer, is the pattern that it forms. Individual notes are meaningful because we hear them in relation to other notes which precede them in a melody so that, for example, they appear to drop or climb, sound 'right' or dissonant (no note is dissonant in itself, only in relation to a sequence of notes), and so that we anticipate where a melody will go next. Understanding internal meaning is a matter of grasping the pattern in a way that allows its twists and turns, as it unfolds through time, to have an experiential effect upon us – new directions surprise us, for example, forcing us to work to re-establish our grasp upon the pattern. We might do this pre-reflectively and may lack the vocabulary to explain what is going on but such understanding can involve reflection and discourse for those so inclined. External meaning, by contrast, involves hearing or interpreting external references in the music: e.g. perceiving a work to be about class struggle or an expression of sexual desire. External meanings are generated in interpretation and often take shape initially in language. Once articulated in language, however, they may form a tacit and unspoken background against which the music is subsequently heard.

I return to Meyer, internal meaning and understanding later. We can develop the idea of interpretation and external meaning, however, by reference to the work of literary theorist, Stanley Fish (1980). Fish challenges the idea that art objects have any single, determinate meaning. The same object, he argues, can always be interpreted in multiple ways. Many of his critics believe this implies that objects can have any meaning, resulting in a woolly form of subjectivism in which the object means something different to each and every person. Fish rebuts this criticism, however, arguing that although objects take on different meanings across different 'interpretative communities', within such communities their meaning is often determinate, both in the sense that it is obvious and in the sense that, where disagreements or ambiguities arise, they can be resolved through argument. The meaning of an object is determined by the stock of taken-for-granted assumptions and interpretative conventions generated, maintained and, over time, transformed through the interaction of members of an interpretative community. Because the meaning of the object depends upon the interpretative conventions of a community it tends to be shared by members of that community. Across different communities, however, or even within the same community across significant periods of time, where conventions differ, no such agreement exists. And there is no legitimate way of deciding between the interpretations or conventions of different communities.

Fish is right, in my view, to seek to avoid the individualistic subjectivism which his critics accuse him of, striving rather to define meaning as intersubjective. However, there is a danger in his account that worlds appear more consensual with respect to meanings, interpretations and understandings than they often are, and conversely that the differences and difficulties of communication and argument between communities are exaggerated. In some cases a world may involve various competing (but not incommensurable) interpretative communities. And as new members enter a world, particularly when they do so in large numbers, the constitutive interpretative conventions of the world can be disturbed and uprooted. In reading accounts of punk, for example, I have been struck by numerous comments to the effect that the music and style were misunderstood as they diffused to wider audiences: e.g. playful mock violence was replaced by the real thing while an emphasis upon fluidity and experimentation in musical and clothing styles was replaced by uniformity as certain designs were misinterpreted as *the* punk style. We must be careful how we interpret such claims. They elevate their authors as true and authentic punks relative to those whom they criticise and may be motivated by this end. However, they also suggest that the original meaning of punk was difficult to sustain as it diffused beyond its original participants, giving rise to different and opposing interpretative communities within the punk world.

The discourses and understandings that shape meaning in a music world may be generated in face-to-face interaction but publications, such as the mainstream music press and the fanzines that flourished during the heyday of punk and post-punk (Spencer 2008), are crucial too (Lopes 2002). Publications provide a common point of reference for potentially large numbers of geographically dispersed enthusiasts, helping to engender shared understandings between them. And some writers have argued that the boundaries of worlds are effectively defined by the circulation of such publications. The boundaries of a world, according to Shibutani (1955: 566–7), 'are set neither by territory nor by formal group membership but by the limits of effective communication'. They 'come into existence with the existence of communicational channels'. Publications are one such important channel.

Music as collective action

The above ideas are integral to the concept of art worlds as Becker develops it. They form a backdrop to the main thrust of his own contribution, however, which is more focused upon the idea that art is collective action. Art is an activity for Becker. It is done. 'Work of art' refers not to an object but to the activity, the work, involved in making the object, and that work is usually performed by many people, in addition to those conventionally regarded as artists. A song, for example, might be written, performed, recorded, produced, packaged, promoted and distributed, with different personnel involved at each stage. Likewise, bands have agents and managers. They need instruments and other equipment, which they neither make nor supply for themselves. And as Danto's and Fish's work suggests, their songs only achieve the public status of songs and music in virtue of being perceived as such by a receptive audience, who also contribute to the process whereby the song acquires a public meaning. Indeed, these songs only generate pleasure and aesthetic experience for an audience who engage with them, orienting to genre and other conventions (see also Dewey 2005). There is no art without an audience who recognise and enjoy it as such, even if, in the limit case, audiences are tiny and identical with the community of artists involved. The key sociological question is how this all comes together. The activities of the multiple contributors to the work of art must be coordinated, incentivised, etc., and the sociologist must explain how this is achieved.

Many of these ideas are echoed with specific reference to music by Christopher Small (1989), who coins the term 'musicking' to capture the web of interactivity which is involved in the making of music and who goes some way to addressing the sociological question of how this collective action is achieved. Becker offers a more comprehensive answer, however, with his notion of art worlds.

There is no single template that captures the details of every case, for Becker. Art worlds vary and he uses the concept to capture and explore this variation. As Strauss says of worlds more generally, they might be big or small; geographically concentrated or dispersed; local, national or international; open or secretive:

> Some are so emergent as to be barely graspable; others are well-established, even well-organised. Some have relatively tight boundaries; others possess permeable boundaries. Some are very hierarchical; some are less so or scarcely at all ... etc. (1973: 121)

However, four features are central to Becker's understanding of art worlds: (1) *networks*; (2) *places*; (3) *conventions*; (4) *resources*. These component elements need to be unpacked.

Networks and resources

Becker uses 'network' in two ways: (1) to indicate the division of labour that is typically involved in the production of an art object; (2) to capture the web of interacting social actors involved in a world and the 'community' they form. All artistic production involves a division of labour between multiple actors, for Becker. A hit single, for example, typically involves input from an artist, engineers, a producer, managers, various record company personnel, sleeve designers, radio deejays, music journalists and adoring fans, to name only the most obvious. Each party, to varying degrees, leaves her mark on the product and enjoys a stake in it but their respective contributions are dependent upon those of the others to reach fruition.

The creation of an art object is, at the same time, the creation of a network in this respect; a network in which actors pool their skills, time, energy and other resources in return for anticipated rewards. This process presupposes a prior network, however, of actors who know who to approach to get things done and whose pre-existing relationships and reputations within the network help to secure cooperation. It is perhaps more accurate to say, therefore, that artistic production activates and simultaneously modifies a pre-existing network.

The interdependence between actors in this process generates power balances which may be mobilised where conflicts of interest arise. Different parties may have different ideas about how a song should sound, for example, and each may be concerned about the impact of a 'wrong-sounding' song upon their reputation or financial return. Such disagreements may be resolved by parties agreeing not to work together and artists could try to do everything themselves. However, the skills of different parties take time and energy (important resources) to acquire, as do the tasks those skills are used for, all of which would draw the disgruntled artist away from their primary passion. Furthermore, third parties, such as record labels, may make their own involvement conditional upon that of particular producers, engineers, etc. Somebody must concede in such standoffs, backing down in the face of the other's threat to withdraw, and that will usually be the actor with the most to lose.

Some power balances are indeed balanced, each party standing to make the same losses if things don't work out. And in some the stakes are not particularly high. In others, however, much is at stake and relations are extremely imbalanced, such that one party is in a much stronger position to call the shots. Numerous rock biographies suggest that it is by no means always the artist who enjoys this dominant position.

On another level, involvement in the networks comprising a music world may be a source of important resources and support, with power imbalances manifesting in marginalisation. In an important analysis of gender relations in Liverpool's indie music world, for example, Sara Cohen identifies women's exclusion from informal networks as a major obstacle to participation (see also Cohen 1991):

> The scene comprises predominantly male groups, cliques or networks engaged in activities shaped by norms and conventions, through which they establish and maintain relationships with other men ... They regularly circulate and exchange information, advice and gossip; instruments, technical support and additional services; music recordings, music journals and other products. Social networks such as these extend out of the local scene to national and international scenes and industries, maintained through face-to-face interaction and communication technologies. (1997: 20)

There are two points here. Cohen's main point is that women are marginalised within informal networks of the local music world. This observation derives its bite, however, from a second observation: that the men involved in the network benefit hugely from it and are enabled to become musicians because of it. This is partly because resources, such as information, instruments and technical know-how flow through the network, giving network members access to them. Musicking requires resources which informal networks afford access to. In addition, however, the network is a resource in its own right; a form of 'social capital' (Coleman 1990). Norms of trust, cooperation and mutual support, cultivated in the network, coupled with an emergent sense of solidarity and collective identity, generate possibilities for musicking that would not otherwise be available. In addition, the network, particularly where dense, may help to reinforce aesthetic preferences, maintain commitment and, linking with the insights of Blumer, Danto and Fish, generate shared conventions of understanding and interpretation which make the music meaningful and give it value.

The first performance by the Banshees, discussed above, for example, was undoubtedly supported by the fact that Siouxsie, Steve Severin and especially Sid Vicious were close friends of the Sex Pistols and well known within the dense network of the early punk world. Audience members were primed both to treat their performance charitably and to hear it as 'punk rebellion' rather than substandard rock 'n' roll. Many audiences would have booed them off within seconds but they were playing to a close-knit in-crowd, to which they belonged, who were sympathetic to what they were trying to do. And of course they *were* trying to do something different.

I return to network effects in Chapter 4, considering some of the supporting evidence for them. Presently, however, I want to add two qualifications. First, none of this precludes the possibility of competition, conflict, factions, power imbalances (as noted above) and power struggles. The evidence for such tensions is overwhelming in almost every music world, including those studied later in this book. Moreover, they can play an important role. Competition between bands or factions, for example, may provide an incentive for those involved to push the boundaries, innovate and rehearse in a way that they would not otherwise do, resulting in new and exciting music. Worlds are neither purely consensual and cosy nor purely conflictual and competitive. They are, as Simmel (1906, 1955) says of individual relations, ambivalent combinations of each, varying across time and context. Second, networks are differentiated structures. As I showed in Chapter 1, individual nodes, subsets of nodes and whole networks each manifest variable properties. Some individuals are better integrated than others and/or occupy different positions; some sub-groups are more cohesive than others; likewise some (whole) networks, etc. It is not networks per se that have the effects I am referring to. Any collective may be viewed as a network. What make the difference are specific network properties. Cooperation is more likely, for example, in dense networks (Coleman 1990).

Places and/as resources

'Every artwork', Becker argues, 'has to be some place' (2004: 17). Musicking must happen somewhere and at some time. Becker focuses upon performance spaces in particular, exploring the way in which they shape both performance and performer. We might add, however, that rehearsal, recording and meeting places are important too, and so are music and record shops. Becker defines place, in this context, as:

> a physical place that has been socially defined; defined by its expected uses, by shared expectations about what kinds of people will be there to take

part in those activities, and by the financial arrangements that underlie all of this. And defined further by a larger social context that both provides opportunities and sets limits to what can happen. A place, so defined, can be as large as a city ... or as small as a night club. (*Ibid.*: 20)

Notice the overlap here with what I said earlier. A place is physical. It involves bricks and mortar or, in the case of a city, a territory. But it has a meaning for those who inhabit and use it, and it gets that meaning in large part from the way in which they use it. It is a space in which they 'play', in every sense of the word, and their play transforms and bestows meaning upon it. A club is often just a set of dingy rooms but they become a club when they are used in particular ways: e.g. to put on bands. And they may become a very special club if, for example, the interaction of their regulars generates a convention and reputation for, for example, stylistic innovation.

Some 'jazz places', Becker observes, facilitate and encourage innovation, allowing both styles and performers to evolve and develop. New techniques and patterns are tried out and perfected. Many jazz places, however, are entertainment focused. Punters want to dance, which limits the rhythm and tempo at which music can be played, and they want to dance to songs which they know, played in a familiar way, which again limits the musicians' scope. This is partly an effect of feedback loops connecting convention, reputation and audience composition. Some clubs develop a reputation for entertainment, for example. This affects the audiences they attract, and the audience, in turn, affects what can be played, further shaping the reputation and performance conventions of the club. This is underwritten, however, by the effect of resources and power balances. Club owners need punters if they are to make a profit. If punters want to dance and be entertained, therefore, that is what club owners must demand from musicians, whose need to eat will often trump their artistic aspirations, resulting in compliance.

Places for innovation often emerge in a context where punters and owners are indifferent, leaving players free to do what they want. Becker notes that innovative jazz clubs were often drinking clubs where, by the early hours, punters were so drunk they didn't care what music was played. In these places, at these times, small numbers of jazz aficionados would gather to play 'real jazz'.

Hinting at the idea of critical mass which I discuss in Chapter 4, moreover, Becker suggests that big cities facilitate innovation more easily than small towns. Where there are more potential punters in a concentrated area, as in a city, he argues, there will be more clubs to meet the demand for them and the competition between those clubs will encourage each to carve out a distinct niche. In addition, in big populations, minorities, such as 'real jazz' lovers, are likely to exist in sufficient numbers to allow clubs to emerge which cater for their esoteric tastes (the existence of these clubs may then further cultivate a preference for 'real jazz' among others whom these clubs manage to convert). As such, furthermore, big cities more often have a number of small avant-garde clubs where fledgling players have an opportunity to practise innovative numbers and styles. They provide training grounds for groundbreaking musicians.

In an otherwise unrelated article, Krenske and McKay (2000) echo this argument with respect to heavy metal clubs in Brisbane, Australia. These clubs tend to be rather generic, incorporating a range of metal sub-genres and with a strong anchor in the mainstream, they argue, because the town and by extension its population of metal enthusiasts is too small to support a greater range of more specialised clubs:

> The heterogeneity of both the patrons and music of Club Thrash can be explained by the relatively small population of Brisbane, the absence of a critical mass that can support distinctive HM [heavy metal] sub-cultures. (Krenske and McKay 2000: 292)

Similarly, writing about UK indie, Wendy Fonarow observes that:

> Because many of the smaller cities, especially those without student unions, have correspondingly smaller youth communities, it quite difficult to attend gigs as frequently there as one can in [larger] cities. (2006: 109)

It will be clear from these observations that a music world's places not only absorb and generate resources, in the form of rent and admission revenue, but count as resources in their own right. Bands need places to rehearse, perform and record. And some places, innovative clubs, for example, provide a rare opportunity for forms of musicking which are important to both individual musicians and the development of the worlds to which they belong.

It is important to add that places may also have a specific socio-demographic profile. Becker, who played in the Chicago jazz clubs in the 1940s and 1950s, notes ethnic divides in particular. The USA was sharply racially segregated at that time and though white musicians sometimes frequented black clubs, where the jazz was deemed more authentic, blacks were prohibited from white venues. Other socio-demographic factors may be important too, however. Many clubs have an age profile, for example (although the significance of age in relation to popular music is changing (Bennett 2013; Bennett and Hodkinson 2012; Smith 2009), and a number of writers have suggested that musical places are often predominantly masculine and relatively inaccessible to women, at least if unaccompanied by men (Bayton 1998; Cohen 1997; McRobbie and Garber 1978). The late-night-drinking holes discussed by Becker, for example, would pose both a physical and a reputational threat to any woman who might be tempted to frequent them. Furthermore, as Cohen's (1997) work suggests, the masculine culture practised in those spaces, which enter into their very constitution as places, actively excludes women in a variety of ways (see also Krenske and McKay 2000). In so far as these places are the key form of access to certain forms of music, it follows that this limits access to those forms of music along socio-demographic lines.

Becker says very little about the physical properties of 'music places'. Other writers, however, including Small (1998) and David Byrne (2012), whose band, Talking Heads, played regularly at CBGB in New York and were part of the city's pioneering punk world, argue that these properties influence musicking in many ways. Byrne, for example, notes that the acoustics in certain venues render certain types of music impossible and others preferable, and he suggests that musicians compose and perform in ways which will suit the venues in which they typically perform.

Place is crucial in relation to punk and post-punk. Both were strongly identified, at least in the first instance, with particular cities – not least London, where punk first took off. These cities were punk and post-punk places. Within these cities, moreover, particular places loomed large. Venues such as the Roxy in London, Liverpool's Eric's, and Manchester's Electric Circus are obvious examples but beyond venues other places were crucial too. Probe records, in Liverpool, was a key haunt for the city's post-punks, for example, and SEX, the boutique run by Vivienne Westwood and Sex Pistols' manager, Malcolm McLaren, played a similar role for many of London's punk pioneers.

Places and networks

As these final comments suggest, places contribute to the formation of networks because they attract lovers of a type of music, drawing these people together and increasing the likelihood that they will meet and both form and maintain ties. Music places are, to borrow Feld's (1981, 1982) term, network 'foci'. Many key players in Liverpool's punk and post-punk worlds met at Eric's, for example, because Eric's was the place to go for punks in Liverpool. And these ties were maintained because punks returned repeatedly to Eric's and kept bumping into one another.

However, foci often exert the pull that they do because they acquire a reputation, and this reputation takes form within an existing network. Foci generate networks and networks allow places to become foci. In addition, a strong reputation increases the inflow of a particular type of punter, allowing a place, whether a shop or a club, to specialise. And by specialising the place better serves its punters, boosting its reputation. Furthermore, networks between punters in focal spaces contribute to the generation of the conventions, culture and atmosphere which mark the space out as a 'place to be'. Places and networks are in these ways mutually constitutive within the context of an emerging music world.

Convention

Cooperation in musical worlds is often aided, Becker observes, by conventions. Conventions are sometimes thought of as shared habits but Becker, drawing upon the work of David Lewis (1969), adds an important relational aspect, stressing that conventions are solutions to 'coordination problems' (Gilmore 1987). They facilitate coordination in situations where a number of different and equally satisfactory lines of interaction are possible but where actors will only achieve their desired outcome if they select the same one. It doesn't really matter whether we drive on the left or right-hand side of the road, for example, but driving will be both arduous and dangerous if we do not 'agree' upon one or the other. Conventions arise when one pattern emerges as the preferred option.

Lewis insists that a course of action is only conventional if those involved recognise it as such and are cognisant of alternatives. I disagree. This precludes deep-rooted patterns of interaction which, if actors think about them at all, they tend to regard as natural. It is a revelation when something we previously assumed to be natural is shown to be a convention but I see no good reason to insist that it wasn't a convention before it was recognised as such. We may follow conventions, as I use that term, with or without recognising them as such.

Music is conventional through and through, for Becker. On one level, different styles of music (and clothing and argot) are rooted in convention. Style, according to Meyer, 'is a replication of patterning, whether in human behaviour or in the artefacts produced by human behaviour, that results from a series of choices made within some set of constraints' (1989: 3). These 'choices' are not made on each occasion of the behaviour, however, or by each individual who enacts them, otherwise there would be no 'replication'. 'Rather they are learned or adopted as part of the historical/cultural circumstances of individuals or groups' (*ibid.*). They are shared and become habitual. More importantly, from the point of view of our discussion of convention hitherto, they facilitate coordination between those involved.

This may be difficult to comprehend with respect to stylistic conventions, particularly those concerning visual style. How do ways of dressing resolve coordination issues? Stylistic conventions are important, however, because they allow members of a world to communicate their belonging to both fellow insiders and outsiders, building and marking out spaces, identities and symbolic boundaries. They signal the existence of a world, affording those who engage in it a shared sense of belonging. Furthermore, adherence to stylistic conventions is often used as a test of commitment which participants in a world use to build trust and solidarity. Participants must conform to stylistic conventions to prove their loyalty to others. In all of these ways stylistic conventions are integral to the interaction which builds and sustains a music world.

Beyond this, on a musical level, stylistic conventions allow musicians to play together more easily. Jazz players can play together because they mutually orient to the conventions of the particular style of jazz they are playing, for example (Faulkner and Becker 2009). And this is not only a matter of style. Convention goes to the heart of musicking. The Western system of notation, with its crotchets and semi-quavers, is or at least was peculiar to the West, for example, along with the twelve tone system (A to G, with associated sharps and flats), the keys, scales, chord configurations, time signatures and rhythms that it transcribes, and the instruments we play. As with stylistic convention, but perhaps to a greater extent, these agreements facilitate coordination between musicians, allowing them to make music together.

Moreover, it is not only the relationship and interaction between players that is coordinated by conventions. It is the relationship between players and audiences:

> By using such a conventional organisation of tones as a scale, the composer can create and manipulate the listener's expectations as to what sounds will follow. He can then delay and frustrate the satisfaction of those expectations, generating tension and release ... Only because artist and audience share knowledge of and experience with the conventions invoked does the art work produce an emotional effect. (Becker 1982: 29–30)

Becker alludes here to important work on musical meaning and pleasure by Leonard Meyer (1956), subsequently developed by David Huron (2007, see also Ball 2011, 254–321). Building upon Dewey's (1894, 1895, 2005) work, both on aesthetics and affect, Meyer argues that when listening to a piece of music we seek to identify patterns, hearing what is being played at one point against the background of what preceded it and anticipating what will come next. Detecting patterns is itself pleasurable and central to the aesthetic experience but this is enhanced in art which, as Becker suggests in the above passage, teases and plays with our expectations. This generates tension in the listener, which it then releases, giving rise to feelings of pleasure. Furthermore, slight dissonances and irregularities challenge our capacity for 'pattern recognition'; a challenge which, according to Dewey (2005), is rewarded, if successful, with feelings of pleasure[4] (Crossley and Bottero 2014).

This only works, however, because and to the extent that composer and audience orient to the same musical conventions and form similar expectations about the way in which musical sequences, having begun, will proceed. It is for this reason, Meyer argues, that we often find unfamiliar genres difficult and unappealing. We do not know their conventions and we therefore find it difficult to pick out their patterns and anticipate their trajectory.

By the same token, however, music which sticks too closely to familiar conventions often lacks appeal because it is too predictable and poses no challenge to our sensory sense-making capacities. It is for this reason, Meyer argues, that the history of music is, in some part, a history of challenges to musical convention – and in the Western art music tradition specifically to harmonic and melodic conventions. To maintain the excitement and pleasure that music generates successful composers have sought to advance the 'experiments' of their predecessors, subverting certain conventions but, at least where successful, thereby establishing new conventions which subsequent composers will feel the need to challenge in a process of constant evolution.

These ideas are very important. In the next chapter I discuss various academic explanations of the emergence of punk. Most have some credence but they all fail to consider the excitement and pleasure of participation; an excitement and pleasure which jump off the pages of autobiographical accounts as factors motivating the iterated interactions which shaped the punk world and allowed it to grow. Musicking and its intrinsic pleasures were only one element in this excitement, alongside others, but they were an important element and we need to be able to understand the pleasure and excitement generated by engagement with music if we are to make sociological sense of any music world (see also Crossley and Bottero 2014). Sociology and aesthetics are or at least should be conjoined aspects of a single perspective.

Convention, structure and constraint

Conventions create opportunities for the artist, in the respect that mastery of them enables the artist to both perform and compose in ways not otherwise possible. Musical creativity is not *ex nihilo*. It requires competence and know-how on behalf of the creator, which is to say, an embodied understanding of musical conventions. But for this same reason, conventions constrain or at least channel creativity.

This is not determinism. Becker argues that most artists, most of the time, follow most conventions. This is largely a matter of habit. Even where actors become aware of and wish to challenge a convention, however, there are costs to doing so which often prove prohibitive, particularly in the case of more entrenched conventions. Conventions reduce the time and effort required to achieve certain ends, and there are therefore time and effort costs to breaking with them. In addition, they often interlock, such that one cannot break with one convention in isolation, multiplying the costs of an unconventional approach. Moreover, some conventions are literally built into the equipment and environments that actors work with, further increasing the costs of innovation. If we want to depart from standard twelve tone music, for example, we immediately encounter the problem that most Western musical instruments and our system of musical notation are designed for this type of music. We would need to design new musical instruments and new systems of notation, which we will then have to persuade musicians to learn, audiences to listen to and so on.

Some composers, such as Harry Partch, have done exactly this, spending months working with particular orchestras, whose players must build their own instruments and then learn how play them. His results are important and fascinating but many would weigh them against the likely results of a more conventional approach:

> Seven or eight months of work finally results in two hours of music which could have been filled with other music after eight to ten hours of rehearsal by trained symphonic musicians playing the standard repertoire. The difference in the resources required measures the strength of the constraint imposed by the conventional system. (Becker 1982: 33)

Becker is not criticising Partch. He is explaining why very few composers challenge convention to the extent that Partch does, and why certain conventions have the power that they do; what he calls 'the power of inertia' (1995).

Another example is Charles Ives. His experiments with polyrhythms and polytonality broke so many conventions that they were originally deemed unplayable. Ives apparently experienced this as a liberation, no longer feeling constrained to write music which could be played. However, Becker speculates that most composers would deem this a prohibitive cost.

It is not only fellow musicians who must be persuaded of a breach of convention, of course. Audiences must be persuaded too if they are to pay to hear it – the acts of listening, interpreting and criticising being the final stages in the making of music – and financial costs are to be recouped. As noted above, musical appreciation generally presupposes familiarity with specific musical conventions. And as Danto's work indicates, avant-garde deviations from convention generally need to be framed by reference to avant-garde theories and conventions if they are to be recognised as 'art', rendered meaningful and thus appreciated.

Again there is no determinism here. Becker credits the composer with the reflexive capacity to become aware of and contemplate breaking the various conventions which structure their practice. They could do it. What usually keeps the convention in place, however, the power of inertia, is the cost of breaking many conventions. Furthermore, he adds that social power balances play a role. Dominant conventions within an art world are usually cherished by prominent figures who have made their name and career by way of those conventions and the prominence of these figures usually means that they are in a position to bring harsh sanctions to bear upon others whose activities they disapprove of. This creates a tendency towards conservation.

Conventions and resources

There is a great deal of discussion in contemporary sociology about the need to take technology and material objects more seriously. Some have gone so far as to suggest that material objects should be regarded as actors in the social world (Latour 2005). I am not persuaded by this latter claim (see Crossley 2011) but technologies, material objects and environments, as Byrne's above-cited reflections on venues suggest, are significant in relation to music. Contemporary rock music is unimaginable in the absence of the electric guitar, for example, and the specific form of post-punk pursued in Sheffield by Cabaret Voltaire, the Human League, Vice Versa and Clock DVA would not have been possible without the synthesiser.

These ideas chime with Becker's art world concept and we need to be mindful of them. His emphasis is different to that of Latour and his colleagues, however, and preferable. First, he tends to think of technologies (e.g. music instruments) as products of human labour and design, and as materialisations of social convention rather than as actors. The piano keyboard reflects the chromatic scale of the Western music tradition, for example. In some part it was responsible for establishing that convention and we need to be mindful of that effect but we gain little by regarding the piano as an actor in its own right and should remain mindful of the web of activities surrounding both its invention and the emergence of the conventions it anchors.

Second, notwithstanding its original design, the meaning of an object is determined in practice by the use to which it is put by actors and by conventions of use. As David Sudnow (1993) argues, the piano only becomes a musical instrument when used as such and generally by one with the skills to use it as such. In some houses a piano is simply a piece of furniture. Moreover, it exists in quite a different way for the person who has to polish than for the person who plays it.

Finally, Becker is concerned with differential levels of access to particular objects. In this respect he deems them not just materialised conventions but also resources. Musicians need access to instruments, rehearsal spaces, etc., if they are to make music and the emergence and flourishing of music worlds will depend in some part upon the availability of such resources. It wasn't the synthesiser per se that enabled the Sheffield post-punk world to take the shape that it did, for example. Synthesisers had existed for several years and were used in progressive rock. It was the *increased availability* of *cheap synthesisers*.

Conclusion: emerging music worlds

'Music', for Becker, involves interaction. It is collective action. Different types of musicking involve different roles but many will involve composers, players, promoters, producers, engineers, instrument makers and the all-important audience who not only pay to participate, funding others, but also, because perception is an active, ordering and generative process, contribute to the shaping of what finally counts as 'the music'. This process requires the use and exchange of resources both directly and in order to facilitate and incentivise participation, and it involves cooperation and coordination on the behalf of participants. Over time participants typically settle upon particular ways of working which makes it easier for them to coordinate and cooperate; they generate conventions. And collective identities form around particular networks, whose members develop their own distinct ways of doing things and of making sense of what they do; their own 'places' for performance and rehearsal; and perhaps also their own distinctive style(s) and ethos. This may happen on a local level, within a town or city, but also at a national or international level, and increasingly in virtual reality too.

Where this happens we may speak of an 'art world' or, as I will put it from this point on, a 'music world'. Music worlds are not always discrete entities. They overlap and nest within one another. But they are sufficiently distinctive for us to recognise and abstract them for purposes of analysis. Punk and post-punk are both examples.

In this chapter I have tried to elaborate upon this notion of music worlds through a discussion of the work of Howard Becker and other relevant writers. The question we must now address is how these worlds come about and how, in particular, punk and post-punk came about. Before I offer my own answer to that question, in Chapter 4, it is necessary to review the range of answers suggested in the available literature.

Notes

1 That is to say, a tendency towards increased in-group interaction. Actors with the attribute or interest are more likely to interact with others who have it than we would predict if there was no such tendency.
2 'King of kinky', weekend section (p. 44), *Guardian* 11/9/10.
3 Brillo pads were a form of cleaning cloth commonly used in the 1960s and 1970s. Brillo boxes were the boxes they came in and were often found stacked up in supermarkets, as washing powder boxes are today. One of Warhol's more famous installations involved a number of wooden boxes, identical to Brillo boxes in external appearance and stacked much as they were stacked in supermarkets.
4 Dewey believes this to be an evolutionary adaptation. Organisms must be good at spotting patterns (i.e. predators and prey) in their environment and organisms which reward themselves (with pleasure) for good perceptual discrimination, thereby sharpening this skill, have an evolutionary advantage.

3

Explaining punk: a review of existing accounts

In this chapter I review a number of theories of punk's emergence, preparing the way for my own account in Chapter 4. All of the theories discussed shed some light upon punk's origins but I will argue that, even in combination, they do not suffice. My purpose in discussing them is twofold. On the one hand I want to take what is useful from them. On the other, critiquing them affords me an opportunity to sketch out ideas that I will build upon in later chapters.

The focus of the chapter is exclusively upon punk. In part this reflects a bias in the literature. Academics have not lined up to explain post-punk as they have punk. An exclusive focus on punk makes sense in explanatory terms too, however, because post-punk grew out of punk, as a further phase of a single process. The transformation from punk to post-punk requires explanation and I discuss that in Chapter 8 but the sociological (if not aesthetic) roots of post-punk lie within punk itself and the discussion in this chapter, though focused upon punk, is therefore relevant to both.

The chapter focuses upon six explanations:

1 Punk was a response to alienation and domination on behalf of working-class youths, bolstered by indignation at the co-optation of previous youth rebellion.
2 Punk was a reaction to the crises (economic, political and social) of UK society in the mid 1970s.
3 Punk was a response to frustration at the state of popular music in the UK in the mid 1970s.
4 Punk was inspired by a number of earlier attempts to recapture the vibrancy and excitement of pop's history.
5 Punk was a response to new opportunities for innovation within the music industry.

6 Punk was the product of Malcolm McLaren's entrepreneurial machinations and/or the charisma of John Lydon.

I discuss each of these in turn. As the first three each suffer a common
problem, however, in that they explain punk by reference to an underlying social strain and the frustration this generated, I pause briefly
between points three and four to discuss strain-based explanations in
more generic terms.

The alienation of working-class youth

The idea that punk was a response to the alienation of working-class
youth is associated with the CCCS, whose concept of subculture was
discussed in Chapter 2. All post-war youth subcultures are a reaction
against and form of resistance to the twofold domination and alienation
of working-class youth according to the CCCS; that is, to their alienation, as members of the working class, from a bourgeois culture which
has achieved dominance and legitimacy ('hegemony') within contemporary capitalism, and their alienation, as young people, from the adult
working-class culture of their parents. Alienated from the cultural environments in which they find themselves, in the school, home, church,
neighbourhood and workplace, working-class youths seek to carve out
their own culture, in their own spaces; a culture which they feel at home
within, which offers them the meaning, identity and status otherwise
lacking in their lives, and which allows them to resist the bourgeois
cultural hegemony and age-based authority structure of working-class
culture that are imposed upon them. The alienation which subcultures
address is mostly discussed in abstract terms by the CCCS. However,
concrete issues, such as the breakup of working-class communities in
the context of urban renewal and problems of boredom and lack of
opportunities for advancement are often noted.

How effective subcultures are at addressing these 'strains', in the
view of the CCCS, is not always clear. In his account Hebdige suggests
that the punks mounted an effective symbolic challenge to bourgeois
hegemony. References by other CCCS members to the 'magical' nature
of subcultural protests at least hint that this resistance goes no further
than the symbolic level, however, and that it is flawed. The CCCS do
not clarify what they mean by 'magical', but, in other accounts, such
as Sartre's (1993) description of emotion as 'magical thought' and
Smelser's (1962) account of magical thinking in his theory of collective
behaviour, magical solutions to problems console those who resort to
them and address subjective symptoms of distress, in the short term,

without tackling the underlying social and material strains which cause this distress.

As understood by the CCCS, then, punk is one in a series of collective responses to alienation on behalf of working-class youth. Moreover, the series itself is not incidental. The perceived threat posed by sub-cultures is dealt with by 'the system', according to the CCCS, firstly through demonisation within the media and the stirring up of 'moral panic' (see Chapter 7) but then, second, through co-optation. Having initially expressed outrage at subcultural figures the media rehabilitate those figures and render them safe by, for example, exploring their 'normal' family backgrounds. They are, it turns out, no threat; just kids being kids. The status quo is safe after all. Furthermore, having initially shunned subcultural innovations in the hope that they will go away, the music and fashion industries begin to draw upon that innovation, reproducing their own, often watered-down and safer versions of it, in an effort to capture the youth market. This has the effect of further diffus-ing subcultural styles but, as the CCCS put it, it equally thereby 'defuses' the challenge. And this is *a provocation occasioning the rise of the next subculture*. The punks were not only seeking to challenge their alienation as working-class youths but also the co-optation and defusion of the sub-cultures which preceded them. They were seeking to reignite the struggle.

Resistance and politics

We see evidence of this latter claim in early interviews with punk pio-neers such as Joe Strummer of the Clash and Paul Weller of the Jam:

> I'm not going to suddenly turn into Rod Stewart just because I got £25 a week. (Strummer, in Dancis 1978: 69)

> What [1960s musicians] once fought against they've now become a part of. (Weller, *ibid.*: 67)

And both singers were politically outspoken throughout the late 1970s and early 1980s. They were perhaps the two most overtly political figures in the first wave of punk, however, and there is a danger in the CCCS account that we impute political meanings and motivations to many who were not politically focused. Punk *did* gesture defiance at the wider world, as the CCCS suggest, resisting incorporation into it. And many punks *were* seeking to revive the rebelliousness evident in much popular music from the mid 1950s onwards, which was widely perceived to be waning in the mid 1970s. However, many early pioneers distanced themselves from the political stance adopted by the likes of Strummer and Weller:

I thought it was nonsense, spouting all this politics, I thought it was parrot fashion. I wasn't interested in politics but I didn't think they [the Clash] were either, they were just muppets. It was a cheap trick to gain some street credibility. And they've all eaten their words since. (Siouxsie, in Savage 2009: 344)

The songs they [the Clash] did before they went political were much better than the ones they did afterwards ... when they started all that political crap, I went right off them. There wasn't any need for it, really. (Vic Goddard, *ibid.*: 368)

The Clash were overtly political because of Bernie's influence. He wanted it to be heavy left-wing anarchy, and Billy [Idol] and I were just not like that ... It was nothing to do with smashing the system (Tony James, *ibid.*: 283)

People say the Damned were a rebellious group, and I think we were, but I didn't know what I was rebelling against ... When [later] we debated things with Crass, they made a lot of sense. That was when I started thinking more politically. (Captain Sensible, *ibid.*: 335)

Furthermore, a comparison of punk and pop lyrics by Dave Laing (1985)[1] suggests that political content was far from ubiquitous (see Figure 3.1). Punk songs seldom focused upon the stock themes of mainstream pop songs: that is, 'romantic and sexual relations' or 'music and dancing'. They introduced a focus upon sexuality. And they were

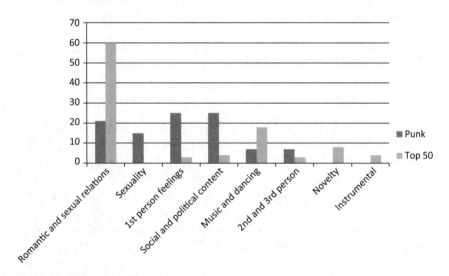

Figure 3.1 Content of punk album lyrics compared with 1976 Top 50 singles (*source:* Laing 1985)

much more focused on both 'first-person feelings' (usually boredom and dissatisfaction) and 'social and political comment'. However, ten out of the sixteen examples of 'social and political comment' that Laing identifies come from the Clash's first album and most of the others were not straightforwardly political in the same way: the Sex Pistols' *EMI*, which is included among the sixteen, for example, is as much a reflection upon their own dealings with the company as it is a critique of the music industry and big business.

The emergence of the punk world opened up an expressive space in which participants could make political claims. And the unrest it involved created an opportunity for what Blumer (1969) calls 'agitators', on both the left and the extreme right of the political spectrum, to recruit punks, channel their frustration into political allegiances and seek to frame punk in political terms. Indeed, certain early influential punk pioneers, such as Jamie Reid, Bernard Rhodes and, to a lesser extent, Malcolm McLaren, brought a political understanding to punk which they attempted both to persuade others of and to frame punk with, as Tony James's above reference to Rhodes suggests (see also Chapter 6). Moreover, the opposition that punks encountered from parents, teachers, local authorities, etc. further served to politicise them by inviting more direct confrontation with 'the establishment'. Their actions took on a political meaning because they transgressed the boundaries of acceptability upheld by various authority figures and those authorities responded, encouraging a more focused and political reply from the punks. However, these desires and the rebellious impulses that fuelled punk were by no means always and certainly not originally political in any straightforward sense. The motivations of participants varied but in so far as there was a shared underlying impetus it was, as the CCCS account also suggests, existential: a 'quest for excitement' (Elias and Dunning 1993), meaning, identity, pleasure, fun, recognition and belonging in a world which seemed to offer none of these.

We should also remember that punk was a music world rather than a social–political movement. It was fuelled by a love of music and the excitement and sensuous pleasure of musicking. Some groups, notably the Clash, expressed a political message in some of their songs but this was not true of even a majority of the early groups, as Laing's survey suggests. And even the Clash are better described as musicians who wrote protest songs rather than political activists. The pioneer punks did not take up instruments and form bands in order to protest their alienation. There were much easier ways of doing that. They could have joined one of the many protest groups of the time, as others did. They came together to make music.

I am not denying that punks gestured defiance at the wider world through their appearance and music, that they carved out their own alternative social space or that they generated a public sphere in which controversial views, including political views, were aired. Nor do I deny that, from an external point of view, this is and punk therefore was political. I should also add that the definition of punk as political certainly shaped its later manifestations both in the UK and perhaps more especially overseas. However, as we have seen, some of punk's most prominent pioneers were resistant to the idea that what they were doing was political. They did not define punk, from the inside, as a political phenomenon. Rather, they perceived their activities to be about making exciting music and having fun. Even their non-conformism, as they understood it, was an existential and aesthetic rather than a political statement. They wanted to be and to be seen to be different from 'the herd'. We might dispute such distinctions and definitions, particularly given the extensive work in sociology on identity politics and 'new social movements' which operate outside of conventional definitions of politics but we must be mindful of them if we believe that it is important to remain faithful to social actors' own intersubjective definitions of their activity in our explanations. Punk or at least certain strands of it became political in my view. It was political in its consequences. But most of its pioneers did not regard themselves to be involved in a political project and their motivations and situational and self-definitions (at the very beginning of punk) were not political in anything but the widest and vaguest sense of the word.

This does not mean that these pioneers were not reacting against their alienation and domination as working-class youths. Again, however, there is very little sense of this in (auto)biographies and band histories. Furthermore, the CCCS's portrayal of punk as a response by specifically working-class youths to their structural location and its effects is highly problematic.

Class and generational conflict?
Even within the CCCS there has been criticism that the focus upon class and age in their account of subcultures ignores the importance of other key social divisions, particularly gender, sexuality and race, and there have been attempts to introduce a focus upon these divisions too (Gilroy 1992, 1993a, 1993b; Hebdige 1988; Jones 1988; McRobbie 1991, 1994; McRobbie and Gerber 1978). I return to these shortly. First, however, it is important to consider whether punk manifested the class and age profile that one would expect given CCCS's explanation of it.

If punk was a response to alienation on behalf of working-class youth and that is to suffice as an explanation of it, then we would expect a large number of working-class youths to have been involved. In fact, however, as numerous critics of the CCCS have noted, this was not the case (Clarke 1990). Only a minority of working-class youths ever become involved in subcultures, of any type, and class-based frustrations do not suffice to explain punk therefore. We need to know why some working-class youths became involved and others did not.

To compound this there is evidence of significant levels of middle-class participation in punk. I present my own evidence of this, with respect to the pioneers of punk, in Chapter 5. Presently, note that Laing's (1985) survey of leading musicians from the early days of punk suggests an even balance between working- and middle-class origins, while Clarke (1990) identifies a strong middle-class presence among punk audiences.

Similar problems arise in relation to age. Later in the book I distinguish older and younger cohorts among the original punks but even the older pioneers were fairly young, a fact which supports the CCCS argument. Only a fraction of adolescents ever became punks, however, challenging the idea that the conditions of youth per se explain punk. Furthermore, there are a number of interesting discussions of ageing punks in the recent literature, suggesting that punk continued to appeal to some individuals beyond their youth and whatever structural conditions attach to youth (Bennett 2006, 2013; Davis 2006).

I am not denying that working-class youths were alienated, nor that some of the frustration this caused was vented in punk songs. The formation of the punk world opened up an expressive space in which any number of frustrations could be vented and explored. However, class and generational conflicts do not explain that formation.

As noted above, moreover, an exclusive focus upon class and youth ignores other significant social divisions, not least those based upon gender, sexuality and race. Might these have played a role in the origin of punk? None of them explain punk, as such, but each shaped it in a way that the standard CCCS account fails to allow for. This point requires brief elaboration.

Gender

McRobbie (1991) views punk as one of a small number of subcultures which were more open to women and more facilitative of female involvement. This view is echoed by a number of other writers (Bayton 1998; Leonard 2007) and explored at some length by Reddington (2012). Women were more involved in the punk world, as musicians, than they had been in previous music worlds. Furthermore, it has been observed by these same writers that female involvement in punk facilitated the articulation of a feminist agenda within it. All female bands, such as the Slits, and female artists such as Siouxsie and Polystyrene, challenged the usually subordinate position of women in music both performatively, through their high-profile involvement, and discursively, in their lyrics. They used their lyrics and profile to raise feminist questions, inspiring others, most famously the later Riot Grrrls, to do the same.

This feminist agenda is important but in contrast to Riot Grrrls nobody suggests that it explains the emergence of punk. Feminism was a voice in the expressive space of the punk world and, as such, shaped that world but frustration at gender inequality was not a cause of punk.

Sexuality

Sexuality is seldom discussed in relation to punk but it was important. Punk appropriated elements of gay and sadomasochist subcultures (e.g. bondage and bumflaps) and as we will see later, gay clubs, because more open to experimentation in clothing and lifestyle, were often important 'punk places' in the early days. In addition, several early punk pioneers were openly gay, bisexual or transgendered and this formed part of the culture. For example, early audiences witnessed the slow but very public transformation of Wayne into Jayne County.

Some early punks, following David Bowie, were bending gender long before the bands of the early 1980s who are famed for this. And, if gay spaces proved a hospitable refuge for the early punks, the punk world reciprocated by affording a safe space for the expression of different sexualities and aspects of gay culture (George 1995; Marshall 2006). Again, however, this is less a clue as to the origin of punk, more a reflection of its open and critical nature qua expressive space. Punk was no more a gay liberation movement than a feminist or class movement but elements of its world did take shape in gay spaces and it reciprocated by affording space to diverse sexual expression. In this way it was shaped by emergent sexual cultures.

Race

Dick Hebdige (1988) makes race central to his account of subculture. He observes the existence of (predominantly) black subcultures, both in the UK context and overseas, and notes their influence upon (predominantly) white subcultures in the UK. First-wave skinheads appropriated ska and Motown, for example, and to some extent also the image of the Jamaican rude boy. Similarly, the beats appropriated jazz and its 'cool'. Black music and subcultures have proved very attractive to whites, Hebdige argues, because they articulate opposition to inequities which white working-class youths themselves experience, albeit in different contexts and forms, and they do so both with style and from a clear position of disadvantage and exploitation – a status which enjoys kudos in the context of resistance. This appropriation of black by white sub-cultures isn't always evident, he continues. It is absent in 'glam rock', for example. But it is evident in the case of punk. His argument in relation to punk is peculiar, however.

It is easy to identify elements of black, particularly Rastafarian and reggae influence in punk; from the Clash's early reggae cover versions and appropriation of the argot of 'rude boys' to the use of the Rastafarian concept of 'Babylon' in such songs as the Ruts' 'Babylon's Burning'. Hebdige, however, focuses upon the differences:

> Reggae and punk were audibly opposed. Where punk depended on the treble, reggae relied on the base. Where punk launched frontal assaults on the established meaning systems, reggae communicated through ellipsis and allusion ... the two forms were rigorously, almost wilfully segregated ... (1988: 68)

Perversely, he interprets this as evidence in support of his claim. Punk style, he suggests, developed 'in antithesis to its apparent sources':

> To use a term from semiotics, we could say that punk includes reggae as a 'present absence' – a black hole around which punk composes itself. (*ibid.*)

In the absence of any supporting evidence or further argument this is an absurd claim. Marked differences between punk and reggae, assuming that punks weren't rebelling against reggae (they weren't), suggest a lack of influence between the two. Or, rather, given that there actually is evidence of *some* influence, it would be more appropriate to argue that some punks borrowed some elements from Jamaican culture while others did not.

Hebdige's literary semiotics, which abstracts punk, as a style, from the network of actors whose interactions gave rise to that style, makes it very difficult for him to capture what is going on. Had he conceptualised punk as emerging within a network he could have recognised the diversity of backgrounds and influences of those involved. Some had grown up among black communities and absorbed elements of their subcultures but many had not and were much more influenced by other sources, such as the glam rock of David Bowie and the New York Dolls. In addition, he might have explored the contexts which brought punks into contact with reggae, such as Don Letts's widely documented DJ sets at seminal punk club, the Roxy, which drew heavily upon reggae (because few punk records existed), and the Rock Against Racism gigs of the late 1970s, which often brought punk and reggae bands and audiences together and which raised issues of racial politics within the punk world (Gilroy 1992; Goodyer 2009; Street 2012).

Furthermore, a focus upon networks would have allowed Hebdige to consider that at least some appropriations were reflexively chosen. When the Clash were considering including reggae numbers in their set, for example, they consulted their friends:

> we went to the pub with the Pistols to discuss it. They didn't think it was such a great idea but we could see the potential to combine it with what we were doing to make something powerful. (Paul Simonon, cited in Gilbert 2005: 134)

Gilbert (*ibid.*: 136) adds that this appropriation might also have been informed by the group's desire to distance themselves from the racist tag which their first single, 'White Riot', had unintentionally invited.

Finally, Hebdige's account obscures the widely observed fact that, while some white punks valued elements of black culture, there is little evidence of participation by black youths in punk, at least prior to Rock Against Racism and the Two-Tone ska-punk hybrid that formed in punk's wake. Moreover, as Gary Clarke (1990) notes, Hebdige is very selective in his discussion of race, focusing more or less exclusively upon Jamaicans and reggae, but omitting Asians and their musical forms, for example, and overlooking racism in white subcultures. Many subcultures have involved strong and explicitly racist elements and this was particularly evident in the 1970s, when the National Front was on the ascendency. Several mainstream punk bands attracted far-right elements in their audiences, with varying degrees of complicity on their own part, and while some mobilised against racism in the context of Rock Against Racism others embraced racist and even fascist agendas.

Crisis

The second explanation I will consider is that punk was a response to economic, political and social crisis. Bruce Dancis (1978) advocates this argument, as does Dick Hebdige (1988), who adds an interesting twist:

> Punks were not only directly *responding* to increasing joblessness, changing moral standards, the rediscovery of poverty, the Depression, etc., they were *dramatising* what had come to be called 'Britain's decline' ... punks appropriated the rhetoric of crisis which had filled the airwaves and the editorials throughout the period and translated it into tangible and visible terms ... The various stylistic ensembles adopted by the punks were undoubtedly expressive of genuine aggression, frustration and anxiety. But these statements ... were cast in a language which was ... current. (87, emphasis in original)

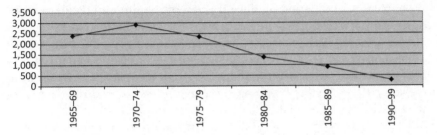

Figure 3.2 Number of strikes in the UK (1965–99; yearly averages)
(*source:* Office for National Satisics 1999)

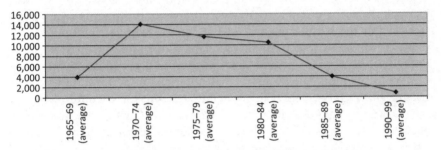

Figure 3.3 Days lost to strikes in the UK (1965–99; yearly averages)
(*source:* Office for National Statistics 1999)

This is an interesting and astute observation which explains, in some part, how and why punk came to symbolise crisis for both its apologists and critics. Furthermore, it hints at why some of those suffering the worst effects of the crisis might have identified with punk and felt that it spoke for them. However, crisis does not suffice to explain punk.

There was a crisis. On the economic front, unemployment had reached unprecedented levels and, defying the 'laws' of Keynesian economic theory, this was combined with record levels of inflation; a state of affairs which forced the government to seek a bail-out from the International Monetary Fund. On the political front this generated a post-1945 peak in levels of industrial action, whether measured in numbers of strikes or numbers of days lost to strikes (see Figures 3.2 and 3.3), and this cascaded as the Conservative government failed to manage a national miners' strike in 1974, prompting them, first, to declare a state of emergency, and, second, to call an early election (which they lost).

At the same time the campaign of the Provisional Irish Republican Army had gathered pace and spread to the British mainland, resulting in bomb attacks in Birmingham and Guilford in 1974 which killed twenty-six people and left many more injured. Meanwhile, the National

Front were accumulating significant levels of support and regularly demonstrating and recruiting in the centres of many major cities, fuelling already existing racial tensions, which spiked in the Notting Hill riots of 1976 (Gilroy 1992). The peace and love of the late 1960s had given way to a new culture of conflict and aggression, a trend further manifest, in the early 1970s, by the bombing campaign of the Angry Brigade and, in the mid 1970s, by escalating levels of football hooliganism.

These crisis conditions and the frustration they generated were explored and articulated in any number of early punk songs. The Clash's 'White Riot', which was famously written after members of the band found themselves caught up in the Notting Hill riots, is an obvious example. Chelsea's 'Right to Work', an anti-union song, is another. In this respect the social upheaval of the 1970s clearly shaped punk. But many of the same objections that I raised to the youth alienation thesis apply here too. Crisis provided inspiration and provocation for songwriters in the punk world but it does not explain the formation of that world. Punk's pioneers did not gravitate together on account of shared views and feelings regarding the crisis. They appear to have had markedly different views about it, including, on the behalf of many, indifference. What brought them together was music.

Aesthetic frustration

A further 'strain' which is often cited as an explanation of punk involves popular music. It is commonly acknowledged that the birth of rock 'n' roll marked a watershed in popular culture (Melly 2008). It was unlike anything that had gone before, exciting teenagers and terrifying their parents in equal measure. Furthermore, from skiffle in the 1950s, which had young working-class men making and buying instruments in their droves, through to the boy-next-door appeal of the Beatles, rock and pop encouraged both participation in music making and identification with performers. Young people felt that pop and rock were *their* musical forms, made by and for them. By the mid 1970s, however, as the innovative glam rock of David Bowie and Marc Bolan gave way to pale imitations, pop music began to stagnate. The mainstream became stodgy and saccharine while the underground was overtaken by progressive ('prog') rock, a form perceived by many would-be punks as pompous, boring and divorced from the experiences of young pop audiences.

The vices and virtues of prog remain an issue of contention in some punk circles but there is a general agreement that, whatever its virtues, it abandoned key values of pop music. It was not music by and for 'people like us'. It was complex in structure. Its musicians were accomplished and their equipment both sophisticated and beyond the financial reach of most. Moreover, though experimental in ways which were attractive to some would-be punks and post-punks, compositions were often grandiose and abstract. They shunned the three-minute format of the rock 'n' roll single in favour of lengthier compositions, sometimes clustered in 'movements' and running across whole albums, aspiring to the format of opera and classical music. And they drew upon literary and academic themes which were unfamiliar to many. 'Saturday Night and I Just Got paid'[2] gave way to 'In the Wake of Poseidon'[3] and 'Tales from Topographic Oceans'.[4]

This state of affairs was a clear cause of frustration for some, including many of those who would go on to pioneer UK punk. Many note how bored and frustrated they had become with the music of their day, prior to punk:

> It was so boring, and apathetic, and nothing going on, and it was frustrating ... I wanted something of my own I could listen to. And I couldn't get anything to listen to that my parents didn't have in their record collection. I didn't want that; I wanted something that was mine. The only way we could do it was by doing it ourselves. (Rat Scabies, in Gimarc 2005: back cover)

> Musically [the mid 1970s] was just dreadful ... appalling ... dominated by real second-ratedness. All the great Sixties heroes had disintegrated into drugs or to nothing. I stopped listening to English music ... even [US music] was getting boring. (Tony Wilson, in Robb 2006: 97)

Lest this sound like post hoc rationalisation, similar grievances are to be found in the archives of the music press for this time, especially in the underground. Contributors to the US zines, *CREEM* and *Who Put the Bomp!*, as Simon Reynolds (2011) notes, for example, regularly called for a return to proper rock 'n' roll values. It was in the latter that musical journalist, Lester Bangs, published his polemic, 'James Taylor Marked for Death', a scathing attack upon what he saw as the betrayal of rock 'n' roll by the musicians of his day (reproduced in Bangs 1987). And this was only one of many articles in which Bangs and others expressed such views.

To give another example, the editorial for the July 1975 issue of the *Hot Flash*, a Manchester-based zine whose associate editor, Martin Hannett, was to become a mover and shaker in the city's punk and post-punk worlds, reads:

> From a variety of pressures – commercial, artistic, historical – ROCK MUSIC has lost the cultural dynamism that steamhammered the 60s and early 70s. ROCK CHANGED SOCIETY ... Now, far too often, the music squeaks in falsetto for a decaying aristocracy of greasy management and gilded

superstars, or mumbles incoherently to cloistered coteries of musicians and self appointed experts jealously guarding their exclusivity ... So where does The Hot Flash come in? We believe it's time to open up a window and let some air into the room; to demystify the scene, bridge the gulf between audience and performers, and have some laughs along the way. (cited in Lee 2002: 111, emphases in original)

Others were predicting the revolution that Hot Flash called for:

The Big show will vanish ... I think the political thing is a possibility. I'm thinking of someone who's 16 who is going to start saying 'Look, all this stuff these bands do with these huge PAs and lights, that's not where it is at. It's down to the people. And I'm going to get out my acoustic guitar and sing revolutionary songs in pubs, working-men's clubs and factories.' (Peter Jenner, cited in Laing 1985: 6)

That is not exactly what happened. The boy was 17 and he didn't reach for his acoustic guitar. He cut his hair short, in a protest against hippies, dyed it green and, ironically, given Peter Jenner's early involvement with them, scrawled 'I Hate' across his Pink Floyd T-shirt. However, punk is in some part both called for and predicted in such pre-punk outbursts.

Later in this chapter I will criticise the strain model that this explanation of punk, along with the previous two, relies upon. Presently, however, note that although frustration at saccharine pop and prog rock are recurrent themes in the biographies of the pioneers and clearly part of the story of punk, the musical context of the mid 1970s was not quite as barren as has been suggested. There were alternatives to prog within the musical underground. More importantly, it was as much positive identification with these alternatives as hostility towards prog and the mainstream that energised the formation of the punk world. An interest in alternative music and fashion, prior to punk, and a heightened interest in music and fashion generally, are striking features in the biographies of many early punks. Indeed, it has been suggested that these alternatives belong squarely within the story of punk. I consider this claim in the next section.

Pockets of noise, violence, androgyny and protest

Music journalists, Jon Savage (2011) and Simon Reynolds (2011), both argue that punk was preceded by a variety of what Savage calls 'pockets of noise, violence, androgyny and protest', each inspired by many of the same frustrations with popular music as punk, and that it drew upon and was inspired by these pockets. UK punk was the latest in a string of attempts to reclaim the rock 'n' roll spirit:

when you delve into punk's prehistory, it becomes clear that punk was a long time a-comin. Finally achieving lift-off after a drawn out process of damp squibs and false starts that dragged on for a good seven years, punk really ought not to have been a big shock.

How something so incremental and rehearsed became a Year Zero Event is hard to reconstruct in hindsight. (Reynolds 2011: 240)

The precursor most often referred to in the literature is the musical world which formed around New York's CBGB nightclub in 1974–75 and which was itself christened 'punk' in a zine of that name. This manifestation of punk differs from the London-based manifestation in important respects but there are parallels and there was a clear channel along which influence could pass. It is sometimes suggested that UK punk was sparked and shaped by this (slightly) earlier US version. I will use this claim to frame my discussion in what follows.

CBGB opened in 1973, quickly becoming a magnet for bands who, contrary to the house rules of most other New York clubs, wanted to play their own material. Among them were several who would later be identified as punk (e.g. Suicide, Wayne County, Television, Patti Smith, Talking Heads, Blondie and the Ramones), and who, through their common involvement at CBGB, shared audiences and began to influence and form ties with one another. Notwithstanding stylistic differences between some a collective identity began to emerge.

This identity became a specifically 'punk' identity when the CBGB bands, along with the Stooges and the MC5 (both from Detroit), were named as such by Legs McNeil, John Holstrom and Ged Dunn, in their fanzine, *Punk*, which ran for fifteen issues between 1976 and 1979. The term 'punk' had first been used in relation to music in *CREEM*, to refer to bands who were rejecting what music journalists perceived to be the polish and pretension of contemporary music trends in preference for a stripped-down, energetic and raw style. It was a derogatory term in US usage at the time because of its homosexual connotation but, perhaps because of this, the authors of *Punk* magazine embraced it.

The extent of the influence of the CBGB bands upon the sound of the early UK punks is difficult to discern. Pistols bassist, Glen Matlock, acknowledges the influence of Richard Hell's 'Blank Generation' upon 'Pretty Vacant' (Matlock 1996), and Hell's early band, Television, cultivated a look based on ripped clothing and spiky hair which was very similar to the style adopted (slightly later) by many UK punks. Moreover, along with the New York Dolls (who slightly pre-date the CBGB scene but became involved in it) and the Ramones, Hells's later bands, the Heartbreakers (formed with ex-New York Dolls, Jerry Nolan and Johnny Thunders) and the Voidoids, would not sound out of place on a compilation of early UK punk.

The time gap between events at CBGB and those in London is small, however. Combined with the big geographical separation and the fact that very few recordings of any New York bands were available until mid 1976 this makes the likelihood of significant influence slim. The Ramones' first LP had a huge impact on many London punks, for example, with Sid Vicious spending whole evenings trying to play along to it, but it wasn't released until April 1976, by which point the Sex Pistols had begun to make their mark, Buzzcocks had formed, and Mick Jones and Tony James were experimenting with London SS. Patti Smith's *Horses* had been released several months earlier and her iconoclasm had excited many proto-punks in the UK. However, there is little suggestion of her slower, arty and poetic style in early UK punk.

These time–space factors were short-circuited, to some extent, by the Sex Pistols' manager, Malcolm McLaren. He met the New York Dolls in 1971 at a New York fashion show, subsequently supplying some of their clothing, and he returned briefly to New York in February 1975 to manage them, during which time he visited CBGB, met the New York punks and found himself particularly impressed by Richard Hell, whose short spiky hair and ripped T-shirts resonated with the boutique owner. McLaren was in a position to broker between the emerging punk world of New York and that which started to take shape in London in late 1975, spearheaded by his very own Sex Pistols. Indeed, he invited both Richard Hell and David Johansen (of the New York Dolls) to front the Sex Pistols (pre John Lydon). Only so much could flow through this relatively thin channel, however, especially as McLaren's involvement in band management was very new at this time and his interests were more focused upon clothing and fashion than music.

The influence of the New York Dolls, the Stooges, the MC5 and the Velvet Underground on the UK punks is much less equivocal. McLaren was bowled over by the Dolls and wanted 'his' band to sound like them. Not that they needed persuading. Steve Jones, in particular, was a fan. Likewise, when Mick Jones and Tony James advertised for a drummer and guitarist for London SS, in July of 1976, they explicitly cited the Dolls as an influence, along with the Stones and Mott the Hoople (Gilbert 2009: 61). Meanwhile, up in Manchester, Steven Morrissey, who would become a key figure in Manchester's punk world, was president of the Dolls' UK fan club. When writing one of many letters of this period, in this case passing opinion on the Pistols' first gig in Manchester, he explicitly drew comparisons with the Dolls, the Heartbreakers (featuring ex-Dolls) and Iggy Pop (of the Stooges). Indeed, it was a comparison with the Stooges in the Pistols' first major gig review, in the *NME*, that prompted many in Manchester to check them out. This was part of the lure for Pete Shelley and Howard Devoto, for example, who travelled from Manchester to London to see the Pistols (twice) within a week of reading the review:

> that was one of the reasons we'd gone to London because they played a Stooges number, and it was an immediate reference point. Nobody else played the Stooges and suddenly here was this band, and we'd been fumbling around trying to play a few numbers off Raw Power ... (Howard Devoto, cited in Lee 2002: 126)

When they arranged for the Pistols to come and play in Manchester, several months later (see Chapter 7), the Stooges link was part of the attraction for many of the small number who turned up:

> I read a review of them in the NME back in 1976, which was the first time I'd heard them mentioned. It said that they played a version of No Fun by the Stooges and me being a big fan of theirs since about 1969/70 I thought I've got to check this out. Because my favourite bands prior to punk had been the proto-Punk bands, Velvet Underground, Flaming Groovies, MC5 ... (Jon the Postman, cited *ibid*.: 126)

> We'd heard about them already through the music press, just as a group that did Stooges' cover versions. There was a photo of a guy with short hair and I was wondering what these 'skinheads' were doing covering Stooges' songs, I wasn't really into the idea. I went along thinking I could heckle or something but I was really bowled over. I got my hair cut soon after, I could see that something was happening (Martin Bramah, cited in Ford, 2003: 16)

My point here is not only that the Pistols sounded like and had been influenced by the Stooges. They do sound like them and music journalist, Nick Kent (2010), who both knew Iggy Pop and played briefly with the Pistols in their early days, claims that he tried to push this influence. However, equally significant is the fact that the Stooges, along with the Dolls, the MC5 and the Velvet Underground cultivated a 'taste community' whose members, upon identifying the Pistols with their heroes, were keen to hear these UK punks. The US bands didn't just influence the UK punks, they formed a common reference point and drew UK enthusiasts into a common orbit.

It is also noteworthy that this enthusiasm inspired the formation of proto-punk bands across the UK. To stick with Manchester, Shelley and Devoto had made various attempts to form bands like their US idols. Indeed, the two met when Devoto placed an advert on their college notice board for musicians inspired by the Velvet Underground's Sister

Ray. Meanwhile, elsewhere in Manchester, two glam rock bands who would later convert to punk, Slaughter and the Dogs and Wild Ram (later renamed Ed Banger and the Nosebleeds), had formed and were beginning to gig. Both claimed a Stooges/MC5 influence, alongside a Bowie/Ronson influence, and the lead singer of Slaughter had green hair!

For the London punks in particular, however, there was another source of influence closer to home. 'Pub rock' involved a small cluster of bands who had carved out a circuit of London pubs to play in. They varied in style but were unified in a self-conscious rejection of the frills and pretentions of both the musical mainstream and the prog underground. They valorised live music, played in small sweaty pubs where the relationship with audiences was immediate, and they too were responsible for cultivating a proto-punk taste community.

Early pub bands were drawn from an older age group to the punks. They were rockers, raised on the R&B of the early 1960s, whose tastes were not catered for by the music industry as it stood and who, as musicians, often found themselves without anywhere to play because a small cabal of promoters, with different tastes and ideas about music, controlled most of London's small venues. As the pubs changed their policies on live music, however, allowing rock bands to play, these rockers found an outlet. They had an alternative to the venues which shunned them. Eventually they formed their own record labels too; the most prominent being Stiff and Chiswick. Furthermore, over time the demographic began to shift, with younger pub bands emerging whose styles, both musical and visual, were more appealing to London's proto-punks; notably, Dr Feelgood, whose sharp and aggressive style impressed and influenced many, and Eddy and the Hot Rods.

Two further pub bands who deserve mention are the 101ers, whose singer, Joe Strummer, would later front the Clash, and Kilburn and the Highroads, whose singer, Ian Dury, has been credited with lending punk certain of its stylistic features. Describing Dury's first encounter with John Lydon's stage performance, Dave Thompson (2009) notes that:

> From the stance to the stare, and all the way down to the razor-blade earrings that Dury had been wearing for years, the king Kilburn might have been looking into a distorted mirror, and it was hard to tell at first whether Rotten, too, was somehow disabled, the way his back twisted and his head twisted, whilst his snarly vocals slurred from a mouth that clearly couldn't be bothered to open too wide.
> Dury was furious. 'They're taking the fucking piss.' (57)

The punk bands and the Pistols in particular avoided playing on the pub circuit initially, according to Savage (1991), because they lacked the musical ability to survive in what was an unforgiving performance environment. They preferred art colleges, where their efforts were treated more charitably and their performance antics and arty gestures appreciated. According to Thompson (2009), however, early punk pioneers were often to be found in the audiences at pub rock gigs, if only because the pub rockers were the closest that many were going to find to live bands playing music that they liked. And when the Sex Pistols began to gravitate away from the art colleges, a number of their early gigs were playing support to such pub bands as the 101ers and Eddy and the Hot Rods. Indeed, in his discussion of 'the London Scene Punk Wise', in the first issue of the UK's first punk fanzine, *Sniffin' Glue*, Mark P includes both Eddy and Hot Rods and fellow pub rock band, Roogalator, among the London punk bands (reproduced in Perry 2009). The boundaries between pub and punk rock were blurred in July 1976.

Beyond pub rock and US punk, Savage (2011) identifies a number of further proto-punk 'pockets', including: late 1960s US garage-psychedelia, which was popularised in the UK musical underground in the early 1970s by Lenny Kaye's *Nuggets* compilation; Krautrock, an experimental synthesiser-based form of music hailing from Germany, which was popular among a number of punk's UK pioneers; and, as noted earlier, reggae, which some punks in racially mixed neighbourhoods had grown up listening to. Finally, we should not discount mainstream influences. The cover versions played by the Sex Pistols in their early performances suggests a Mod influence, for example, and the glam rock of David Bowie, Roxy Music and Marc Bolan had a huge influence.

The 'pockets' identified by Savage and Reynolds do not explain punk but they hint at various mechanisms involved in its emergence. On one level, the excitement they generated was a stimulus to many would-be punks, inciting them to want to make music. On a further level, many of these pockets directly influenced the form which punk music took and those which didn't, such as Krautrock and reggae, were very influential on the first wave of post-punk (see Chapter 8). Most importantly, however, the tastes and enthusiasm cultivated by these pockets and the events, stalls and shops which emerged to cater for such tastes were 'foci' (Feld 1981, 1982) which pulled would-be punks into the same orbit, enabling them to meet, form ties and start their own bands. As I will argue in the next chapter, this process of network formation was crucial to punk's emergence.

In addition to the musical undercurrents that influenced punk and post-punk, a number of writers have identified links with trends in other arts and in particular with Situationism, a European art and political movement whose members sought to create objects and events ('situations') which would shock audiences into questioning what they took for granted in everyday life (Marcus 2001; Plant 1992). There is some evidence for this. Much early punk artwork and performance echoes Situationism and there are identifiable lines of connection. Jamie Reid, a friend of Sex Pistols' manager, Malcolm McLaren, who designed many early Pistols' record sleeves and promotional posters also published the first English-language anthology of Situationist writing and founded his own Situationist press (Suburban Press). And both McLaren and Clash manager, Bernard Rhodes, were interested in Situationism. McLaren visited Paris with Reid in 1968, for example, in the immediate aftermath of uprisings in which the Situationists were involved (McLaren and Reid had instigated a sit-in at their own art college shortly before this). Likewise in Manchester, Tony Wilson is said to have issued many of the bands whom he signed to Factory Records with an anthology of Situationist writings. The name of the Haçienda nightclub was taken (by Joy Division manager, Rob Gretton) from this book. Furthermore, Wilson borrowed 'Durutti Column' from a Situationist poster, to name a band he managed, and borrowed the Situationist idea of an artwork which destroys other artworks for their first album sleeve – *The Return of the Durutti Column* had a sandpaper sleeve which, Wilson claimed, would destroy any other records it was stacked next to.

However, the younger, less 'arty' musicians with whom these agitators worked weren't always as impressed by continental art movements and philosophy. John Lydon, who is often held to have been closer to Jamie Reid than most, is forthright:

> All the talk about French Situationists being associated with punk is bollocks. It's nonsense. Now that really is coffee table book stuff ... nonsense for arty French students. (Lydon 2003: 3)

Similarly, numerous accounts suggest that Wilson met with bemusement and derision from most when handing out his 'little green book'. And he enjoyed a degree of ironic detachment from his own adherence:

> Wilson, a Situationist? Give me a break. He was just a fan. Been lucky enough to score acid at university from a couple of guys who were translators of [leading Situationists] Vaneigem and Debord. Connected with and fell for the sheer fun of it. And of course bored all his friends rigid with this shit, including giving them this book as a welcome-aboard present. (Wilson 2002: 18)

This is not to deny that Wilson was indeed a 'fan' nor that he, Reid, Rhodes, McLaren and others perceived punk through a Situationist lens and used their influence to feed Situationist ideas into it. As I argued with respect to politics above, however, this only amounted to one voice within the expressive space of the punk world and the success of these 'agitators' in persuading others of their cause was uneven at best.

Strain theories and micro-mobilisation contexts

Attempts to explain punk by reference to the alienation of working-class youth, crisis or frustration at the state of popular music each suffer a common problem. Sociologists established many years ago that strains and frustrations do not explain even explicit political uprisings because such strains are ubiquitous and political mobilisation is not, and because no correlation can be found between deterioration in social conditions and increases in protest (Crossley 2002; McAdam *et al.* 1988). Indeed, protest often increases as conditions improve. Feeling frustrated at something does not automatically trigger action. Many people feel frustrated without doing anything, prompting the sociological question of why and how some people, in some contexts, do. This objection applies equally to the idea that punk might be explained by the excitement generated by the pockets of innovation and rebellion referred to above. Excitement is not action and we need to explain how the former was translated into the latter in the context of the birth of punk.

To properly explain collective action we must attend to its 'micro-mobilisation context' (McAdam *et al.* 1988); that is, to the process whereby mobilisation was achieved in a specific time–space through the interactions of specifiable actors. We must abandon loose and abstract generalisations in favour of a more concrete focus. Doing this, moreover, will address a further problem in the accounts considered above; namely, that the conditions they point to affected huge numbers of people across the UK when punk started and for several months remained localised within a small area of London. Why not Manchester, Liverpool or a small fishing village in the Scottish Highlands?

I explore punk's micro-mobilisation in Chapters 5–6. In the next section of this chapter I want to consider another factor which has figured strongly in post-strain sociological theories of collective action: opportunity. I am not convinced that this played a big role in relation to punk but the idea resonates with the concept of music worlds and we should briefly consider it.

Opportunity structures

In an important paper entitled 'Why 1955?' Richard Peterson (1990) asks why rock 'n' roll took off when it did and not earlier or later. He considers but rejects the idea that it was due to a talented and innovative cohort of artists who happened to come along at that time, arguing that talented and innovative artists can be found in every birth cohort. Likewise, he dismisses the effect of the baby boom, which increased demand for popular music. The baby boomers did not become consumers of music until after the emergence of rock 'n' roll, he argues, so they cannot be a factor in its emergence.

Instead, he argues that the mid 1950s saw a temporary break in the domination exercised over the recording industry by an oligopoly of conservatively inclined record companies. This afforded innovators an opportunity to break through and the result was rock 'n' roll. In 'Why 1955?' Peterson explains this temporary break by reference to a series of interconnected changes in law and technology. For example, the shift from shellac to vinyl records in the late 1940s opened up the possibility of mail order distribution, because vinyl records were tougher, thereby boosting the trade of small, independent record labels who previously lacked affordable means of getting their product to customers. Independent labels were important, in turn, because they were inclined to sign up more innovative acts in an effort to carve out a niche for themselves. In addition, legal changes allowed the number of radio stations to grow and loosened the control which the major record companies exercised over radio play lists, affording the independent labels greater marketing opportunities. And this process was further enhanced by the fact that new radio stations, like independent labels, were seeking out new and innovative music to make a niche for themselves. Rock 'n' roll emerged when it did, according to Peterson, because it was championed by independent labels and radio stations who themselves enjoyed greater opportunities for success in the mid 1950s.

This argument builds upon earlier work in which Peterson and David Berger (1975) demonstrate an inverse relationship between innovation and concentration of ownership within the music industry. Oligopoly is the industry norm, they argue, and it tends to stifle innovation because dominant firms are inclined to play safe, only releasing songs which fall within narrow musical parameters that are assumed to have broad demographic appeal. Occasionally, however, smaller, independent companies, pursuing their own market niche through new and innovative acts, manage to break through, temporarily dislodging this conservative oligopoly.

This argument predicts unmet demand in music markets. Whatever the role of the music industry in shaping tastes, Peterson and Berger argue, stifling innovation in production creates dissatisfied audiences on the look-out for something different. This is evidenced by the enthusiasm and speed with which such innovations as rock 'n' roll are embraced.

Peterson and Berger test their thesis by looking at the US top 10 between 1948 and 1973. For each year they identify two indicators of market concentration:

1 The number of firms and labels represented in the top 10.
2 The proportion of hits released by the four and eight biggest firms respectively (the so-called four-firm and eight-firm ratios).

Alongside a content analysis of lyrics, they identify five indicators of musical innovation – the number of:

1 records which make the Top 10;
2 number 1 records;
3 new artists (i.e. artists who have not previously charted) in the Top ten;
4 established artists in the Top 10; and
5 cover versions in the Top 10.[5]

If they are right, they hypothesise, then increases in innovation will be correlated with decreases in concentration. This is what they find. Specifically, innovation rises and concentration decreases in the mid 1950s, at the point where rock 'n' roll took off.

This thesis has been subject to extensive retesting and critique (e.g. Burnett 1992; Christianen 1995; Dowd 2004, 2007; Lopes 1992; Rothenbuhler and Dimmick 1982). Most critics argue that Peterson and Berger are correct with respect to the 1950s but that the major record labels ('majors') learned from their mistakes during this period and changed their strategy in a way which confounds the thesis for the late 1960s onwards. Although they profited from rock 'n' roll, it is argued, the majors realised that they had been slow to catch on and could have missed out. Consequently, they began to build a range of different types of relationship with smaller labels, which allowed them to keep their ear closer to the ground and profit more immediately and successfully from innovations, without having to take too many risks or incur too many losses. In some cases they set up their own smaller labels, which operated relatively independently. In others they struck distribution deals with independent labels, sometimes securing the right to transfer successful artists to their own labels, blurring the distinction between major and independent labels and vastly increasing the ratio of labels to (underlying) firms. This had the effect of decoupling concentration and innovation such that, while the critics find evidence of re-oligopolisation in the music industry from the 1960s onwards, as predicted by Peterson and Berger, their studies find no evidence of the corresponding reduction in innovation which Peterson and Berger also predict.

I would add three methodological observations to this critique. First, with the possible exception of their content analyses, Peterson and Berger's indicators of innovation are better described as indicators of chart turnover. A high number of songs in the chart in any one year is not necessarily indicative of innovation because the songs may all emulate an established template. Likewise, new acts may simply replicate old acts and are not necessarily innovative.

Second, in so far as Peterson and Berger do identify innovation their analysis is less focused upon its emergence than upon its breakthrough into the mainstream pop world, which is only one of several (pop) music worlds. Apart from an early paper on jazz by Peterson (1967), they do not consider underground music worlds, which are often important spaces of innovation, some of which later break into the mainstream. While the industry conditions that Peterson and Berger examine may help to explain such breakthroughs, they are looking in the wrong place for the source of innovation.

In addition, note that the reservoir of 'unmet demand' referred to by Peterson and Berger might be met in underground worlds whose participants not only prefer the music therein but also cherish its underground status. Sociologists and music journalists have repeatedly found evidence of this from early studies of jazz (Riesman 1950), through more recent studies of club culture (Thornton 1995), indie (Fonarow 2006), hip hop (Jeffries 2011) and dubstep:

> whenever I ventured into the genre's forums ... I kept bumping into people who said it was dead ... When I say 'dead', what I mean – of course – is that it's topping the charts, selling out arenas, putting out compilations (here comes *100% Dubstep Vol 2*), conquering America and shaping some of the biggest pop records around ... It's the kind of 'dead' that most people could live with. (Jonze 2011: 4)

I do not have space to discuss the whys and wherefores of this preference. It is no doubt complex and multifaceted. But it should alert us to the dangers of focusing upon the top 10 alone when exploring and seeking to explain musical innovation.

Third, while 'Why 1955?' defines opportunities for innovation broadly the exclusive focus upon industry concentration in the earlier paper only captures one element of opportunity. It ignores the role of the media (e.g. radio playlists), for example, which is crucial if innovations are to diffuse and breakthrough into the mainstream (see Chapter 7). Furthermore, even 'Why 1955?' doesn't capture every significant element in the opportunity structure. It ignores the impact of cultural policy at both local and national levels, for example, which Street (2012) and Cohen (2007) have each shown to have significant effects.

Given these criticisms, it would be inappropriate to seek an explanation of punk in the concentration ratios of the music industry in the mid 1970s. At best such considerations might tell us something about how punk broke into the mainstream. Punk did break into the mainstream, however. Much of its impact was on account of this. And post-punk was, in some part, a response to this mainstreaming. For these reasons it would be interesting to briefly consider the possible role of opportunity structures in punk's mainstream breakthrough in the mid 1970s.

According to Laing, punk emerged at a time when ownership and control within the music industry was highly concentrated:

> In 1976 two-thirds of the British record market was shared between six major transnational companies … not only did they originate recordings by signing artists and putting them into the studio, they also manufactured discs and tapes and then distributed and promoted them to shops. Each controlled three of the four main aspects of the record business, while EMI had a stake in the fourth – retailing – through its chain of HMV record shops. (1985: 1)

Furthermore, he notes that these figures do not include the role of the majors in the manufacture and distribution of the products of smaller labels. When this is taken into consideration 'it was estimated that EMI handled about one-third of all records sold in Britain during the mid-1970s' (*ibid*). This conflicts with what we would expect at the point of an innovation such as punk, on the basis of Peterson and Berger's work.

That punk emerged in the context of oligopoly would not surprise critics of Peterson and Berger, such as Dowd (2004, 2007) and Lopes (1992). As noted above, they believe that the majors changed strategies in the late 1960s, working with a proliferating number of smaller labels who took on the risks of signing innovative acts. This begs the question: did the increase in number of such labels immediately prior to punk, stimulate a more aggressive search for new talent and innovation from which punk benefited?

To test this idea I surveyed the number of both labels and new (to the charts) labels represented in the UK Top 40 every year between 1965 and 1984 (using McAleer 2009 as my source). This survey shows an increase in labels in general, as Lopes and Dowd predict, but this increase falters towards the end of the 1970s, at the point when punk was taking off.

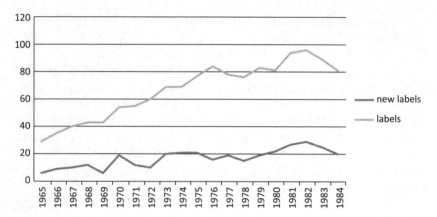

Figure 3.4 Number of labels and new (to the charts) labels represented in the UK Top 40 (1965–84)
(*source:* figures derived from McAleer 2009)

In addition, in contrast to what one would predict on the basis of the theories of both Peterson and Berger and their critics, many of the first-wave punk bands signed to major labels: e.g. the Sex Pistols to EMI, the Clash to CBS and the Banshees to Polydor. The Damned were an exception. They signed to the pioneering pub-rock indie, Stiff. And Buzzcocks extended punk's DIY ethos when they released their seminal EP (*Spiral Scratch*) on their own label. As I discuss in Chapter 10, this triggered a massive boom in independent labels. However, the first wave of mainstream punk was a major-label affair.

Interestingly, moreover, Figure 3.4 suggests that the indie boom triggered by *Spiral Scratch* did not impact significantly upon the mainstream. There is a slight increase in new labels during the late 1970s and early 1980s but it is only slight and we cannot read too much into it given the general upward gradient and bumpiness of the trend over the whole period.

However, following Peterson and Berger, I also surveyed the number of acts and new acts represented in the Top 40 over this same period and my findings, represented in Figure 3.5, are interesting. We see a slump at the end of the 1960s both in number of acts in general making the chart and also in the number of new acts making it, followed by a rise in both in the mid 1970s (although the percentage of new artists among all charting artists remains stable). The mid 1970s rise begins too early to be explained by punk but the late 1960s slump bears out the subjective experience of many proto-punks, that music was in a slump in the early 1970s (turnover certainly slowed), and the rise in 1974–75 may indicate

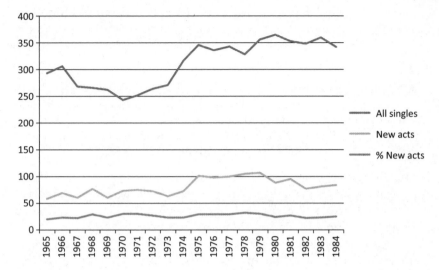

Figure 3.5 Acts, new acts and percentage of all acts which are new in the UK Top 40 (1965–84)

(*source:* figures derived from McAleer 2009)

a response on behalf of the record companies, seeking to find new acts to revitalise the market. If so, given its timing, this would have opened up opportunities for punk bands.

Furthermore, my earlier discussion indicates that some music journalists were becoming frustrated with the pop world in the mid 1970s and were looking for 'the next big thing'. This too may have translated into increased opportunities (for mainstream exposure) for the emerging punk world. This is very speculative but if true it would be important.

Fagin meets the Antichrist

The final theory that I will consider centres upon the contributions of two individuals: Malcolm McLaren and John Lydon ('Johnny Rotten'). McLaren claimed responsibility for punk on various occasions, calling it his invention. The narrative of the first Sex Pistols' film, the *Great Rock 'n' Roll Swindle*, largely tells the story from this point of view, for example, and its soundtrack LP includes a song, 'God Save the Queen (Symphony)', in which McLaren explains how he did it: 'Find yourself four boys ... make sure they hate each other ... make sure they can't play' and so on. Like a latter-day Fagin, he gathered urchins from the streets and sent them out to do his work.

It's not clear to what extent McLaren actually believed this but it per-
sists to this day as an explanation of punk and there is a credible theory,
postulated by George Melly, regarding the role of the entrepreneur in
promoting musical innovation:

> A local enthusiasm for some form of music gradually crystallises around
> a particular group or artist. At this point an entrepreneur, sometimes
> a local enthusiast with an eye to the big chance, sometimes an outsider
> led towards the scene by apparently fortuitous accident, recognises the
> commercial potential [and brings it to fruition]. (2008: 41)

In an interesting twist, Melly's discussion centres upon Larry Parnes
(manager of Billy Fury and Tommy Steele), who was a hero and role
model to McLaren. Numerous associates describe his admiration for
and identification with Parnes (Macleay 2010; Savage 1991).

The other chief contender for 'the individual who invented punk' is
John Lydon. According to many accounts, punk's first pioneers, the Sex
Pistols, were indistinguishable from the pub and glam bands whom they
emulated until Lydon, with his green hair, 'I hate Pink Floyd' T-shirt and
spiky charisma joined them. Lydon, it is claimed, was the ingredient that
turned pub into punk rock. He was the innovative spark which gave rise
to punk and its charismatic leader:

> without Johnny Rotten, the outsider, firing the starting pistol, bringing a
> certain something that no one can quite put a finger on to an otherwise
> barely happening party, it wouldn't be overstating the case to suggest that
> there'll be no punk movement of any significance in Britain whatsoever.
> (Johnstone 2006: 22–3)

> I know Malcolm McLaren and I know John and believe me, Lydon is the
> original. Malcolm learned so much more from Lydon than Lydon ever
> learned from Malcolm. I love Malcolm, but Lydon was a martyr for his
> generation. He blew away an era past and entered an era about to come
> on us all.
>   [...]

> Lydon ... let an entire generation be themselves. Lydon isn't a pop star,
> he's a fucking religion. Lydon is our Jesus Christ ... (McGee 2006)

Again resonating with such accounts, Melly (2008) has a theory of charisma too. He suggests, however, that this 'magic halo emanating from
objects, people and places which gives them power over and above
their measurable qualities' (43) is less an effect of the person than of
the music and often of the atmosphere of the small-club situation in
which it is performed. Furthermore, he links this to his theory of the
entrepreneur. Speaking of Tommy Steele, for example, he suggests that:

'Parnes and John Kennedy ... recognised his charisma and believed they could exploit it commercially' (*ibid.*: 47). Charisma must be exploited to be effective, in other words, and that is the role of the entrepreneur.

Following the logic of Melly's account we might argue that McLaren needed Lydon (or someone like him), Lydon needed McLaren (or someone like him) and that the emergence of punk required both. I agree but suggest, in addition, that McLaren and Rotten each depended upon a wider network to achieve their magic and that our analysis must focus upon this network. Individuals and their qualities are important to the story of punk and Lydon and McLaren are particularly important. However, they were not the only ones who could have served the function that they did in punk's emergence. Others might have played their roles had circumstances been different. More importantly, it was 'circumstances', for which read social processes and dynamics involving a wider set of people, that gave each the opportunity to play the role that he did. Each capitalised upon a situation which was irreducible to his own actions and intentions and which neither appears to have foreseen. They had the nous and talent to seize upon an opportunity but that opportunity was created for them as an unintended consequence of the interactions of others.

McLaren could only sell what there was to sell and only to punters actively seeking these goods, for example. Furthermore, most accounts suggest that he only became interested in actively managing the Sex Pistols after his above-mentioned trip to New York persuaded him that it might be exciting and profitable to do so. Before this point, his involvement was half-hearted and subordinated to his desire to succeed in fashion. McLaren was made by punk as much as he made it.

In addition, a number of key turning points in punk's history, often attributed to McLaren's cunning, were beyond his control and initially misread and mismanaged by him. The infamous Bill Grundy interview (see Chapter 7), for example, which played a key role in diffusing and popularising punk and which established McLaren's reputation for generating 'cash from chaos' was anything but a part of his master plan. The interview only came about as the result of a last-minute schedule change. It was arranged by EMI. And McLaren was initially furious about the band's behaviour, believing they had wasted an opportunity and possibly put an end to their career. It was only later that he realised what a trick he had pulled.

A similar story holds for Rotten's charisma. Charisma is relative to specific audiences, an effect of interaction between performer and audience. Charismatic figures are often only charismatic to certain audiences, indicating that their charisma depends upon the receptivity of that audience. Rotten's charisma depended for its existence upon an initially very specific audience who were receptive to his unconventional approach. He was a spark but could only create a fire in conjunction with the combustible material which his fellow travellers in the proto-punk world collectively formed. To fans of Iggy Pop he was amazing. To fans of Yes and the Bay City Rollers he was rude and talentless. And of course his performance was not only his performance. He needed a band and also other bands who collectively cultivated and maintained an audience and atmosphere.

Social movement scholars sometimes analyse the pull that movements exert at certain points in time by reference to 'framing' (Crossley 2002). A movement attracts adherents when its message is framed in a way which resonates with pre-existing interests, identities and concerns. The punks' above-mentioned appropriation of the discourse of crisis was a masterstroke in this respect because it allowed them to seem to speak directly to many people's experience. And Rotten's charisma worked in much the same way. He encapsulated something which an initially very small audience identified with. This made him an inspiration and a pioneer but he could only play this role in relation to a network of enthusiasts who identified that something in him, and the story of punk is therefore as much about that network as about Rotten himself.

Conclusion

In this chapter I have discussed strains and inspirations which impacted upon punk's pioneers and also opportunities which may have allowed them to take their innovations into the mainstream. These factors are important but they are general and abstract. They tell us about the broad social conditions in which punk emerged; conditions affecting huge numbers of people who had nothing to do with punk as well as the tiny minority who did. Theories focused upon individuals, such as Rotten and McLaren, help to narrow and concretise our focus to some extent but they pose a different problem. Whatever the qualities of punk's leading personalities they are far from unique and, as such, do not explain punk either. McLaren wasn't the only opportunistic wheeler-dealer in Chelsea in the mid 1970s, let alone in the UK, and Lydon wasn't the only charismatic rebel. To properly explain punk we must look beyond these general background considerations to the microcosm in which punk emerged, its micro-mobilisation context, and to the social mechanisms at work in that context. That is the task of the next three chapters.

Notes

1 The study is problematic because it compares punk album tracks with pop singles. In addition it relies upon content analysis, which ignores the meanings perceived by audiences.
2 The opening line to 'Rip It Up', first recorded by Little Richard in 1956.
3 King Crimson's second LP.
4 Yes's sixth studio LP.
5 It was not uncommon in the 1940s and early 1950s for record companies to immediately release a cover version of one of the songs of their rivals if it was successful.

4

Theorising micro-mobilisation: critical mass, collective effervescence, social networks and social space

In the previous chapter I suggested that whatever strains, inspirations, opportunities and personalities may have played a role in punk's emergence, a full explanation must focus upon its micro-mobilisation context. In this chapter I take a first step towards doing this by outlining a theory of micro-mobilisation which, I will argue in the next chapter, explains the emergence of punk in London between late 1975 and the end of 1976. My argument is that *music worlds emerge as an effect of collective effervescence within a networked critical mass of actors who are defined by shared interests of some sort*. This argument rests upon four claims:

1 The number of potential participants for a collective action must exceed a particular threshold (critical mass) if that action is to be triggered.
2 This is more likely in large concentrated populations, such as big cities, because, all things being equal, potential participants exist in greater numbers within larger general populations.
3 Mass is not sufficient. Members of a mass must be connected, forming a network, and collective action is more likely to succeed where that network has particular properties (specified below).
4 The cultural innovation sometimes involved in collective action (and certainly in the emergence of punk) is not reducible to the individual creativity of those involved but rather entails interaction, mutual influence and mutual stimulation between them, a form of collective creativity which Durkheim (1974) dubs 'collective effervescence'.

This explanation emphasises the agency of the pioneers involved in a music world. They make the world. However, the concepts 'critical mass', 'social network' and 'collective effervescence' identify relational mechanisms beyond the control of those involved, which are also important. They point to the sociological equivalent of a 'chemical reaction', triggered by actors coming together, which constitutes them as a creative collective that is greater than the sum of its parts. They facilitate collective action and also the creative energy constitutive of a music world.

In this chapter I outline these ideas, deferring a discussion of their application to the emergence of the London punk world until Chapter 5. I briefly discuss their significance for post-punk in Chapter 8.

Critical mass

A critical mass of participants is important in the generation of music worlds for reasons of both motivation and resourcing. In relation to motivation it has been argued that an individual's willingness to participate in collective action is sometimes dependent upon the number of others doing so and that different actors have different thresholds in this respect (Granovetter 1978; Schelling 1995). This might mean an upper limit, with some actors withdrawing from an action when too many others become involved. However, we are more concerned with lower limits that individuals like to see exceeded before they will become involved.

This may be a matter of atmosphere. Smaller crowds may fail to generate the buzz necessary to make participation exciting and intrinsically rewarding. It may be a matter of protection. Individuals may feel vulnerable participating in actions that very few others see fit to join. And cross-cutting these two factors, it may be because larger numbers help to generate a feel and situational definition of being part of something exciting and meaningful. Large crowds and 'have you heard' conversations about bands can lend them an extra layer of significance and excitement, a sense that there is more happening than simply a band playing music. That a band or cluster of bands is exciting to some makes them more exciting to others.

This affects bands as well as audiences. Many quickly tire of playing in empty venues. It also affects promoters, managers, venue owners and zine writers, who often have a financial investment in big numbers. Small audiences yield small profits or losses. Even where incentives are not economic, however, it is difficult to remain enthusiastic about performances which generate little perceptible enthusiasm among others.

David Riesman (1950) captures something of this in an early study of a world of 'hot jazz' enthusiasts on a university campus. Meeting other enthusiasts, he argues, affirmed the preferences of those involved, giving them an identity and allowing and encouraging them to further explore their love of jazz, enhancing their experience of it. Collectively they were able to transcend their individual powers, organising gigs and dances and recruiting sufficient audiences to make them successful. Moreover, each became a resource for the others, as they exchanged knowledge, information and records. In addition, competition was an important driver. Status contests, focused upon knowledge of, commitment to and involvement in jazz motivated all involved to invest further in it, increasing its perceived importance and enhancing their experience of it.

The link between resources and critical mass is developed in the work of Gerald Marwell and Pamela Oliver (1993; see also Crossley and Ibrahim 2012; Kim and Bearman 1997; Marwell *et al*. 1988; Oliver *et al*. 1985; Oliver and Marwell 1988). Their work is focused upon very different forms of collective action to those I am analysing and rests upon a number of questionable theoretical assumptions.[1] However, their core claims are important.

They argue that an actor's availability for participation in collective action depends upon their being able to pay whatever costs (e.g. time, money, effort, etc.) are required and their anticipation that the projected benefits of the action (e.g. enjoyment) will outweigh those costs. Sometimes the potential for collective action does not come to fruition because potential participants either cannot afford the costs or feel that they outweigh projected benefits. They feel that it is not worth it.

The formation of a musical world requires that a number of actors buy and learn to play musical instruments, for example, which takes time and effort as well as money. It requires that bands rehearse, putting in the hours and sacrificing time and energy that might be put to other purposes. Furthermore, it requires that rehearsal spaces are sought out and paid for, gigs arranged and promoted, equipment bought or hired and transported, etc. A brief musical performance presupposes a considerable investment of time, effort and money.

As the number of potential participants increases, however, assuming they can pool their resources without reducing individual benefits, the cost–benefit ratio shifts in favour of benefits and therefore action. By pooling resources actors can reduce individual costs, making participation more affordable, more profitable and therefore more likely. The number of participants which switches the ratio in favour of collective action is the 'critical mass' for action according to Marwell and Oliver.

There is no exact figure for critical mass because different actors have different levels of resources to contribute and different levels of interest (objective or subjective)[2] in the outcome. Specifically, Marwell and Oliver envisage 'big investors' who may reduce the number of participants necessary to form a critical mass because they either have a greater interest in an outcome, such that they are prepared to pay more, or have more resources, such that their relative costs are lower. A manager who is prepared to pay for equipment and rehearsal space from their own pocket during a band's early days or a promoter who is prepared to suffer losses on early gigs which young bands themselves could not afford might each qualify as 'big investors' in this sense.

Big investors can be very important in music worlds. However, they can only do so much because roles must often be distributed across different people. Bands usually need skills (a resource) in a variety of instruments, for example, but also different players in possession of those skills. A multi-instrumentalist is no substitute for a full-size band when various instruments must be played simultaneously. Likewise, although the same small pool of musicians may form different combinations for different purposes the need for variety in a music world generally requires a range of different bands, involving different musicians. Finally, the contribution that audiences make must be distributed across a (preferably large) number of them and cannot be concentrated into a small number of super-keen fans.

However, individual costs can be reduced through bigger numbers and the likelihood of collective action thereby increased. Bands will find life easier and more sustainable, for example, if they can find others willing to take on management, promotion and roadie duties, sharing the costs involved. This may be a matter of individuals taking on specified roles but it may equally be a matter of individuals chipping in where they can. The audience member who arranges for the band to play at her local or rehearse at her church hall, is one example; the individual who elects to run a zine, inadvertently taking on a promoting role for a number of bands, is another.

In addition, where multiple bands cluster they often benefit by sharing equipment, knowledge, rehearsal spaces and support slots. A considerable amount of time, money and energy is saved for all involved when bands cooperate in this way. Furthermore, each can help to establish venues and audiences for the others. The first London-based pub rock band, Eggs over Easy, reduced the costs for subsequent bands, for example, by doing the work of persuading landlords and audiences that live rock music in pubs was a good idea. They created a resource (venues and audiences) which other bands could share. This does not preclude

competition between bands but that too, as Riesman's work suggests
(see above), is often an important benefit because it spurs bands on and
encourages them to do what they might not otherwise do; rehearsing
harder, innovating, seeking a distinct sound and identity, etc.

Likewise big audiences: not only do bigger audiences make a greater
contribution to the confidence and enthusiasm of performers, they make
a band more attractive to venues, who will profit from them. And in
some cases, a proportion of that money will find its way back to the
bands, lessening the financial costs they bear in performing, funding the
purchase of better equipment, etc.

In the city

Turning now to the second of the four claims outlined at the outset of
the chapter, Marwell and Oliver (1993) claim that actors with sufficient
levels of interest and the right combination of resources for collective
action are more likely to be found in bigger, concentrated populations.
The logic of this argument mirrors that of sampling in survey research.
If I want a random sample of a population but I also want to capture
significant numbers of a particular minority within that sample (e.g.
drummers), then I need a very big sample because minorities will occur
in a random sample in the proportion in which they occur in the wider
population. If 1 per cent of the population are drummers, for example,
then I cannot hope to get one in my sample if that sample contains fewer
than one hundred people. And so it is in collective action. When those
with the necessary interests and resources comprise a small proportion
of the population they only reach the critical mass necessary for collective action in very big populations. Thus, the search for suitable band
mates is more likely to be successful in the context of a bigger, geographically concentrated population. One may struggle to find a drummer in
a small village but in a larger town the search should be easier and even
more so in a big city.

This claim is problematic. It does not allow for targeted resource
generation. Groups of friends who form bands often decide who will
play what before anyone can play anything, acquiring the skills and
equipment they require from scratch. Bands may form within very
small populations in this way and do not need to rely upon finding
other musicians in the wider population. In addition, the claim rests
upon the problematic assumption that resource holders (e.g. drummers)
are randomly geographically distributed. They are not. Musicians and
music lovers gravitate towards certain places and become concentrated
there. If I wanted to find a drummer, I wouldn't search randomly in

the general population. I would enquire at music and record shops, rehearsal spaces, gigs, etc.

However, the basic point is important and helps us to make sense of the geographical distribution of punk and post-punk. It suggests that most forms of collective action are more likely in large urban centres, the size and diversity of whose populations increase the likelihood that it will contain a critical mass of actors with the required resources and levels of interest to form a music world. We might add, furthermore, that this effect is amplified by feedback. Where critical mass in a city facilitates the formation a music world the city will acquire a reputation for music, which will then attract enthusiasts from further afield, increasing mass in the city and draining it from surrounding areas. As Cohen's (2007) work suggests, even some cities (Liverpool) lose out to others (London) as an effect of musicians migrating in search of opportunities.

These arguments are not so specific as to identify London as the necessary epicentre of punk's emergence nor Manchester, Liverpool and Sheffield as key sites for its subsequent spread and mutation into post-punk. However, they suggest that if something like punk or post-punk was ever going to happen then these are among the likely places where it would.

The importance of population size for music has been noted in a number of the studies considered earlier in this book. Riesman's work on hot jazz (see above), for example, focuses upon the role of the university campus in generating a critical mass of enthusiasts, contrasting this state of affairs with that in the small towns from which some of his enthusiasts came:

> Sometimes these are young men – strikingly enough there are very few hot jazz girls, save in an occasional 'symbiotic' relation to a hot jazz boy – who grew up as somewhat rebellious individuals in a small high school where they stood almost alone in their musical orientation. Then they came to university, they found many other such people and for the first time experienced the security and also the threat of peers who shared their outlook. (1950: 369)

Similarly, when discussing music places in Chapter 2 I noted that Fonarow (2006) observes an association between indie music and university towns, explaining this in terms of the size of their youth populations; that Krenske and McKay (2000) bemoan the limited options for heavy metal in Brisbane, explaining this as an effect of a small population whose subset of metal heads is not big enough to support the diverse range of metal clubs found in other cities; and that Becker (2004) hints at the same idea when he observes that big cities typically have the audiences to support more specialised jazz clubs.

There are many similar arguments about critical mass to be found in the sociological literature, particularly in relation to social movements (e.g. Crossley and Ibrahim 2012; Tilly 1978). Two very relevant studies for our purposes, however, are Judith Blau's (1989) investigation of elite cultural provision and Claude Fischer's (1975, 1982, 1995) investigation of urban subcultures.

Blau observes that while the number of popular cultural facilities, such as cinemas, found in a town grows in a linear fashion as a function of population size, elite facilities (e.g. opera and ballet) manifest a threshold effect. Below a given population size there are none but where the threshold is crossed a city will typically offer several. She explains this by reference to critical mass. Elite facilities are only economically feasible, she notes, where a big enough audience can be found, and given that high-art consumers are a minority, that means only in the largest cities where that minority is large.

Though her focus is elite culture, Blau's argument applies to any cultural form with limited appeal, including underground forms of popular music such as early punk, and so do three of her further observations. First, she notes that the establishment of one elite cultural facility often lowers the costs for subsequent developments, thereby increasingly their likelihood. This happens because the first facility incurs costs of sourcing and establishing a supply of various services and raw materials which subsequent developments can tap into without incurring the same costs. Second, she argues that cultural tastes tend to come in what she calls 'packages'. A taste for alternative music often coincides with a taste for alternative clothing and lifestyles, for example, such that where we find one, we will often find the others. This, she notes, encourages outlets for those tastes to cluster geographically. Finally, she notes that meeting the demand for a minority cultural form through provision of facilities often further increases it by exposing and recruiting neophytes. Punk clubs will usually only emerge where a critical mass of punks are found and demand is sufficient but the existence of punk clubs will generate further demand for punk in the area by recruiting and converting previously uninterested actors.

Fischer's (1975, 1982, 1995) contribution arises in a critique of the often repeated claim that big cities destroy communities. A city is not a community, Fischer argues, but rather a patchwork of many communities, each of which serves the specialised interests, identities and needs of its members. Furthermore, it is only in cities that such specialised communities emerge. There are several reasons for this but population size is central among them because it increases the probability that actors with minority interests will find and hook up with a sufficient number of likeminded alters to form their own 'social world':

> The very numbers of people ... means that they are more likely to reach the 'critical mass' it takes to become worlds unto themselves. (Fischer 1982: 12)

Punks in a big city will converge and form a punk world because they exist in big enough numbers to do so. Punks in small towns will often be isolated and expected to fit in with the general community.

Actors are drawn together by pre-existing similarities in this process, creating a homophilous pattern of interaction but their similarities to one another and also their differences from others are amplified, according to Fischer, as interaction between them generates a distinctive social world. Moreover, homophily is further reinforced as tensions between different co-located worlds drive their members inwards. Identification with one's own world is intensified in the context of hostility to and from other worlds. Of course actors often belong to several different worlds simultaneously, serving, as Simmel (1955) observes, as a point of intersection between them. Nevertheless, levels of intersection between and closure around worlds vary. Some worlds may be relatively insulated from others.

Collective effervescence

The discussion has already moved beyond the idea of critical mass, touching upon the third of the claims I began the chapter with, regarding social networks. 'Critical mass' is a misnomer if 'mass' suggests mere aggregation. A mass only makes a difference if its members: pool and exchange resources, communicate, cooperate, coordinate, etc. If they do not interact and form a network, then their size is irrelevant and they can have no effect. This is why cities are important; not because of their population sizes per se, which are easily matched by the combined populations of a number of smaller towns, but because that population is concentrated into a relatively small geographical area, increasing the likelihood that actors who share interests will come into contact and join forces. In what follows I discuss the importance of networks and connection in more detail. I begin by briefly outlining the creative dynamics of collective effervescence before turning to network structure.

Music worlds are not created from scratch, on the basis of a master plan, even if strategies abound when they begin to take shape. Bands and stylistic innovations take shape within a web of interaction whose participants encourage, stimulate and provoke one another without any sense, initially, of where this is taking them. A pattern of interaction 'catches on' among them which they find fun and exciting, incentivising them to continue and drawing others in. With time and particularly as external bodies become interested they may begin to conceive of what they are involved in as a 'project', orienting to it in a more reflexive and strategic manner, but that is not how things begin.

This hurly-burly of interaction and collective creativity is nicely captured by Durkheim's (1951, 1974) concept of collective effervescence, at least where he uses that concept to think about change.[3] Collective effervescence refers to a transformation in patterns of interaction within a community which stimulates and excites those involved and which breaks down old conventions, generating new ones and also new identities, ideas and values:

> It is in fact in such moments of collective ferment that are born the great ideas upon which civilisations rest. The periods of creation or renewal occur when men for various reasons are led into a closer relationship with each other, when reunions and assemblies are most frequent, relationships better maintained and the exchange of ideas most active. Such was the great crisis of Christendom ... Such were the Reformation and Renaissance ... the Socialist upheavals of the nineteenth century. (Durkheim 1974: 91–2)

Durkheim does not unpack this process in detail but a number of writers have discussed the potentially creative and generative aspect of social interaction; the way in which it can lead participants in unexpected directions, causing them to act and think in new and different ways which surprise them (e.g. Joas 1996; Mead 1967; Merleau-Ponty 1962). One action stimulates another, which stimulates another and so on in a process whose outcome cannot be known in advance and which may carry all involved into new cultural territory.

Of course many interactions and interaction outcomes, whatever their unpredictability, are constrained by conventions and norms which are enforced both externally, by outsiders, and internally, by way of the reflexive self-monitoring and self-control of those involved. However, as Blumer (1969) suggests, these constraints are sometimes temporarily and partially suspended, affording imagination and creativity a greater role and allowing interaction to follow new and innovative paths. Inter-actors play with and combine conventions, transforming them and giving rise to new cultural forms. In many cases these cultural experiments fizzle out, leaving no lasting legacy, but in some cases they gather momentum and acquire traction, drawing in new participants, generating collective identity and instituting change. Collective effervescence gives rise to durable social worlds which make a lasting impact.

Collective effervescence is only possible, however, where actors interact, and the likelihood of it achieving an impact is affected by the properties of the network in which such interactions are embedded and which they reproduce and transform.

Networks and collective action

Whatever the spontaneous and unintended nature of the early phases of the process whereby new and novel worlds emerge it requires coordination. Participants must know when and where events are taking place. Half-formed bands must be able to find suitable members to complete their line ups. And the style and stories which give the world its distinct identity must be diffused. This is only possible if all involved belong to a social network. It is not necessary for everybody to be in direct contact but each must be at least indirectly connected, through third parties. In other words, to use a concept defined in the Introduction, *the network of key participants must comprise a single component.*

Furthermore, coordination is better achieved when information passes quickly through the network, allowing recipients time to respond, and is not subject to the distortion which inevitably arises when messages are relayed through multiple intermediaries. Information about gigs is of little value after the event or when significant details such as location are missing or miscommunicated. Such problems are less likely, all things being equal, when, to use another concept defined in the Introduction, *average path lengths are short.*

Short path lengths are more likely, as Marwell and Oliver note, when a network is either *dense*[4] or *highly degree centralised.*[5] High density shortens path lengths because it involves more ties and thus both more direct connection and more bridges shortening the path between nodes which are not directly connected. High degree centralisation has a similar effect because 'hubs', to which most nodes connect, serve as 'junction boxes', linking everybody to everybody else.

High density has added importance, however, because it tends to increase cooperation and trust (Burt 2005; Coleman 1988, 1990). When actors know that their alters know one another they are aware that breaches of trust and lack of cooperation will earn them a bad reputation which, in turn, may result in them becoming isolated within the network and cut off from important alters. The significance of this will vary according to their dependence upon those alters for valued goods and resources but in dense networks, where most are well connected, their investment in the network is likely to be high and a bad reputation therefore best avoided.

This, in turn, is important because numerous studies of social capital show that cooperation and trust allow actors, both individually and collectively, to act in ways that would not otherwise be possible (Burt 2005; Coleman 1988, 1990; Gould 1991; Halpern 2004). In our case, for example, cooperation and trust might allow and encourage bands to share equipment and rehearsal space, include one another in support slots, recommend one another to venues and promoters, and pass on information and contacts.

In addition, the collective protection and support which cohesive networks can offer in the face of hostility from outsiders (Gould 1991; McAdam 1988), which was evident in relation to punk, from attacks on the street to media-led moral crusades (see Chapter 7), is very important. Participants need the support of others to cope with such attacks and maintain their commitment to their style. Furthermore, they may be more inclined to take on the risks associated with cultural innovation, putting themselves on the line, when they can trust that their action will be supported by others.

It is important to qualify these remarks by recognising, as Riesman's (1950) discussion of the hot jazz world shows, that competition too may be rife in dense networks and that this is also important because it motivates participants to work harder at what they do, innovating and taking risks in pursuit of status. Different bands and artists each want to be top dog and their respective attempts to stay one step ahead of the others contribute to the dynamism and excitement of the network. Dense networks can generate both competition and cooperation, contributing to the generation of exciting and innovative music on both counts.

Coleman (1988, 1990) and Burt (2005) both suggest that cooperation and trust emerge in dense networks for strategic reasons. Actors cooperate and keep to their word, at least where interaction has given rise to norms of cooperation and trust, because the costs of doing otherwise are high. Blumer (1969) and Mead (1967) each suggest a different picture. Blumer suggests that participation in collective activity, particularly when galvanised by shared symbols and rituals, can generate an *esprit de corps*; a lived and embodied sense of solidarity which persuades the individual to pursue the interests of the collective, even, in some cases, where it conflicts with their individual interests. Mead adds to this in two respects. First, he suggests that norms of cooperation and trust are often internalised as a sense of duty which informs an individual's action irrespective of utilitarian considerations. Second, he draws a distinction between what he calls 'economic relations', in which considerations of cost and benefit are paramount, and 'religious relations', which involve a sense of shared purpose, empathy and *esprit de corps*. Many relations, he suggests, involve an element of both, and the former, in particular, may lead to the latter. Strategically motivated interaction drives those involved to find out more about one another and seek to understand one another's perspectives, which, in turn, can generate empathy and *esprit de corps* between them (see also Simmel 1955). Mead is surely right to recognise both types of relation and the possibility of their coexistence. It would be naive to assume that cooperation in music worlds is always and only motivated by a sense of *esprit de corps* but no less naive to suppose that such feelings are never in play and that cooperation is only ever a matter of perceived individual gain.

Density and the related property of network closure[6] are also important if deviant cultural patterns, such as those which emerged in the context of punk and post-punk, are to be established and maintained. Sociolinguistic studies, for example, point to the role of dense ties in maintaining local variations in language use (Milroy 1987) and Elizabeth Bott's (1957) seminal study of kinship networks points to the insulation that density affords their members from external cultural changes.

We can understand this, in part, by reference to Blumer's (1986) work on worlds, discussed in Chapter 2, which suggests that actors collectively define their situations and frame their experiences in interaction with one another, negotiating appropriate courses of action. We derive our sense of normality from the behaviour of others around us and, as Mead (1967) observes, achieve a sense and valuation of self by assuming the perspective of others towards ourselves, whether that be particular others in our network or, more abstractly, the general view of the network as a whole (what Mead calls the view of 'the generalised other'). When a high proportion of the network are in regular contact with one another this will tend to result in relative homogeneity because short paths will allow ideas and practices to diffuse quickly, without distortion, and because, being tied to a high proportion of others in the network, nodes are exposed to the same influence from multiple different sources, increasing their exposure and giving the impression that whatever is being diffused is important. Closure further contributes to this, in the case of deviant cultural formation and transmission, because a relative absence of ties to the outside minimises the likelihood of countervailing influences which might reassert wider norms or water down an emerging consensus. The network has little anchorage in the world outside of itself.

In addition, when conventions are valued by network members they tend to be reinforced by sanctions, both positive and negative, which encourage adherence. This becomes particularly significant when a network is dense and closed because the actor, having few ties outside the network and a large proportion within it, is highly dependent upon the network for a range of goods and particularly sensitive to sanctions by its members.

Developing this point, Coleman (1988) suggests that dense and closed networks are fertile ground for the cultivation of 'deviant' incentive structures which encourage participants to make sacrifices for their world and its values which are incomprehensible to the outsider (his examples are suicide missions and the commitment of athletes). Achieving status within a particular network can motivate actors to do all manner of things, valued within the network, which strike outsiders as peculiar or wrong.

On another level, much work on social movements suggests that networks are key mechanisms in recruitment to collective action (Fernandez and McAdam 1988). This can work in two ways. Ties to alters who are opposed to involvement can inhibit an actor's recruitment, while ties to activists increase its likelihood, often both providing a direct channel of recruitment and shaping the way in which actors perceive involvement (Kitts 2000; McAdam 1986; McAdam and Paulsen 1993; Passy 2001, 2003; Snow et al. 1980, 1983). A tie to somebody else who is involved encourages assimilation of a positive participant identity (Passy 2001, 2003). Similarly, activists have been shown to be more likely to cease participation when their close associates do so (Sandel 1999).

Finally, networks are important channels for the diffusion of cultural repertoires and enthusiasm (Edwards 2014; Hedström 1994; Hedström et al. 2000). This can be a matter of raising awareness of something which would otherwise pass unnoticed but it is often a matter of increasing the likelihood of uptake for cultural practices which are widely known about but not yet widely adopted. Actors who are unsure what they think about a new phenomenon and whether they want to participate are more likely to be swayed if they know of others who have become involved, especially if those others seem to be benefiting from their involvement: e.g. having a good time and not suffering any obvious difficulties.

A focus upon networks does not preclude the possibility that individual actors enjoy disproportionate influence. However, it suggests that any such influence will be mediated through network position. Networks are not undifferentiated social wholes. Each individual is situated, by means of their pattern of ties, within the network and the position which they occupy (which may reflect their strategic manoeuvring within it but not always and never exclusively) affects their capacity to act and enjoy influence. Some of the opportunities and constraints generated by a network are enjoyed/endured equally by all in it but others are specific to nodes in particular positions. Furthermore, actors bring statuses and resources into the network, from outside, which may impact upon it. This point requires elaboration.

Status homophily and social space

The CCCS conception of punk, discussed in Chapters 2 and 3, put a strong emphasis upon its class and age base. I questioned this but there is a danger with the concept of music worlds that such social divisions are overlooked. In this section I guard against this by considering the role of homophily and 'social space' in the process of world formation. I base my ideas on the work of Peter Blau (1974, 1977) and its development in the work of Miller McPherson (2004) and Noah Mark (1998, 2003) (see also Crossley 2014; Hield and Crossley 2014).

Blau observes that similarities in status and resources between individuals, along with geographical proximity (which in turn is affected by status and resources), tends to increase the likelihood both that they will come into contact and that they will form ties when they do. Lazarsfeld and Merton (1964) call this 'status homophily', contrasting it with 'value homophily'; that is, the increased likelihood that we will come into contact and form ties with others who share our values, tastes or ideas (see also McPherson *et al.* 2001).

It is tempting to think of status and value homophily as competing principles of network formation and that may sometimes be the case. However, as Mark (1998, 2003) suggests, status and taste often go together. Tastes, he argues, are acquired by way of social influence within networks, and as networks tend to manifest status homophily, individuals who share similar statuses therefore often also share tastes. Liking for a particular type of music may be prevalent among a particular ethnic group, for example, because that form of music originated among members of that group and, in virtue of homophilous networks, spread disproportionately to others in that group.

It is important when considering this argument to be sensitive to different types of tie. Adolescents usually have strong ties to adults (their parents), for example, but often seek actively to mark themselves out from such alters by way of their tastes. Dressing or liking the same music as your dad is regarded as a serious character flaw by many adolescents, regardless of the intensity of the tie and the emotional and financial interdependence it involves (although there is some evidence of intergenerational transmission of tastes and music world involvement – see Bennett 2013; Hield and Crossley 2014; Smith 2012). However, building upon Mark's argument, it is very likely that the social networks in which emerging music worlds take shape and through which participation diffuses will be characterised by status homophily, at least in their early stages, giving worlds distinctive demographic profiles (Crossley 2014). We would expect punk's pioneers, because they were connected, to be socially similar to one another. And we would expect punk to have spread initially to others who shared those similarities.

It is for this same reason that types of music tend to become associated with particular places: e.g. country music with Nashville; Motown with Detroit; ragtime with New Orleans; bebop with New York, etc. As a city acquires a reputation for a type of music, this can trigger a self-fulfilling prophecy: musicians in that style are attracted to the city by its reputation, helping it to fulfil that reputation. In its early stages, however, a city will often became associated with a type of music because the taste for a particular type of music catches on within local networks. As noted above, geographical proximity, alongside social similarity, significantly increases the likelihood of ties between individuals such that networks are often geographically clustered and so too are the cultures which flow through them.

Mark expresses his version of this argument in terms of 'social space', a concept he also borrows from Blau. The differences in status and resources which affect the likelihood of actors forming ties can each be thought of as parameters (or axes) of a multidimensional space in which every individual in the relevant population has a location. For example, a 40-year-old white male who earns £20k per year will be at notch 40 along the age dimension, 20 along the income axis and, though this is more difficult to envisage in terms of axes, at the white and male poles of the ethnicity and gender axes respectively. We can visualise this for the age and income parameters (see Figure 4.1).

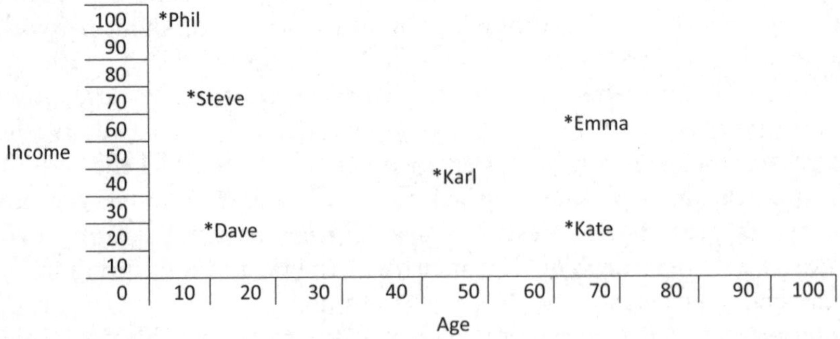

Figure 4.1 Visualising social space

Actors can be considered more or less socially distant from one another according to their respective positions from this perspective. High and low earners are distant on the income axis, for example, though they may be close on other axes. And proximity in social space indicates the likelihood that two actors will meet and form a positive tie, at least if we factor geographical proximity in. The closer two individuals come in both geographical and social space, the more likely that they will form ties.

It is not only individuals who can be located in social space. If participation in a particular music world is strongly associated with specific parameters of social space, then we may locate that world too. Focusing exclusively upon continuous parameters such as age and income, Mark suggests that we do this by taking average values and standard deviations.[7] If the average jazz fan is 60, for example, with a standard deviation of 10, then jazz is located between 50 and 70 along the age parameter, and if the average income for jazz fans is £50,000, with a standard deviation of £15,000, then jazz is located between £35,000 and £65,000 on the income parameter. Putting these two together allows us to visualise the location of jazz within social space (see Figure 4.2).

How well this idea works in practice is not yet clear. However, it is suggestive. We can think of music worlds as forming not only in specific geographical locations but also in specific locations in social space. And such clustering occurs for the same reason in both cases: because taste and participation are influenced by networks and networks are shaped by proximity (geographical and social).

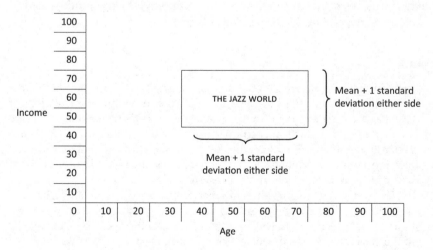

Figure 4.2 Locating music worlds in social space

Conclusion

In this chapter I have outlined a theory of the emergence of music worlds. Music worlds are a form of collective action and they arise through a process of mobilisation and collective effervescence. This is only possible, however, where a critical mass of interested individuals are connected to one another in a social network, or at least where sufficient interest among appropriately resourced individuals within a network can be mustered. Where a music world is new, innovative and/or catering to minority tastes this is more likely to happen in a big city because the greater population size of a city means that most minorities exist in greater numbers within it and are therefore more likely to hit critical mass.

The minorities in question may be defined by their tastes (e.g. fans of the New York Dolls and Stooges), and there is a body of literature exploring the way in which similarities in taste tend to draw people together into networks. Feld's (1981, 1982) notion of 'foci', discussed in Chapter 2, for example, predicts that individuals' tastes will draw them to common spaces (e.g. music venues) at common times (e.g. when particular bands are playing) thereby increasing their likelihood of meeting and forming ties. Similarities in social status and resources also pull people together, however, and, given that network contacts also influence taste, this can lead to some music worlds having a distinct social–demographic profile. Music worlds, like individuals, are located in social space.

That is the theory. In the next chapter I consider whether and to what extent it is born out in relation to the emergence of the punk world in London between late 1975 and the end of 1976.

Notes

1 Marwell and Oliver are rational action theorists. They assume that actors make all of their decisions on the basis of often quite complex calculations of cost–benefit, only acting in ways which are to their individual benefit. There are many problems with this approach (for my own criticisms, see Crossley 2002, 2011). If we relax some of the assumptions of the model, however, then it becomes more plausible. The critical mass model works perfectly well with a more relaxed model and is persuasive in my view.

2 'Objective interest' implies that an actor stands to gain from an action in a tangible way. 'Subjective interest' implies curiosity and psychological captivation. I may have an (objective) interest in reform of the tax laws, for example, in the sense that I would benefit from reform, even if, subjectively, I really couldn't care less. Conversely, I might be compelled to seek out the result of a

sporting contest (subjective interest), even though I don't stand to gain from it, whatever it is (objective interest).

3 In his essay, 'Value Judgements and Judgements of Reality', Durkheim (1974) suggests that new systems of ideas and belief come into being through collective effervescence. In *Elementary Forms of the Religious Life*, however, he argues that collective effervescence functions to conserve existing belief systems and group formations (Durkheim 1915). These accounts are not incompatible. What gives life to a group and its beliefs is sometimes also necessary to revivify and perpetuate them.

4 That is, when a high number of the potential ties in a network are actually realised.

5 That is, when a high proportion of ties within a network centre upon a small number of 'hubs'.

6 A network cluster is closed to the extent that there are few ties connecting it to nodes and clusters outside of itself.

7 Actually Mark suggests that we plot 1.5 standard deviations either side of the mean but I am simplifying for sake of illustration.

Micro-mobilisation and the network structure of the London punk world

This chapter has two aims. First, to demonstrate how the theory of micro-mobilisation outlined in Chapter 4 applies to and explains the emergence of punk in London during 1976. Second, preparing for what follows in Chapter 6, to offer a preliminary analysis of the social network which underpinned the London punk world.

The theory of micro-mobilisation begins with the claim that the collective action generative of a music world requires a critical mass of suitably motivated and resourced potential participants. This begs a question in relation to punk. The theorists of critical mass discussed in the previous chapter all assume that the tastes and identities which define the members of a critical mass pre-exist their combination in a mass, even if the mass does subsequently recruit new members and generate new cultural forms and identities. There were, by definition, no punks prior to the emergence of punk, however, so who were punk's pioneers?

Proto-punks and critical mass

Building upon arguments in Chapter 3, I suggest that punk's pioneers were characterised by their disillusionment with mainstream music and attachment to underground alternatives, such as the Stooges and New York Dolls. They were drawn to the rebellious side of music, its edge and capacity to challenge but felt let down by the artists of the mid 1970s. They were in search of something more; something which some had found in one or more of the alternative 'pockets' identified by Savage and Reynolds (see Chapter 3). They were people who went to gigs, not just at major venues but in art schools and small sweaty pubs; who frequented record shops catering to their specialised tastes; and who aspired to look 'different', hanging out in underground and counter-cultural clothing outlets such as those found on London's Kings Road.

London was by no means unique in having such individuals however. Insofar as the capital's proto-punks were shaped by the frustrations and anxieties caused by the socio-economic crisis which beset the UK in the mid 1970s, or indeed by the more general alienation of working class youth, as discussed in Chapter 3, they were hardly alone. The other cities discussed in this book and many others beside were equally as badly affected. Furthermore, in my discussion of dissatis-faction with contemporary music in Chapter 3 I drew upon evidence from Manchester, among other places, demonstrating that dissatisfac-tion with the music of the mid 1970s was not uniquely concentrated in London either. I quoted from a scathing editorial piece in the Manchester zine, *Hot Flash*, for example, written by Martin Hannett, who would become a major player in Manchester's punk and post-punk worlds. Similarly, I discussed evidence of significant interest, in Manchester, in the various alternative musical 'pockets' referred to above and particularly in the New York Dolls, Stooges and MC5 – who were the most influential bands in relation to the sound of the London punks. Finally, I referred to bands (Slaughter and the Dogs, Wild Ram) and attempts to form bands (e.g. by Howard Devoto and Pete Shelley) reflecting these influences.

Manchester was by no means the only city outside of London where such proto-punk initiatives were stirring. Liverpool developed a thriv-ing pub rock scene during the mid 1970s and in a number of cases, as in London, the bands involved had strong ties to the local art college, adding an element of style and playfulness. Deaf School, formed in 1973, who have been deemed central to much that followed in Liverpool's punk and post-punk worlds, and who played a minor role in the story of London punk,[1] are the obvious example, but Albert Dock and the Cod Warriors (who supported the Sex Pistols on the latter's first Liverpool gig) also fit this bill.

Similarly, as I discuss in Chapter 8, Sheffield's Musical Vomit were described as the first punks by X-Ray-Spex singer, Polystyrene, who saw them in 1974, and Sheffield's seminal post-punks, Cabaret Voltaire, formed in 1973, two years before the formation of the Sex Pistols. Their experimental music making was every bit as challenging as punk – albeit in a different way – and was influenced by Krautrock, one of the 'pockets' identified by Savage.

These examples do not prove the existence of a critical mass in the three cities mentioned and it is difficult to address this issue because we do not know how many potential participants would constitute a critical mass. I identify seventy-five key figures in the London punk world (below) and various first-hand accounts suggest that attendance at Sex Pistols gigs seldom exceeded 100 – at least where the band were headlining – but it is impossible to be any more precise. Furthermore, we do not know how many proto-punks there were in each of the three abovementioned cities. However, the speed with which a punk world took shape in Manchester after the Pistols played their first gig in the city in June 1976 (see Chapters 8 and 9) suggests that it already had enough proto-punks at that point. This begs a question: why did punk emerge in London and not Manchester?

There are many reasons, not least the concentration of record labels and music media in the capital. London is a culturally privileged area; a site of cultural dominance. Whatever happens there stands a much greater chance of coming to the attention of major players who have the resources to market and publicise it, hugely boosting its chances of success. Furthermore, this both increases the incentive for local talent to try their hand and generates an incentive for bands from elsewhere to move to the capital, boosting its pool of motivated talent and draining the regions (Cohen 2007).

I cannot rule this out as a factor. As we will see in Chapter 7, the London-based music press played a significant role in the rise of punk, lending events publicity and a cultural legitimacy which similar undercurrents elsewhere would probably not have achieved. However, as I discuss in the next chapter, something was happening in London at this time, initially independently of the music press and prior to any involvement by the major record labels; and though proto-punk developments were taking shape in Manchester, Liverpool and Sheffield, none were as advanced as these London-based stirrings.

In addition, we should not overstate the significance of the geopolitics of the music industry. During the 1960s Liverpool was a key site of musical innovation and activity, in the form of Merseybeat, for example, and it was Birmingham which gave the world heavy metal, in the late 1960s and early 1970s (Cope 2010). Both of these examples suggest that the cultural dominance of the capital does not preclude other cities taking the lead. In addition, though London's punk world was the first and remains the best known, Manchester very quickly rose to prominence, demonstrating that it possessed all of the ingredients necessary to lead the way, as it subsequently did in relation to both the early phase of post-punk and the dance world of the early 1990s – with Liverpool and Sheffield being similarly prominent in both cases. This brings us back to the question: why London?

Social networks

The key factor was 'social networks'. Manchester had a critical mass of proto-punks in the mid 1970s, who assembled to generate a punk world within months of first making contact with the London punks, but they were not connected to one another before this point and, as such, were incapable of collective action. They were not interacting, influencing one another and generating the collective effervescence which, in the London context, gave rise to punk. This began to happen in the final months of 1976. Manchester's proto-punks converged in a network and collectively generated a punk world. But the process of network formation began later than in London and, as a consequence, so too did the formation of a punk world.

We see this if we compare the networks of key punk 'movers and shakers' in London and Manchester respectively, as they were at the beginning of June 1976, weeks before the Sex Pistols first visited Manchester (see Chapter 1 for details on these data). There is a difference in the number of nodes between the two networks (London = 75, Manchester = 56) but this reflects the fact that I am looking at a subset of the Manchester network here rather than any real difference in numbers. More important is the fact that 91 per cent of nodes in the London network form a single component, with only 3 isolates and one further component, whereas the Manchester network comprises 17 isolates and a further 12 distinct components, the biggest of which includes only 24 per cent of nodes in the network (see Figures 5.1 and 5.2). Manchester's proto-punks were not in contact, were not communicating and were neither influencing one another not coordinating their activities. They were in no position to build a music world.

Unsurprisingly, there is also a large difference in both density (0.15 in London, 0.04 in Manchester) and average degree (9.09 in London, 2.5 in Manchester). And while most path lengths for Manchester are undefined (because no path exists between nodes), the path lengths for London's main component point to a compact network: 16 per cent of pairs are directly connected, 51 per cent are separated by only 2 degrees ('friends of friends') and a further 29 per cent are separated by only 3 degrees ('friends of friends of friends'). Information, innovation and ideas did not have far to travel in this network, such that they could travel more quickly and with less risk of distortion. Furthermore, members of the London network had many more proto-punk contacts which, as I discuss below, afforded them support and stimulation, encouraging their involvement in the emerging punk world. They had a proto-punk reference group with whom to both cooperate and compete.

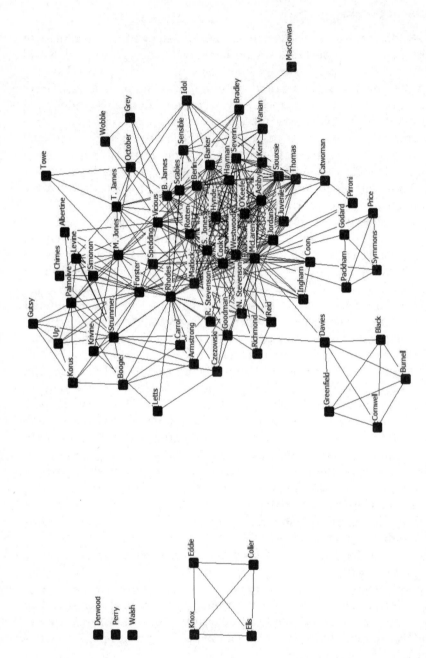

Figure 5.1 London's proto-punk network (June 1976)

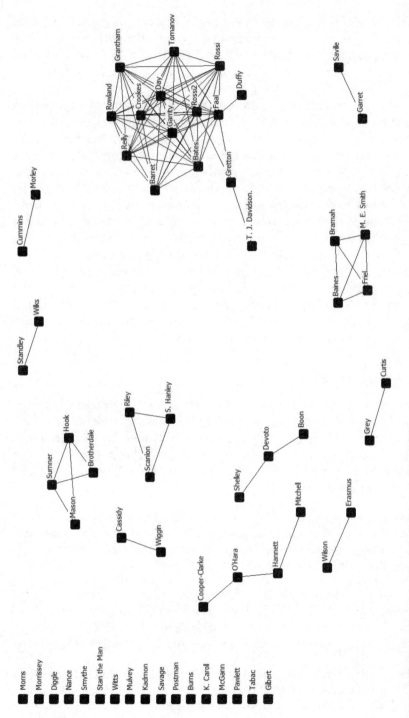

Figure 5.2 Manchester's proto-punk network (June 1976)

The closure of the London network is difficult to gauge. I assume that many of those involved had ties outside of the network, as I have defined it, to alters who had little or nothing to do with punk. However, first-hand accounts suggest that, particularly as punk gathered momentum, actors devoted increasing amounts of their time and energy to it, inevitably therefore spending more time with their punk associates than with outsiders. Moreover, it is evident that punk contacts loomed larger within their subjective lives, as a reference group and source of inspiration. The London punks weren't literally cut off from the rest of the world, like members of a remote rural commune, but they were increasingly focused upon the activities of the punk world such that their ties to and interactions with fellow punks assumed priority over other ties.

The London network was a large, dense and relatively closed component, with short path lengths; exactly the properties that I identified as conducive to collective action in Chapter 4. In Manchester, by contrast, there was no network connecting proto-punks. This is why punk took shape in London. This begs a further question of why London had a network and Manchester, at this point in time, did not? I return to that question in Chapter 6. Presently I want to explore the London network further, beginning with its qualitative 'content'.

Ties of mutual influence

That ties in the London network were serving to create, recruit to and expand a distinct music world is evident from many first-hand accounts. Slits drummer, Palmolive, for example, recalls how her conversion to punk was due to her boyfriend, Joe Strummer, who in June 1976 was poached from pub rock band, the 101ers, by Mick Jones and Bernard Rhodes, to play in the Clash:

> A lot of it was to do with Joe Strummer ... We'd been living together for about two years at the time and he was really into [punk] I was curious and really tired of the hippy scene and I wanted a change, rather than necessarily that change. I thought, yeah, it sounds fun, I didn't really give it too much thought ... it was exciting. (Palmolive, in Howe 2009: 9)

Strummer himself had undergone something of a conversion upon contact with the punk network and with Bernard Rhodes in particular. His first contact was when the Sex Pistols played support to the 101ers:

> The next few weeks saw modifications in Strummer's outward bearing: his voice became a slurred cockney grunt and his demeanour grew rougher. His characteristic gentleness was buried deep in a subcutaneous

layer ... Within a few weeks, Joe was looking, talking and thanks to Bernie thinking like a member of the group who were already recognisable as The Clash. (Gilbert 2005: 92)

Rhodes had a harder time persuading Mick Jones to chop his hippie locks and adopt the characteristic short hair of the punks. Social influence seemingly verged upon coercion in this case:

> Bernie nearly through a party when Mick got his hair cut ... It was a struggle. Mick, Mick, Mick ... everyone was saying it. Get your fucking hair cut. You had to drag him along. I don't think he ever liked it. (*ibid.*: 147)

And when Bob 'Derwood' Andrews, an isolate in the London network in June 1976, was poached from a non-punk band for Generation X, in December of 1976, his new band-mates pleaded with him to ditch his flares and cut his hair:

> We rehearsed him every night for a week, and on Friday night he still had long hair and flared trousers. We were begging him. The afternoon before the gig he says 'Okay'. We took him down to the hairdresser's and had his hair cut off in the nick of time. (Tony James, in Savage 2009: 282)

Captain Sensible needed no such persuasion, however, having grasped that a haircut was a rite of passage into this exciting world:

> I had to cut my hair off; that was part of it. It was safety in numbers. Everyone in this circle was kind of a different persuasion at the time from what was normal. The cutting-the-hair thing was part of it. (Captain Sensible, in Robb 2006: 136)

Influence was only one dynamic in the ties comprising the network, however. In addition there was support. When future Slits guitarist, Viv Albertine, began learning guitar and playing in a band, for example, she was helped by her old friend, Keith Levine (who played in the first line up of the Clash), and her then boyfriend, Mick Jones (the Clash). Albertine was equally galvanised by competition in the network, however. She had to learn quickly because other bands, not least the Sex Pistols, were storming ahead:

> There was a period when I was learning to play the guitar when I sometimes wouldn't go to their [Sex Pistols'] gigs, thinking I must get on with my own thing, there was this very strong rivalry thing, which was really weird. I don't know why you couldn't take the evening off. (Viv Albertine, in Savage 2009: 287–8)

Likewise between certain members of the Pistols and the Clash

> Joe and I felt like The Pistols were the opposition. The others, Mick and
> Paul, were saying 'No, they're our comrades in arms'. (Terry Chimes, in
> Gilbert 2009: 95)

And between their fans:

> There was great rivalry at the time cos the BOY crowd were very much
> into the Clash, and we were the elitists, the Sex Pistols bunch, and we very
> much frowned on the Clash and a lot of other bands who were around.
> (Jordan, in Savage 2009: 46)

Furthermore, in pubs, bars, bedrooms and squats there were endless conversations in which ideas and inspiration were exchanged. Individuals
were sparking off one another and collectively generating the ideas and
style that would define punk. As Glen Matlock says of the early Sex
Pistols:

> We'd work out which songs to cover by kicking about ideas in the pub.
> Anybody was allowed to chip in. Sometimes Bernie would offer ideas,
> sometimes Jamie Reid. It was a collective consciousness. Key words would
> get bandied around, in-vogue words like nihilism, and themes and attitudes
> would be assessed. A whole evening's conversation would be devoted to
> what constitutes being 'actionary' as opposed to 'reactionary' ... Bernard
> was incorrigible, he'd talk the hind legs of a donkey and then discuss why
> it wouldn't budge. However, from there we'd find songs which would
> express an idea. (Matlock 1996, 78)

And perhaps above all, contact between members of the network was
generating collective excitement along the lines suggested by Durkheim's
concept of collective effervescence:

> we started to convert everybody who would listen, telling them about this
> great band that was playing every week ... each time the Pistols played
> the audience doubled ... 15 people and then it would be 30, 60 until
> there were 100 for a key gig at the Nashville. (Steve Severin, in Paytress
> 2003: 31)

> I saw them play once, and by the next gig I was working for them. I closed
> down my stall on the Kings Road, and the following week we were at
> Malcolm and Vivien's flat, designing posters ... It all happened really
> quick. (Nils Stevenson, in Robb 2006: 148)

> I walked into this pub in west London and I saw my first Pistols gig. It was
> one of the best, maddest things I'd ever seen. That's when I totally knew
> that I was in the right place at the right time. It was one of the highest
> points of my life. (Keith Levine, *ibid.*: 162).

> I saw the Clash at Rehearsal Rehearsals in Camden. After that I was never the same ... I came back and cut up all my clothes and sprayed all my clothes (Ari Up, *ibid.*: 196)

Examples of each of the interaction dynamics identified above (support, coercion, competition, mobilisation, etc.) could be multiplied many times over. They only hint at the full extent of what was going on. However, the process is clear. Disillusionment with contemporary music and the inspiration provided by such bands as the Stooges was being turned into something else, something new, as an effect of interaction and mutual influence within a network.

Network structure

The discussion so far has focused exclusively upon whole network properties, ignoring the different positions that actors occupy. In what follows, turning now to the (London) network as it was in December 1976, I focus upon these positions. This will allow me to further consider one of the theories of the origin of punk introduced in Chapter 3, regarding Malcolm McLaren and John Lydon. And it will prepare the way for my analysis of the formation and evolution of the network in Chapter 6. My analysis comes in three stages, beginning with a reflection on the centrality of certain nodes.

Centralities

To say that punk was created by and in a network is not to deny that some nodes in that network were more central than others and it would be instructive to briefly consider who the most central nodes were. This is interesting in its own right and also a useful way of following up claims concerning the importance of Malcolm McLaren and John Lydon. In Chapter 3 I criticised accounts which reduce punk to either McLaren's machinations or Lydon's spiky charisma but I conceded that both may have played a part. And insofar as they did, I suggested, this must have been mediated through the network. Discovering that McLaren and Lydon were central to the punk network would not prove that argument but it would be consistent with it and would suggest that their entrepreneurial skills and charisma, respectively, were well placed in the network to have the effect often attributed to them.

As noted in Chapter 1, there are many measures of centrality, each of which conceptualises it in a different way. Here I focus upon the three introduced in that chapter: degree, closeness and betweenness. Degree, it will be recalled, is the number of ties enjoyed by each node. Table 5.1

Table 5.1 The degree 'top five'

Rank position	Name	Degree (% of highest possible degree)	Standard deviations above the mean
1	Malcolm McLaren	46 (61)	3.6
2	Bernard Rhodes	36 (48)	2.5
3	Glen Matlock	32 (43)	2.09
4	Steve Jones	31 (41)	1.9
5	John Lydon	30 (40)	1.8

Note: Mean = 12.67
Standard deviation = 9.23

lists the five nodes with the highest degree (for December 1976). It suggests that McLaren and Lydon were each very central. Both have a degree more than one standard deviation above the mean (McLaren's is almost four times the mean). McLaren is connected to 61 per cent of the network and Lydon to 40 per cent.

However, Lydon has a similar degree to other members of the Sex Pistols, Glen Matlock and Steve Jones, suggesting that his centrality comes from the band rather than anything independent of it (Pistols' drummer, Paul Cook, comes in 7th place, just under their future bassist, Sid Vicious, who was a key punk 'face' at this time). This interpretation is reinforced by a comparison of their respective profiles of ties: they were connected to the same people (see below). Even if his impact was greater, therefore, on account of his presence and charisma, it was dependent upon his involvement in the band.

I will suggest in the next chapter that McLaren too owed much of his centrality to his involvement with the Pistols. His much higher degree suggests that something else was at play as well, however. My reading, which is discussed in more detail in the next chapter, suggests that two factors were at play. First, as the Pistols began to take off and other punk bands began to form, McLaren, who had been very impressed with what he saw at CBGB in New York, recognised the importance of having a number of punk bands in play alongside the Pistols if any were to succeed, wanted control over these bands and therefore approached several with offers of gigs and rehearsal space. This generated ties for him over and above those directly generated by his involvement with the Pistols. Second, his offers were often accepted because he was a useful man to know. As a businessman he had resources, including money, entrepreneurial skills and contacts outside of the punk world which could help a fledgling band to take off and he enjoyed some notoriety in underground circles as the man who had (briefly) managed the New

York Dolls, supplied their clothes and who ran a trendy counter-cultural boutique on the King's Road. Where these properties didn't directly attract people to him they certainly encouraged people to take him up on his offers.

It is interesting, to make a final observation on the degree rankings, that Bernard Rhodes, manager of the Clash, is at number two. Rhodes didn't have the same status as McLaren but he too was a mover and shaker. He was an old friend of McLaren's who competed with him to find and manage a band who would lead the punk revolution. And like McLaren he made his resources available to a number of young bands.

Managers and other 'support personnel' typically enjoy a high degree because they control important scarce resources, work simultaneously with a large number of bands and often seek out such bands in order to carve out a role for themselves. McLaren and Rhodes are key examples for the London punk world during the period examined here but others, such as Andy Czezowski, would fit the pattern if I extended my analysis into 1977. Czezowski, who managed both the Damned and Generation X at early stages in their careers, enjoys a degree slightly above the mean in my December 1976 network but in 1977 he opened seminal UK punk club, The Roxy, and became a very central player.

High degree centrality would be less impressive and less indicative of influence if a node's ties were concentrated in a particular 'neighbourhood' of a network, with other neighbourhoods lying beyond their purview and influence. We can check for this by examining closeness, a measure based upon the cumulative path lengths linking every node to every other node in the network. Looking at Table 5.2, which records the 'top five' actors for closeness, we find exactly the same ranking, with similarly large deviations from the mean. In other words, the influence of the actors discussed above is reflected not only in their number of ties

Table 5.2 The closeness 'top five'

Rank position	Name	Normalised closeness	Standard deviations above the mean
1	Malcolm McLaren	72.54	3.21
2	Bernard Rhodes	61.67	1.87
3	Glen Matlock	61.16	1.8
4	Steve Jones	60.66	1.74
5	John Lydon	60.16	1.68

Note: Mean = 46.6
Standard deviation = 8.07

Table 5.3 The betweenness 'top five'

Rank position	Name	Normalised betweenness	Standard deviations above the mean
1	Malcolm McLaren	29.42	6.79
2	Bernard Rhodes	13.09	2.79
3	Chris Spedding	11.03	2.29
4	Dai Davies	10.37	2.13
5	Sid Vicious	6.39	1.16

Note: Mean = 1.66
Standard deviation = 4.09

but in the relative shortness of the paths linking them to all others in the network.

'Betweenness' measures how often a node lies in the shortest path connecting any two others. This is important because it affords an actor the opportunity to play a brokerage role. By connecting otherwise unconnected nodes they are in a position to control the flow of ideas and resources and/or claim credit for ideas which, in fact, they are only passing on (Burt 1992, 2005). When McLaren returned from New York, for example, he brought back ideas to London which, in some cases, he could claim as his own. And as the London world took off he was able to use his link with New York to bring The Heartbreakers across the Atlantic to tour with the Pistols, helping them to (re)launch their careers, boosting the profile of the tour by including them and profiting in the process. There is plenty of anecdotal evidence to suggest that he and Rhodes were wheeling and dealing within the London world in much the same way but this begs the question whether they enjoyed the elevated level of betweenness which would have facilitated this. Table 5.3 suggests that they did.

It is interesting, however, that the other actors in the top five for betweenness are different than for closeness and degree. Chris Spedding was a musician. He produced the Sex Pistols' first demo and played with the Vibrators at the first punk festival at the 100 Club in London in September 1976. Dai Davies was an old associate of McLaren and manager of the Stranglers. On one level the elevated betweenness of these actors reinforces my point about the significance of support personnel. In the case of Spedding and Davies, however, their high betweenness also reminds us of the dangers of relying exclusively upon numerical properties when analysing a network. Both have high betweenness because they connect an otherwise separate band (in Spedding's case the

Vibrators, in Davies' the Stranglers) to the main component. In theory any communication between the band and the rest of the component has to go through them, affording them a favourable balance of power. In this case, however, the theory doesn't apply, partly because the strict definition of a tie that I have used ignores casual contact. The Stranglers were certainly on talking terms with Joe Strummer, for example, because they had played with the 101ers on the pub circuit. They didn't need to go through Davies to make contact with other punks therefore. More significantly, however, the power balance captured by betweenness only favours the broker to the extent that the parties that they bridge need one another, which doesn't hold in this case. Davies and Spedding undoubtedly did much to launch the careers of the Stranglers and the Vibrators, respectively, but forging an association with the growing punk world was only a very tiny element in this contribution and would probably have been achieved without them. Furthermore, from the other side, neither the Stranglers nor the Vibrators were very popular within the wider punk network, such that the brokers achieved nothing for themselves in that world by bringing their bands into it. While the betweenness ranking tells us something important about McLaren's and Rhodes' respective positions in the network, therefore, this does not hold for Davies or Spedding.

Similarly, Sid Vicious's high betweenness is not indicative of any 'moving and shaking' in the network. His high betweenness reflects the fact that he drifted between a number of bands in the early days of punk, accumulating ties to their other members but never really settling. His contacts might have been a useful resource to him if he had enjoyed the nous to use them strategically, as McLaren and Rhodes did, but there is no evidence that he did. Central actors need intention and strategic know-how to take advantage of their network position. Vicious had neither, nor was he in possession of valued resources which might have consolidated his position.

However, to return to Lydon and McLaren, their elevated centrality is significant because it would have positioned them to exercise the influence that it is often claimed they did. This is not to say that either of them plotted punk *ex nihilo* as part of a grand master plan, nor that they were the only influential participants in the early punk world. But it lends to support to the claim that they were important.

Core and periphery

Centrality rankings are important. However, a focus upon individual nodes can obscure deeper structures. Specifically, nodes sometimes occupy one of a limited number of positions in a network which it is fruitful to analyse and model. A relatively simple model that is often tested on networks is the core–periphery model, which assumes that all nodes in the network fall into one of two positions. Core nodes form a cohesive subgroup within the network. They are densely connected to one another. Peripheral nodes, at least in the classic form of this structure, are more densely tied, as a group, to the core than to one another but in both cases density is much lower than within the core.

The first-hand accounts that I have drawn upon in researching this book offer good reason to suppose that we will find a structure akin to this in our network. The Sex Pistols, along with McLaren, Rhodes and the Bromley Contingent (see below), seem to form a highly cohesive grouping who were very much at the centre of things. I have therefore tested for a core–periphery structure using a pre-established routine in the Ucinet software package. The results, which are given in Table 5.4, include both a list of core and periphery memberships and a table which records densities within and between the two groups.

The density matrix in this case suggests that there is a strong core–periphery structure. Seventy-three per cent of all possible ties among the twenty-five members of the core are realised, compared to only 9 per cent within the periphery, and the periphery enjoy a more dense connection (12 per cent) to the core than between themselves. Membership of the core is revealing but not surprising. It includes four key managers;[2] members of the Sex Pistols and Bromley Contingent; the journalists, Caroline Coon and Jonh [so spelled] Ingham; and photographer, Ray Stevenson, who took many of the early celebrated photographs of the Pistols and their entourage. The inclusion of the latter three is unsurprising given their respective levels of involvement but it is significant nonetheless. Punk's 'PR department' was nested in its very core. The only person who may seem out of place is Mick Jones, who is separated from other members of the Clash. He was a mover and shaker in the early history of punk, however, as I show in the next chapter. His inclusion reflects this.

The existence of a core–periphery structure is important because it points to possible lines of division in the punk world and suggests that all was not equal therein. There was an 'inner circle' within the inner circle. As such, furthermore, it helps us to explain complaints of 'cliquiness' and exclusion levelled by certain of punk's pioneers, including members of both the Damned and the Stranglers:

Us [the Damned] and the Stranglers were always shunned from the punk group. (Captain Sensible, in Savage 2009: 334)

There was that incident with Paul Simonon at Dingwalls, which didn't help with us and the punk elite. The other bands were a bit pissed off that

Table 5.4 Core–periphery density table for the London network (December 1976)

	Core	Periphery
Core (n = 25)	0.73	0.12
Periphery (n = 50)		0.09

Core membership: Malcolm McLaren, Bernard Rhodes, Andy Czezowski, Steve Jones, Paul Cook, John Lydon, Sid Vicious, Glen Matlock, Mick Jones, Siouxsie Sioux, Steve Severin, Debbie Juvenile, Simon Barker, Linda Ashby, Berlin, Jordan, Nils Stevenson, Norah Forster, Vivienne Westwood, Tracey O'Keefe, Simone Thomas, Sharon Hayman, Ray Stevenson, Jonh Ingham, Caroline Coon.

Periphery membership: Joe Strummer, Paul Simonon, John Grey, Don Letts, Sue Catwoman, Billy Idol, Chrissie Hynde, Dave Vanian, Captain Sensible, Rat Scabies, Brian James, Tony James, Palmolive, Suzy Gutsy, Keith Levine, Terry Chimes, Jah Wobble, Marco Pirroni, Viv Albertine, Vic Godard, Rob Symmons, Mark Price, Paul Packham, Gene October, John Towe, Ari Up, Chris Spedding, Nick Kent, John Krivine, Derwood, Sophie Richmond, Jamie Reid, Kate Korus, Shanne Bradley, Shane MacGowan, Dai Davies, Jet Black, J. J. Burnell, Hugh Cornwell, Dave Greenfield, Pat Collier, John Ellis, Eddie Edwards, Knox, Dave Goodman, Mark Perry, Steve Walsh, Ted Carrol, Roger Armstrong, Boogie.

> we had been chosen to represent London ... We were the first people to play with the Ramones and Patti Smith, and that pissed a few people off. We were out of the inner circle after that. That did us immense favours in the long term. We evolved on our own ... (J. J. Burnel of the Stranglers, in Robb 2006: 199–200)

The Damned and Stranglers belonged to punk's inner circle by my definition but not to the inner circle of the inner circle, and they could see that. Their proximity to what Burnel calls 'the punk elite' allowed them to see that they were excluded from it.

Blockmodelling the network

To push this structural analysis further we can blockmodel a network. Blockmodelling involves grouping ('blocking') nodes which occupy an 'equivalent' position in the network and then exploring relations between blocks. There are different forms of equivalence for these purposes. I will use 'structural equivalence'. Any two nodes are perfectly structurally equivalent when they are tied to exactly the same alters. Perfection is rare, however, and so we group nodes which have a similar pattern of ties. This is the most useful definition of 'equivalence' for my purposes because the London punk world was small, informal and centred upon individual identities. Who knew who was important and structural equivalence captures this.

Table 5.5 Densities within and between blocks

	Block one	Block two	Block three	Block four	Block five	Block six	Block seven	Block eight	Block nine
Block one	0.91	1	0.7	0.05	0.08	0	0.13	0.1	0.02
Block two		1	1	0.09	0.28	0	0.75	0	0.04
Block three			1	0.28	0.8	1	0.88	0.25	0.04
Block four				0.6	0.09	0.03	0.08	0	0.01
Block five					0.67	0	0.01	0.2	0.01
Block six						0.4	0.04	0	0.04
Block seven							0.14	0	0.05
Block eight								0.6	0
Block nine									0.22

There are different ways of approaching a blockmodel, whose pros and cons are contested (e.g. Saunders 2008). Because I only had vague hunches about the underlying structure of the network I opted for an exploratory, inductive approach. I began by searching for structurally equivalent 'blocks' using a hierarchical clustering algorithm.[3] This measures levels of dissimilarity in tie profiles between every possible pair of nodes, grouping those which are most similar in successive nested clusters and inviting the analyst to decide a meaningful cut-off point, thereby determining the overall number of clusters. I decided upon a nine block model.

I outline and interpret block membership shortly. First, however, we must consider the relations between the blocks. If a member of one block has a tie to a member of another, then the blocks themselves are tied. We can explore inter-block ties more exactly, however, by calculating the density of ties within and between blocks (see Table 5.5).

It is usual to further simplify the model by deeming blocks either connected or not in accordance with a threshold value. Again I opted for an inductive approach in doing this, looking for a threshold which afforded an interpretable and meaningful model. On this basis I decided to set the threshold at 0.25. The resulting network is visualised in Figure 5.3.

Blocks two and three, occupied by members of the Sex Pistols (block two) and the managers, Malcolm McLaren and Bernard Rhodes (block three), respectively, clearly occupy central positions in the network. They have a much higher number of ties than other blocks (degree centrality). Indeed, all ties in the model involve one or the other of them. Furthermore, Block Three is the only block which has direct ties to every other node in its component, such that it is closer to all other blocks

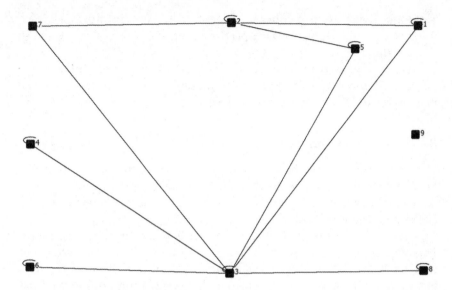

Figure 5.3 A blockmodel of the London network

than they are to one another (closeness centrality). And it bridges many of the other blocks, providing the only link between them (betweenness centrality). Movement of information, ideas or resources between blocks will usually go through block three.

Centrality isn't always an advantage. However, it can be and in this case, given what I said about McLaren and Rhodes above, it is. The social structure of the punk world in December 1976 was centred, in part, upon the Sex Pistols and more especially upon McLaren and Rhodes. This is not to say that either block was individually responsible for punk. They were important because of their pattern of connection to others. All the same, however, the punk world centred upon them.

Two other properties of the model require brief elaboration. First, note that block nine is an isolate. There were no isolates in the original network by December (see Chapter 6), so this is an effect of the threshold value I have used. Block nine does enjoy some connection to the main component but not much. More importantly, the position of its members within the network is extremely marginal. Second, all blocks except two (Seven and Nine) have an internal density which meets the 0.25 threshold, a fact indicated by the circular arrow (showing self-connection) which orbits the nodes in Figure 5.3. This means that all blocks, except Seven and Nine, are relatively cohesive groupings. They might therefore represent competing 'factions' within the punk world.

Seven and Nine are not cohesive, by contrast. Their members are each in similar network positions, respectively, but they are not connected to one another.

We can now start to interpret the blocks. Some of what follows will make more sense after the evolution of the network has been discussed in Chapter 6. However, we can make a start.

Block one: faces and face-makers

Members: Sid Vicious, Siouxsie Sioux, Steve Severin, Debbie Juvenile, Simon Barker, Linda Ashby, Berlin, Jordan, Vivienne Westwood, Tracey O'Keefe, Simone Thomas, Sharon Hayman, Ray Stevenson, Jonh Ingham, Caroline Coon.

Interpretation: this block includes most early punk 'faces', including the Bromley Contingent (a group of Sex Pistols' fans who became almost as famous as the group itself), Jordan and Sid Vicious. It also includes Ray Stevenson, who took many of the most famous photographs of the early punks; Vivienne Westwood, who designed many of their clothes; and the journalists, Jonh Ingham and Caroline Coon. The block captures punk's 'faces' and face-makers.

Block two: 'the young guns'

Members: Steve Jones, Paul Cook, John Lydon, Glen Matlock.

Interpretation: this is the first line-up of the Sex Pistols. The 'young guns' enjoyed a high number of ties in the network, which in their case we can interpret as a sign of their popularity and status.

Block three: 'move and shake'

Members: Malcolm McLaren, Bernard Rhodes.

Interpretation: it is no surprise that McLaren and Rhodes occupy this very central position. As noted above, they were key movers and shakers. The similarity between their positions is explained by their tendency to pass management of bands between them (see Chapter 6).

Block four: 'the squatters'

Members: Joe Strummer, Paul Simonon, Palmolive, Suzy Gutsy, Keith Levine, Terry Chimes, Viv Albertine, Ari Up, Norah Forster, Kate Korus, Steve Walsh.

Interpretation: members of the Clash (who became the Pistols' chief competition in the punk vanguard), The Slits and the Flowers of Romance, pulled together by their involvement in these bands, romantic ties and cohabitation of central London squats. They are less central to the network than one might expect because most became involved in punk a little later than others and because they formed a relatively independent camp within the punk world.

Block five: 'The competition'

Members: Andy Czezowski, Mick Jones, Chrissie Hynde, Dave Vanian, Captain Sensible, Brian James, Tony James, Nick Kent, Shanne Bradley.
Interpretation: this cluster is basically the Damned, London SS (an early punk band, formed by Mick Jones and Tony James, who never played live but who auditioned a significant proportion of others in the network at some point, thereby drawing many others into the emerging punk world) and two further bands involving members of both: Masters of the Backside and the Subterraneans. It is perhaps surprising to see Mick Jones and Tony James in this cluster. They are better known for their membership of the Clash and Chelsea/Generation X respectively. However, they spent much of the pre-history of punk together in London SS, collecting ties to other proto-punks (see Chapter 6). In the very early days of punk members of this block were the greatest potential competition for the Pistols.

Block six: 'the support act'

Members: Vic Godard, Rob Symmons, Mark Price, Paul Packham, Bob Carrol, Roger Armstrong.
Interpretation: this block comprises two constituencies: members of Subway Sect and Bob Carrol and Roger Armstrong, who launched Chiswick Records and were old friends of McLaren and Rhodes. On the face of it these two constituencies have little in common. What unifies them, however, is the fact that both were relatively marginal to the punk world and were connected to it, primarily, by way of McLaren and Rhodes (who each took a turn at managing Subway Sect during the first six months of the band's existence).

Block seven: 'the foot soldiers'

Members: Catwoman, Nils Stevenson, Marco Pirroni, Chris Spedding, Sophie Richmond, Jamie Reid, Dave Goodman, Boogie.

Interpretation: incumbents of this position were close associates of either McLaren or the Pistols. Each worked with McLaren and/or the Pistols at some point (Stevenson, Spedding, Richmond, Reid, Goodman, Boogie) or were close fans of the Pistols from outside the Bromley Contingent (Catwoman, Pirroni).

Block eight: 'Acme of Chelsea'

Members: Don Letts, Billy Idol, Gene October, John Towe, John Krivine, Bob 'Derwood' Andrews.
Interpretation: this block is the band, Chelsea, minus Tony James, plus Don Letts. James's position has already been discussed. Letts occupies this position because he was working in John Krivine's shop, Acme Attractions, which, like the boutique run by McLaren and Vivienne Westwood (SEX), was a key punk 'place'. Later he became the DJ at The Roxy and briefly managed the Slits.

Block nine: 'the outsiders'

Members: John Grey, Jah Wobble, Shane MacGowan, Pat Collier, John Ellis, Eddie Edwards, Ian 'Knox' Carnochan, Mark Perry, Dai Davies, Jet Black, JJ Burnell, Hugh Cornwell, Dave Greenfield.
Interpretation: this block includes two pub rock bands who became involved in punk: the Stranglers and the Vibrators. Along with other members of the block their position in the network is marginal, with relatively few connections.

My discussion of the evolution of the London punk network, in Chapter 6, will put further meat upon this skeleton. For present purposes, as a final step in this preliminary analysis, I want to consider the London punk world's location in 'social space' (see Chapter 4).

Locating punk in social space

On the basis of the various theories discussed in Chapter 3 we would expect the majority of the London network members to be:

- young;
- working class;
- male;
- white.

In what follows I will discuss the extent to which these various expectations are borne out.

Table 5.6 Age, gender and role in the London punk world

	Face	Musician	Support role
Average age	18	19	26
	(n = 11)	(n = 38)	(n = 16)
Male	5	37	14
Female	9	7	3

The age range for those protagonists on whom I have been able to find data (n=65), as of January 1975, runs from 12 to 36, with a mean of 21 and a standard deviation of 5. A majority of those involved were under 20 and only three were over 30. The network in which the punk world took shape, therefore, was characterised by age homophily and that world is located at the younger end of social space's age parameter.

To further this analysis I divided my sample into three groups: (1) those who at any time played in a band; (2) those who (only ever) played a support role; (3) those who were only ever prominent audience members ('faces'). As Table 5.6 shows, those who played a support role in the punk world, though still young by most standards, were on average significantly older than the musicians and faces. It is not clear to what extent this reflects conventions regarding the age of performers within the world and to what extent it reflects the fact that slightly older individuals are more likely to have the resources and be more willing to take on a support role but (auto)biographical sources suggest that both factors played a role.

The age of the majority of network participants renders their social class ambiguous. Do we classify them according to their parents' occupation or their own? And if we choose their own, where do would-be musicians and managers fit in a class schema? Given the difficulties posed by this latter question I looked at parental occupation. I was able to find sufficient data on 35 of the 75 participants. Of these, 23 (66 per cent) came from non-manual backgrounds and would therefore be regarded as 'middle class' in most class schemas. However, I noted considerable heterogeneity within the manual/non-manual categories which is not adequately captured by this binary divide and problematises it. A (very) small number of the middle-class participants were public school educated with very well-to-do parents, for example, whereas most were children of clerical workers, whose incomes may not have been as high as those of a skilled manual worker. Likewise, the working-class sample included some from 'respectable' and apparently affluent manual backgrounds but others who were from very poor backgrounds.

Coming at this from a different angle, I sought out evidence of involvement in post-compulsory education. Excluding those who were still in compulsory education I found evidence regarding 45 of the overall sample. Of these, 23 (53 per cent) were either in or had enjoyed some form of post-compulsory education, which in many cases meant art college.

It is difficult to draw any strong conclusions from this but I suggest that my evidence supports Laing's (1985) contention, discussed in Chapter 3, that the class base of punk was mixed. Furthermore, it lends some support to those who argue that art schools were breeding grounds for punk (Frith and Horne 1987), an observation which Clarke (1990) uses to challenge the CCCS portrayal of punk as a street-level working-class subculture. However, it is important to acknowledge, as Melly (2008) argues, that art colleges were often refuges for working-class kids who aspired to something more than manual work. My data contradict this somewhat: 68 per cent of those attending post-compulsory education were from non-manual backgrounds and 61 per cent of those from non-manual backgrounds attended post-compulsory education. However, the number of cases for which I had both pieces of information was very small and the association is not statistically significant. In addition, my data do not suggest that art colleges were the main context in which punk took shape (see also Chapter 6). They are only part of the story.

Turning to gender, 19 (25 per cent) of the nodes are female. This is a sufficiently large minority, when compared against available figures on female involvement in other music worlds (e.g. Bayton 1998; Cohen 1997; Finnegan 1989; Leonard 2007), to lend support to those who claim that punk allowed for greater female involvement in music (e.g. Reddington 2012). However, women are still in the minority and, as Table 5.4 indicates, they were disproportionately likely to be 'faces' rather than musicians or organisers. This is not to deny that a higher proportion of female artists emerged as the punk world expanded, nor to downplay the significance of the women included here. It does warn us against overstating the feminist credentials of the early punk world however.

I was unable to gather systematic data on ethnicity. However, a combination of photographic evidence and published personal testimony suggests that the early London punk world was almost exclusively white. Some of the early punks had grown up in predominantly black areas and, as Hebdige (1988) suggests, some were drawn to and influenced by black, particularly Jamaican culture. However, the feeling was not mutual. Most young blacks in London did not come into contact with punk during 1976; those that did, as punk began to spread in 1977, largely shunned it; and with only a few exceptions there was no black involvement in the formative punk network identified in my survey.

To summarise, the formative punk world had a distinct age and ethnic profile –young and white. Its gender profile was more mixed but still male dominated. Contrary to the CCCS conception of subcultures, however, its class base was mixed. The punk world straddled class boundaries.

This does not mean that class was irrelevant. Some working-class punks made their class identities central to their music and class tensions, at least as subjectively felt by participants, were sometimes played out within the punk world. Tensions between John Lydon and Glen Matlock (of the Sex Pistols) are sometimes portrayed as a clash of class backgrounds, for example, and the latter's reticence with respect to certain of the more radical early punk gestures are sometimes explained by reference to his being middle class. (He wasn't by any standard definition but he did pass the 11+, attend a grammar school and later art college.) Likewise, class meanings and identities were often attached to the perceived elitism of the Bromley Contingent:

> Siouxsie standing down the front in her £200 bondage suit, in amongst all these urchins in clothes that didn't cost anything. I thought that was gross. She came up to me once, and she was always dressed in expensive gear, and she said 'Captain you're not a real punk and the Damned never will be.' And she walked off. Silly cow. (Captain Sensible, in Savage 2009: 330)

Such observations underline the mixed-class composition of punk, however, and its ambiguous position along the class parameter of social space.

Conclusions and a further question

The central argument of this chapter has been that punk took shape in London, rather than other cities such as Manchester and Liverpool, which appear to have had their own critical mass of proto-punks, because the critical mass of proto-punks in the capital formed a network and a network, as I explained in Chapter 4, is a crucial prerequisite of any form of collective action. This explanation begs a further question, however; namely, why were London's proto-punks connected in a network or at least how did their network form? The final section of this chapter has suggested certain broad parameters that were important. The punk network was almost exclusively young and white, reflecting wider patterns of status homophily; and women were under-represented, particularly in musical and organisational roles, reflecting more subtle forms of exclusion. This would describe many networks, however, and the question therefore remains as to how a specifically proto-punk network formed in London between 1975 and 1976. I address this question in the next chapter.

Notes

1 Mick Jones (of the Clash) and Tony James (Generation X) first met Bernard Rhodes (Clash manager) at a Deaf School gig.
2 McLaren, Rhodes, Czezowski and Pistols' road manager, Nils Stevenson (who later managed the Banshees).
3 I derived a (Euclidean) distance matrix from my original adjacency matrix. I clustered the nodes using Ward's hierarchical (agglomerative) clustering algorithm. I decided upon the number of blocks by visually inspecting the resulting dendrogram.

6

The evolution of the London network

In the previous chapter I argued that London's punk world was the effect of interaction and collective effervescence within a critical and connected mass of underground music enthusiasts. In this chapter I track the evolution of this world and the network which underpinned it. I investigate the formation of ties between pioneer punks, the emergence of punk's stylistic conventions and the broader relational dynamics and division of labour between protagonists.

The main body of the chapter comprises a narrative account. Network graphs and measures will be referred to but only in so far as they inform my discursive attempt to fit the process of punk's emergence together. In the penultimate section of the chapter, however, I quantify certain of the mechanisms and processes referred to in this narrative account. The chapter ends by reconsidering a question raised in Chapter 5: why London?

Network evolution

My account is structured around six snapshots (t_{1-6}) from different time points between January 1975 and December 1976. The node set of the network is held constant across this period. My focus is the growth of ties between nodes. The time points were selected on two bases: data availability and turning points in the evolutionary process which I detected in the wider literature.

(t_1) January 1975
At the beginning of January, 1975, the network is highly fragmented, comprising 30 components, 21 of which are isolates (see Figure 6.1). The main component, to the right of the graph, includes: Malcolm McLaren, Bernard Rhodes, Andy Czezowski, John Krivine, Don Letts,

Dai Davies and Nils Stevenson. Between them these men would manage most of the key early punk bands, including: the Sex Pistols, the Clash, the Damned, Siouxsie and the Banshees, the Stranglers, Subway Sect and the Slits. Few of these bands existed in even embryonic form at this stage, however. Only one, the Strand (who would become the Sex Pistols), was connected to the managerial hub. 'Punk' was unheard of. The connection between these future managers is important, however. Their managerial input was an important resource for the abovementioned bands and their availability and willingness to take on a managerial role was in some part an effect of mutual influence and competition between them. They learned of the emerging punk world from one another and were inspired to become involved by their shared excitement about it.

Apart from Letts, who worked in Krivine's shop, Acme Attractions, and Davies, who was established in music management/promotion (with a tie to soundman, Dave Goodman), they were all wheeler-dealers in the Chelsea area. And with the exception of Rhodes, who had met McLaren at a bowling alley in the mid 1960s, and Davies, who knew McLaren from their student days, all had met in the course of their local wheeler-dealing.

Though not punk-band managers, Ted Carroll and Roger Armstrong, who also belong to the main component, should be added to this list of wheeler-dealers. In 1976 they would launch Chiswick, an independent record label with some punk and several pub rock bands on its roster. At this time, however, they ran a record stall frequented by many who were drawn to the proto-punk sounds of pub rock and US garage bands. Their stall was one of very few outlets in the UK which catered to such tastes and as such they both helped to nurture proto-punk musical tastes and drew proto-punks into a common orbit. Shane MacGowan was a regular punter, as were Joe Strummer, Brian James and Malcolm McLaren. The latter bought rock 'n' roll classics from the stall for his shop's jukebox. Furthermore, Caroll and Armstrong had helped Rhodes and McLaren sell T-shirts, which the latter had designed for the occasion, with Vivienne Westwood, at a rock 'n' roll revival show at Wembley in 1972.

Nils Stevenson too ran a small market stall and, significantly, had contacts in the music business. He was dating June Bolan, ex-wife of Marc and one-time secretary to Syd Barratt. Furthermore, through his photographer brother, Ray, who had photographed and was friendly with both Marc Bolan and David Bowie, he had mixed in the inner circle of the glam rock world. He, his brother and June Bolan, like Dai Davies, had knowledge of the music business that McLaren would later draw upon.

It was rumoured that Rhodes too had previous experience in the music business but he was moving in the rag trade at the time, as were Krivine, Westwood and McLaren, with Czezowski working as an accountant for the latter three. Westwood and McLaren, who were romantically linked at the time, co-owned a shop on the King's Road. The shop began life as Let it Rock, becoming Too Fast to Live, Too Young to Die, then SEX and finally Seditionaries. It included future punk 'face', Jordan, among its regular staff, with Glen Matlock as the Saturday boy and Chrissie Hynde having worked there during early 1974. Steve Jones and Paul Cook, who had met at school, had visited the shop with a view to stealing what took their fancy and Jones, the more frequent visitor, had struck up a relationship with McLaren, who sometimes paid him for doing odd jobs.

Hynde, who also briefly worked at the *NME* and knew *Sounds* journalist, Jonh Ingham, had been introduced to McLaren by her then boyfriend, Nick Kent, a rising star at the *NME* who had written a piece on the shop and on McLaren's involvement with the New York Dolls (he supplied some of their clothing) in the spring of 1974. She, Kent and Ingham were not the only music industry contacts in the main component at the time, however. *Melody Maker* journalist, Caroline Coon, used the shop, as did Chris Spedding, a musician who had just gone solo following a period with the Sharks (whose fans included Mick Jones). Furthermore, Spedding's girlfriend, Norah Forster (heiress to a large German newspaper business), who was also a shop regular, was well connected in the music industry.

Forster's daughter, Ari, who was only 12 in 1974, was yet to develop her involvement in music but she would; as would Jones and Cook. They were in the process of putting together the Strand (named after the Roxy Music song). Jones sang, Cook played drums and their friend, Wally Nightingale, played guitar. When Matlock, who played bass, started work at the shop in late 1974, McLaren suggested that they team up, which they did. It was also around this time that Jones asked McLaren to manage the band. He agreed but was initially very half-hearted.

As a regular habitué of McLaren's shop, Jones was ahead of the game. So too was Marco Pirroni, who spent much of his money there, hanging around to the point where 'I realised they must be getting sick of me' (Savage 2009: 354). In the course of 1975, however, as McLaren and Westwood became more adventurous and less teddy-boy focused in their designs and as word got around, the shop, along with Acme Attractions, became a key haunt for proto-punks. The clothing they sold, like the records that Carroll and Armstrong stocked, were not widely available. Those with underground tastes in clothing had few alternatives. This was the gravity that pulled many proto-punks into McLaren's orbit.

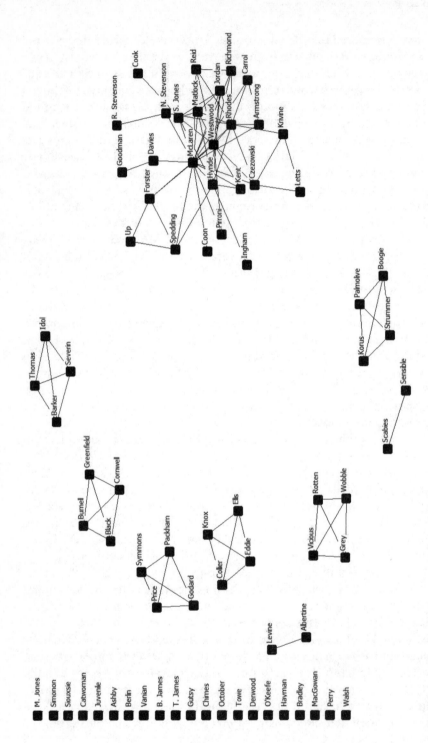

Figure 6.1 The London network (January 1975)

Alongside its rag trade entrepreneurs and musos, the main component has a cluster of artist-ideologues. McLaren counts among these, having enrolled at seven art colleges during his youth and having been a sometime admirer of the Situationists. He was egged on in this respect by Jamie Reid, who was running a Situationist publishing outfit (Suburban Press) and producing a regular pamphlet with his girlfriend, Sophie Richmond, who he had met through political activity. Reid and Richmond were both far-left activists and Reid in particular, when he later came into contact with them, imparted some of this to the younger punks:

> I used to talk to John [Lydon] a lot ... about Suburban Press, about situationism.
> The Sex Pistols seemed the perfect vehicle to communicate ideas that had been formulated, and to get them across very direct to people who weren't getting the message from left-wing politics. (Jamie Reid, in Savage 2009: 441–2)

Likewise Bernard Rhodes. When he started to come into contact with young proto-punks, again slightly later in our story, he was keen to impart his philosophical, aesthetic and political views:

> Bernie was my worst nightmare. He would ring my house ... I would be on the phone for three hours, sitting on the phone for three hours whilst Bernie asked me why I wasn't reading Jean-Paul Sartre? ... Why didn't I leave my parents and live with a hooker over Christmas? Toughen up! ... 'I need you to go to your local newsagent and buy *Gay News* and *Spare Rib*, the lesbian magazine. You need to toughen up' ... Bernie gave me a reading list and I would go and get the books from the library and read them all. (Tony James, in Robb 2006: 123–4)

> Me and Bernie struck up a friendship straight away. It was like he knew everything and I knew nothing. And he said 'You don't know nothing' to me and [Tony James]. He always talked like that. He made you think about things in a different way. (Mick Jones, *ibid*.: 123)

If the first wave of punk had a political orientation and betrayed a Situationist influence, then it was in no small part due to the influence of these 'agitators'. The agitator, according to Blumer (1969), stirs up and seeks to exploit 'social unrest', providing others with a political interpretation of their previously inarticulate frustrations and encouraging them to protest. How successful McLaren *et al.* were at doing this in relation to their protégés is not always clear, as discussed in Chapter 3, but they tried.

Described thus, the main component is a rag bag of wheeler-dealers, musos, politicos, art students and young people attracted to the more rebellious and underground elements of pop culture, all pulled together by McLaren and his shop. But punk was fashioned from a fusion of just these elements and that is why McLaren and his shop were so important. By pursuing his fancies in a haphazard manner he unintentionally generated a network around himself in which representatives of business, music, fashion, far-left politics, avant-garde philosophy and art all came into contact, exchanging ideas and resources. Those involved at this stage could never have created punk on their own. Indeed, it is often reported that McLaren showed little enthusiasm for music at this point. His disillusionment with contemporary music trends (as a devotee of 1950s rock 'n' roll) had turned to disinterest. And there is no reason to suppose that many of his colleagues were especially interested either. However, it was the combination of their resources, ideas and inclinations, with the energy, charisma, determination and talent of the young would-be musicians with whom they were soon to make contact, that would make punk.

Apart from the main component and the high number of actors who were isolates at this point, there are seven smaller components at t_1. One comprises the members of the Guilford Stranglers, who had begun to gig on the pub rock circuit and were in the process of dropping 'Guilford' from their name. They were all relatively experienced musicians, albeit with rather different backgrounds, ranging from Jean-Jacques Burnell's classical training, through Jet Black's experience as a jazz drummer to Johnny Sox, the R&B band that Hugh Cornwell had been playing in. Black had met Cornwell when he responded to the latter's 'drummer wanted' advert in *Melody Maker* and Greenfield had been recruited in the same way. Burnell was picked up by Black when hitchhiking and became involved from there. By the end of 1974 they had gelled into a band and by the end of 1975 they would enjoy a high profile on the pub rock circuit.

Another component comprises the musicians who would later form the Vibrators. At this point they were members of other bands. Pat Collier and John Ellis played in a pub rock band, Bazooka Joe. Ian Carnochan (aka Knox) was playing in a band called Lipstick. And John 'Eddie' Edwards was an occasional roadie for both Lipstick and Bazooka Joe. All had met through mutual involvement on the pub rock circuit.

In addition, the future members of Subway Sect had begun jamming. Only Rob Symmons, who met the other three school friends when he joined their sixth form, had begun to learn an instrument (guitar). The others 'bashed tambourines and things' in imitation of Dr Feelgood and early R&B (Vic Goddard, in Savage 2009: 363). But the ties and the musical interest were there.

Meanwhile, Joe Strummer had returned to London after a period in Newport and moved into a squat at 101 Walterton Road. It was here that he became involved in the 101ers, one of the pub rock bands who prefigured punk, and it was in the squats in the Maida Hill area more generally that he met a number of his significant punk others, including: his one time girlfriend, Paloma Romero (later renamed 'Palmolive' by Paul Simonon), who would play in both the Flowers of Romance and the Slits, in addition to various post-punk bands; John Tiberi ('Boogie'), who would work as a road manager for the 101ers and later both the Clash and the Sex Pistols; and Kate Korus, who was to play in the very first line up of the Slits with Palmolive. Korus and Tiberi were romantically attached for a while, so the four formed a cohesive unit.

The role of the various squats which had emerged in diverse loca-tions around central London from the late 1960s is often underplayed in the story of punk, when compared to the shops on the King's Road, but they were important punk places. They were network foci, drawing likeminded actors together, and also resources, providing spaces where several punk pioneers lived, rehearsed, crashed after late-night gigs and, as time went on, plotted their revolution.

The other small components comprise actors who had met and made friends either at school, art college or work. Keith Levine, who is linked to Viv Albertine, Billy Idol, who is linked to members of what became the Bromley Contingent, and Captain Sensible, who met Rat Scabies when both were employed as cleaners at Croydon's Fairfield Hall in December of 1974, all already played guitar at this stage. And Sensible was playing in proto-punk garage-band, Johnny Moped.

Finally, 'the four Johns' are assembled at this point: John Lydon (aka Johnny Rotten) was a childhood friend of John Grey and had met both John Wardle (Jah Wobble) and John Simon Ritchie (aka John Beverly, aka Sid Vicious) at college. All were passionate about pop music and its underground tributaries, with Lydon leaning variously in the direction of reggae, Krautrock and Captain Beefheart, while Vicious was a huge fan of Marc Bolan and David Bowie. However, none were involved in making music and none had plans in that direction.

(t₂) January–June 1975

The situation only changed slightly in the first half of 1975 but the changes were significant. The Sex Pistols, having been briefly known as 'the Strand' and then 'the Swankers' became QT Jones and the Sex Pistols, a name which McLaren recommended and which advertised his newly renamed shop: SEX. McLaren had less involvement with the band during early 1975, however, as he was in the USA working with the New York Dolls – their career was in terminal decline and his intervention proved fatal but he was both a friend (having supplied their clothes) and devotee of the band and wanted to help. He left Bernard Rhodes in charge of the Pistols, opening the door for Rhodes and Jamie Reid to make their impression on the band.

When he returned to London, however, McLaren was newly enthused about music. He had been inspired by his CBGB experience, particularly Richard Hell, and had new plans for and greater interest in his band. His first thought was to recruit either Hell or Johnny Thunders to front the Pistols. Both refused but he was still able to channel innovation from New York, claiming it as his own. Furthermore, his association with the Dolls was an important source of status among the young, alternative music fans in his circle. In network terms he was a bridge between the New York punks and his London associates, plugging and exploiting a 'structural hole' (Burt 1992).

It was also at this time that McLaren pushed for Wally Nightingale to be dropped from the Pistols, being briefly replaced by McLaren's friend, *NME* journalist, Nick Kent. Kent claims that he was instrumental in changing the musical direction of the band, who up to that point were mainly rehearsing Faces and Who covers. He was a friend of Iggy Pop and a big fan of the Stooges, and he suggested that the Pistols follow their example. In addition, he had acquired a pre-release recording of Jonathan Richmond's 'Road Runner', which he played the band and which, along with the Stooges' No Fun, they recorded:

> Matlock became enamoured of two tracks on that tape –'Pablo Picasso' and 'Road Runner'– and started pushing to feature the latter in the Pistols' repertoire. I in turn became increasingly insistent about covering 'No Fun' … my contribution to their musical development … stripping away all the retro silliness and pointing them towards the future. (Kent 2010: 244)

Meanwhile, elsewhere in the network significant connections were being made. Mick Jones had played in a number of bands through the early 1970s, including Mott the Hoople copyists, Schoolgirl, and the Delinquents, a band influenced by Mott, the New York Dolls, the Stooges, the Flaming Groovies, the MC5 and Chris Spedding's band, the Sharks. A press release of the time described their sound as 'loud and punky', in a 'Mott–Sharks' vein (Gilbert 2009: 42). In early 1975 a 'friend', having sacked him from a third band, Little Queenie, introduced Jones to Tony James. The two set about forming a new band: London SS.

(t₃) July–September 1975

London SS never played a gig. However, they were the common root of at least four of the major bands of the early punk world. Mick Jones was to play in the Clash. Tony James played in Chelsea and co-founded Generation X. And shortly after forming they acquired a third member, Brian James, who would later form the Damned. Before joining London SS Brian James had played in an MC5 influenced band called Bastard. He met Jones and (Tony) James when he responded to an advert they had placed in *Melody Maker* calling for a guitarist influenced by 'Stones, NY Dolls, Mott etc.' with 'a great rock 'n' roll image' (Gilbert 2009: 61).

No less significant than this meeting was a chance encounter on 2 August when Jones and (Tony) James went to the Nashville to check out a new Liverpool-based band: Deaf School. They began chatting to a man who, it turned out, had designed the T-shirt (bought at SEX) that Jones was wearing: Bernard Rhodes. Jones and James told Rhodes about London SS and he offered to manage them, an arrangement which revved up as summer turned to autumn and Rhodes's relationship to McLaren, newly enthused about music and resuming control of *his* band, became increasingly competitive. McLaren had a band, so did Rhodes. Game on. And not only for the managers:

> I think we realised that we had to move fast, 'cos there was an undercurrent of all these people coming up, who were going to start bands. You could feel something was going to happen.
> When we advertised for a guitarist Mick Jones turned up, just to see what was going on. (Paul Cook (Sex Pistols), in Savage 2009: 166)

Nobody was clear what they were racing towards but they were beginning to race all the same. And the connection of London SS to the main component, via Rhodes, was key to this. Members of the two bands came to know of one another via their competitive managers, long before they knew one another, and this provoked competition between them.

The Pistols too made a significant step forward at this point. They found their singer: John Lydon. Or, rather, Bernard Rhodes found him, wandering down the King's Road. He had short, spiky green hair and a ripped Pink Floyd T-shirt, held together with safety pins, which he had modified with the words 'I Hate'. Rhodes took him to SEX, where he later mimed to two Alice Cooper songs from the jukebox and got the job. Rotten had shopped at SEX but did not hang around it as others, including his friend, Sid Vicious, were beginning to do. Vicious had struck up a relationship with Vivienne Westwood in this context and she had championed him, unsuccessfully, for the job of the band's lead singer.

Moreover, further connections were being made outside of the main component. Old friends Steve Severin and Simon Barker formed ties with both Siouxsie Sioux and Berlin, forming the nucleus of punk's infamous 'faces': the Bromley Contingent. Barker first met Sioux, briefly, on a train platform in Bromley during the summer of 1975, when he was out with a couple of her old friends. They met again, however, with Severin this time, at a Roxy Music concert in September, clicking and becoming friends (Sioux and Severin would become romantically involved). Sioux shared Barker's and Severin's taste for Bolan, Bowie and Roxy but wasn't much of a gig goer before coming under their influence. For her own part, however, she had discovered a number of small clubs which they would frequent, including the lesbian bar, Louise's, which would become the punk elite's headquarters for a while. Furthermore, she had shopped at SEX, finding herself drawn to many of Vivienne Westwood's proto-punk designs. Westwood, in turn, was to consider Siouxsie and her friends wonderful adverts for her designs. This arrangement took shape a little later, however.

Berlin joined this group of friends after he spotted Barker's then girlfriend, Simone Thomas, in the street. Impressed with her appearance, he followed her and started a conversation. Both were big fans of Bowie and they clicked. Thomas subsequently introduced Berlin to Barker. In addition to face-to-face meeting they elected to write to one another and it was by letter that Berlin received an invitation to a party that would bring him into the circle: 'The Nuremberg Rally Re-union Party, dress in Nazi uniform or drag' (Marshall 2007: 26). In the later months of 1975 this circle of friends began to bond around their shared love of Bowie, the Velvet Underground and their own cultural experiments. Famously, for example, Sioux took Berlin into a bar on a dog lead and asked for a bowl of water for him. Berlin barked and the two were thrown out.

It is impossible to identify a single point at which this network became a punk world. The conventions and interactions to which the label 'punk' was applied were constantly evolving in the early years. However, with the addition of Rotten to the Pistols, the connection of London SS to the main component (with the consequent competition and mutual sense that something was happening) and the formation of the nucleus of the Bromley Contingent, with their outré experiments in clothing and penchant for Nazi and sexually transgressive imagery, the pieces were falling into place. The big change, however, was to begin in the final quarter of 1975.

(t₄) October 1975–March 1976

On 6 November 1975 the Sex Pistols played their first gig at St Martin's art college, which was just opposite the rehearsal rooms in Denmark St which McLaren had secured for them. They supported Bazooka Joe, whose members, bar one, were not keen and pulled the plug after 20 minutes. Bazooka bassist, Stuart Goddard, was impressed, however, and began a personal transformation that led to his rebirth as Adam Ant: 'After seeing the Pistols I wanted to do something different, be someone else' (Ant 2006: 82).

The St Martin's gig was the first of many in late 1975 and early 1976, mostly at art colleges, and claims of conversion at these events are widespread in the accounts I have read. The various elements that went into a Pistols' gig, from the raw and unpolished sound, through the charisma of Rotten, the visual impact of Westwood–McLaren designs and the aesthetic–political gestures of Reid and Rhodes, to the sheer chaos that resulted from the humour and incompetence of those involved, proved a heady mix which resonated with a small but passionate and growing crowd who experienced something in it which moved and inspired them.

The most significant new converts were the Bromley Contingent, who also grew over this period, adding other early Pistols' followers to their ranks and also several habitués of Louise's. The most notable among the latter was Linda Ashby, a professional dominatrix who had reputedly 'punished' countless members of the British establishment. She had a flat in Westminster and it became a place where the Bromley Contingent and the Pistols would crash after nights out.

The nucleus of the Bromley Contingent first encountered the Pistols when Barker unintentionally caught one of their gigs at Ravensborne College of Art in December 1975 – Severin was with him but managed to miss the band. Barker thought that they were fantastic and he and Severin noticed that McLaren and Westwood, whose shop they were becoming very keen on, were involved with the band. They decided to rally the troops for the next gig and became both regular attendees at gigs and close friends of the band, often travelling with them to more distant gigs and introducing unfamiliar audiences to punk's emerging visual style. When the media wanted visual evidence of punk for their readers it was invariably the Bromley Contingent who filled the slot.

Relations were cemented at Louise's, Linda Ashby's flat and SEX, as well as 'Berlin Baby Bondage Party', an after-show party which Barker organised at Berlin's house, when Berlin's parents were away. Crossing paths in these various places before, after and between gigs, the Contingent became close allies of the Pistols and key faces of the early punk world. Gigs weren't everything for the Contingent, however.

As Debbi Wilson (aka Debbi Juvenile), who met fellow Contingent members at early Pistols' gigs, put it:

> People think the early days of punk were all banging along at Sex Pistols gigs, but the early days for me were camping it up and down Park Lane with a gang of trannies, and looning about. (Wilson, in Savage 2009: 284)

Another (unrelated) early convert was Shanne Bradley, who first saw the Pistols when they blagged their way onto the bill at St Albans Art College in November of 1975. She began to follow the band, booking them for two further gigs at St Albans and becoming very friendly with Rotten for a while. She also became friends with Rat Scabies and Captain Sensible, later booking the Damned, and she hooked up with fellow 'early riser', Shane MacGowan. He had been converted to punk after seeing the Pistols support the 101ers (he was a big fan of pub rock at the time):

> I just couldn't believe it. This was the band I'd been waiting for. I thought 'this is what I'm all about'. So I started following them. (MacGowan, cited in Merrick 2001: 17)

When Bradley attempted to put her first band, the Launderettes, together, MacGowan auditioned. The rest of the band were not impressed with his Iggy-influenced performance but she was and, in addition to becoming romantically attached, they went on in 1977 to form the Nipple Erectors. During the latter part of 1976 they were often seen at punk gigs bound together by a dog lead.

New recruits to the punk world often became recruiters, spreading the word about punk and the Pistols through their own personal networks, swelling the ranks of the regulars and creating, through mutual influence in their interactions, the stylistic conventions which defined punk at this very early stage. As Dave Goodman, who joined the Pistols as their regular soundman in March 1976, observes:

> Fans would bring friends along. You could spot the newcomers by their initial apprehension and reluctance to join the pulsating mass in the front of the stage but, once they did, they experienced something that was really a new form of self-expression. The next week they would be back with a marked change in appearance and attitude, often bringing more friends with them. (Goodman 2006: 19)

Goodman worked closely with Nils Stevenson, whom McLaren had persuaded the previous month to take on road management. McLaren was working the office but the group were increasingly on the road and beginning to play outside of London and he needed someone to travel with them and do the organisational work. Stevenson, in turn, recruited his brother, Ray, to be the band's photographer; a brief which extended to snapping the Bromley Contingent and other punk faces sporting McLaren/Westwood designs. Ray Stevenson snapped his way through the early punk period, producing many iconic images and a celebrated visual document of the early punk world which fed back into that world, contributing to its self-consciousness (Stevenson 1980; Stevenson and Stevenson 1999). For his part, Goodman was responsible for a number of early recordings of the Pistols, which helped to cement their reputation, and also helped to build their live sound. As an experienced soundman he knew the tricks of the trade.

A particularly significant early gig was in February 1976, when the Pistols supported Eddie and the Hot Rods at the Marquee. It generated an *NME* review in which Steve Jones is quoted as saying 'Actually, we're not into music. We're into chaos.' The quote resonated with many, both within and outside of London (see Chapter 7), cultivating wider interest in the Pistols. Within London, *Sounds* journalist, Jonh Ingham, who 'must have read the review five times' (in Savage 2009: 486), decided to check the band out. He was an instant convert. Having seen the band a few times he:

> said to myself, there is no point in writing about this analytically. The point is to encourage this, because we need it.
>
> We're going to appeal to some kid about nineteen, reading Sounds in the suburbs, who is as bored with the situation as I am. And is looking to get excited ... I saw it is a propaganda, far more than analysis. (Ingham, in Savage 2009: 492)

Ingham had worked with Greil Marcus on *CREEM* and *Who Put the Bomp?*, zines which had been expressing frustration at contemporary music in the USA in the early 1970s (see Chapter 3) and he shared that frustration. Now he had spotted a solution. At his first gig, moreover, he bumped into fellow journalist, Caroline Coon, a friend of a friend whom he had met once or twice. Coon had first heard about the band in November of 1975 at SEX. She was a regular at the shop and had been following the Pistols from an early stage:

> meeting Jonh Ingham was wonderful. For the first few months we were competitors, but you couldn't publish it, and when we realised we couldn't publish stuff, we weren't in competition anymore; but we would unite to get the story across, so we used to go to gigs a lot more together. (Coon, *ibid.*: 477)

Coon and Ingham became co-conspirators on the propaganda wing of the emerging punk world. They were romantically tied for a while and also gradually became friends with some of punk's protagonists. They wrote many of the key early pieces on punk, which shaped it as a social world, influencing the perceptions, conceptions and actions of insiders and outsiders alike, while also bringing many outsiders inside. Indeed, although the word 'punk' had been used in the aforementioned review of the Marquee gig (written by Neil Spencer), Coon is often credited with christening UK punk in a celebrated article of August 1976. Sometime later she would act as a caretaker manager for the Clash, and Ingham would assume the managerial reigns for Generation X.

It was at the Marquee gig that Vic Goddard and his friends first encountered the Sex Pistols. They stumbled upon the gig by chance and were hugely excited by what they saw and heard. They were regular attendees after that and, in time, became friendly with the band and with McLaren. He encouraged them to continue with their band (Subway Sect) and briefly managed them, putting up some money for rehearsal space.

London SS, meanwhile, were busy. An advert in Melody Maker brought Rat Scabies, later of the Damned, into the fold and drew various other drummers into the punk orbit, including Topper Headon and Terry Chimes, each of whom would drum for the Clash at one point in time, and John Towe, who would later drum in both Chelsea and Generation X, with Tony James. Another applicant was Roland Hot, who brought along his friend, Paul Simonon. Simonon did not play an instrument and had no interest in playing in a band. He was an art student who wanted to paint. Bernard Rhodes felt that he had the look, however, and suggested that Jones might do better to form a band with him rather than James. Sometime later, when Jones bumped into Simonon in the street, this is what he did.

It was also around this time that Jones started at Hammersmith and Chelsea School of Art, where he met Viv Albertine. They bonded over a mutual love of music and became romantically attached. Through Albertine, moreover, Jones met Keith Levine, who would also try out for London SS and play in the early Clash line-up.

If Rhodes was responsible for drawing Jones away from (Tony) James then McLaren, who was looking to manage a number of bands and recreate the excitement of CBGB in London, was responsible for drawing Brian James away from London SS. He met James through Rhodes, along with Scabies and Scabies' friend, Captain Sensible. He invited them to join a band he was putting together with Chrissie Hynde and Nick Kent, the former of whom had also enjoyed some involvement with London SS. They were called Masters of the Backside and in McLaren's imagination their live performances would involve Hynde whipping the musicians with a cane. Hynde had her own ideas however. Having borrowed a guitar and amp from Chris Spedding, whom she knew from her time at SEX, she was practising vociferously and looking to form her own band. She jammed regularly with Mick Jones over a brief period until the Clash began to consume more of his time and energy.

Shanne Bradley too was briefly drafted into the Masters. Under Captain Sensible's instruction she began to learn the bass, playing briefly in Johnny Moped, whom the Captain was still temping with at the time. Another 'Master' was Dave Vanian. This would have been the first time that Vanian made contact with his future colleagues in the Damned. However, he was approached to audition for the Damned sometime later, after Scabies spotted him at a Sex Pistols' gig, which is where McLaren had first made his acquaintance too.

Between the inevitable break-up of the Masters and the formation of the Damned, Scabies (Brian) James and the Captain, along with Nick Kent, played a couple of gigs as the Subterraneans. Kent was quickly ejected, however, Vanian recruited, and the Damned were born. When Sensible and Scabies bumped into McLaren's accountant, Andy Czezowski, at a Pistols' gig, moreover, they acquired both a manager and a rehearsal space. Czezowski had the keys to a property owned by John Krivine.

As Brian James was drifting in the direction of the Damned and Bernie Rhodes was persuading Mick Jones to form a band independently of Tony James, Tony himself had made a new contact who was to prove central to his own punk success. Chasing up yet another ad (for a guitarist influenced by the Who and the Yardbirds) in *Melody Maker*, he met and clicked with Billy Idol, a close friend of Steve Severin and member of the Bromley Contingent. With John Towe, who James had met when the former auditioned for London SS, he and Idol were to form the nucleus of the first line-up of Chelsea and then Generation X.

Their involvement in Chelsea came about because Idol had responded to another Melody Maker ad, placed by Gene October and John Krivine. October had begun hanging around both SEX and Acme Attractions, getting to know McLaren sufficiently well that he was invited to a Pistols' gig and getting to know Krivine sufficiently well that he was invited to head up an as yet non-existent band. The next step was the advert, which brought in Idol, who brought in James, who brought in Towe, and Chelsea were born. But not for long. By December, Idol, James and Towe had quit the band and formed Generation X. This is jumping ahead, however.

It was during this time that the Stranglers, who were still playing on the pub circuit, signed Dai Davies and Derek Savage as their management team. Savage had been advertising for bands in *Melody Maker* and soon after he joined forces with Davies. This union was significant on two counts. First, Davies and Savage were experienced managers who got the Stranglers good gigs. They supported the Ramones on the latter's first London gig, for example, and they supported Patti Smith on three occasions in 1976. Given the importance of Smith and the Ramones in the increasingly influential US punk world this was a big deal. Second, because Davies knew McLaren, the Stranglers were made more aware of the growing punk world and had an entrée to it. The early stirrings of punk might have passed Davies by as an industry insider but as a friend of McLaren he was in a better position to spot how the tides were turning and to align his band so that they would benefit.

Another band who had spotted the changing tide were the newly formed Vibrators. Pat Collier had already left Bazooka Joe by the time the Sex Pistols supported them but he and Eddie had both been at the gig, as had John Ellis, who was still in the band. It is not clear whether it was this event or Stuart Goddard's departure which inspired the three to team up with Knox to form the Vibrators. And it is widely agreed that the Vibrators' music did not take on a punky aspect until sometime later. However, by February 1976 the Vibrators were rehearsing. They played their first gig at Hornsey Art College, supporting the Stranglers, in the March.

A distinct musical world was beginning to take shape (Figure 6.2). There was competition and rivalry. However, in most cases it was tempered by cooperation, a growing web of friendships and a flourishing collective identity. Although the Pistols and London SS were competitors, for example, Steve Jones lent Bernard Rhodes a large amount of equipment for London SS auditions and Glen Matlock helped out by filling in on bass.

The impact of the Pistols' gigs upon the network during this period is illustrated in Figure 6.3, which plots changes in the properties of the network across the period studied. There is a big change between September 1975 and March 1976. Both the size of the main component and average degree rise sharply, while the number of components drops (equally sharply).

(t_5) April–June 1976

In April, Rhodes, Jones and Simonon, aware that they needed a singer for their band, decided to poach Joe Strummer from the 101ers. They had seen the 101ers play on numerous occasions, not least supporting Deaf School on the night that Jones first met Rhodes, and they,

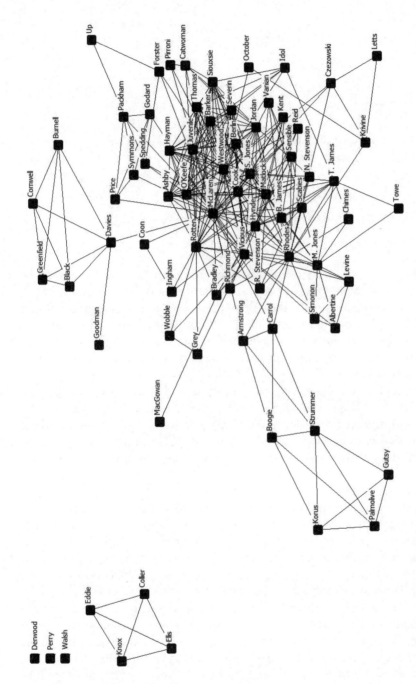

Figure 6.2 The London network (March 1976)

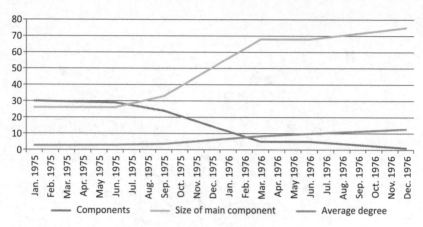

Figure 6.3 Key network changes (January 1975–December 1976)

like many others, were impressed by Strummer's presence and style. It was a difficult decision for Strummer because the 101ers were in the process of recording their first single – for Ted Carrol's and Roger Amstrong's new Chiswick label. Strummer had seen the Pistols a couple of times, however, when they supported the 101ers, and he had come to the conclusion that pub rockers 'were like yesterday's paper, we were over'.[1]

At this point, moreover, the Pistols recorded their first demo, produced by SEX habitué, Chris Spedding. The recording was disappointing, prompting Dave Goodman to rework some of the material in his own studio. Goodman, as noted above, added an important element to the Pistols' early sound. However, the Spedding tapes were a start.

(t₆) July–December 1976

In July the Clash and the Damned played their first proper gigs, in each case supporting the Pistols, and the first issue of *Sniffin Glue*, the first UK punk zine, was published (Perry 2009). Started by Mark Perry, *Sniffin Glue* was originally intended as a fanzine for the Ramones and some of the more exciting bands on the pub rock circuit, such as Eddie and the Hot Rods. When Perry saw the Sex Pistols and the other London-based punk bands, however, he shifted focus. Moreover, over time he drafted in punk world insiders, including Steve Walsh (with whom he briefly formed a band), who were better connected and could get interviews with such bands as the Clash. Roger Armstrong had agreed to stock and sell the fanzine on his stall, as he did for a number of other fanzines, including Shane MacGowan's one-off: *Bondage*. Indeed, it was

Armstrong who suggested the fanzine idea to Perry. Many other zines were to follow, throughout the UK, and another key element of punk's DIY culture was born: spreading the word and providing a vehicle for insider criticism and debate.

As noted in Chapter 2, publications are often a crucial element in the generation of a music world, partly because they extend networks and therefore the flow of styles, meanings, identities, etc., but also because they are key contexts where those meanings, styles and identities are generated. Music and bands are discussed and criticised, meanings attributed to them and boundaries drawn around them, bringing lived-through events and processes into discursive consciousness for a large number of people (by its final issue on 12 September 1977 *Sniffin Glue*'s print run had grown from 100 to 20,000 (Perry 2009), and provided a common reference point for the further discussions of participants).

Meanwhile, punk was beginning to attract attention further afield. The Pistols played in Paris in September, taking the Bromley Contingent with them. And, independently of this, a French promoter and record stallowner, Marc Zermati, who was involved in a garage-pub revival in France and connected to UK events through Chrissie Hynde (who lived in France and became involved in his network briefly during early 1976) and Ted Armstrong (who bought records from him), organised a punk festival at Mont-de-Marsan during August. With one exception the British bands on the bill were pub rather than punk rockers and accounts suggest that the French bands were too. However, the Damned played and the festival indicates that the idea and identity of punk were taking off.

Events during their trip to France pushed the relationship between the Damned and their manager, Andy Czezowsky, to breaking point, and they parted company. The band had formed ties with Nick Lowe's manager, Jake Riviera, while at the festival, however, and he offered to become their manager. This was fortuitous for the band because Riviera had just co-founded a new record label, Stiff, and the Damned were to become one of its first signings. They would release their first single, the first ever UK punk single, 'New Rose', in October 1976. All was not lost for Czezowsky either, however. He was approached by Gene October, who was unhappy with John Krivine's management of Chelsea (October knew Czezowsky through Krivine). Czezowsky therefore took over management duties and, when the other members of the band parted company with October, recruiting Bob 'Derwood' Andrews and forming Generation X, he briefly managed Generation X too. Furthermore, eager for gigs, October pointed Czezowsky in the direction of a suitable venue: a former gay club called Chaguarama's.

Renamed and hosting Generation X on its opening night (21 December 1976), the Roxy would become the seminal punk club during 1977 and Czezowsky, as its manager, would become a key punk player.

One month after the French festival, McLaren and Rhodes held their own, London-based festival at the 100 Club (20 and 21 September). The Pistols, the Clash, the Damned and Buzzcocks, all big names in the punk world by this time, were on the bill, alongside: Subway Sect, who made their debut; Chris Spedding, who teamed up with the Vibrators, having been introduced to them by 100 Club owner, Ron Watts; and Stinky Toys, a previously unknown French band whom McLaren had met when the Pistols played Paris. Still, however, there was a spare slot on the bill.

McLaren happened to mention this to Siouxsie in Louise's, two or three weeks before the festival. 'We've got a band', Siouxsie replied, confessing later to Jon Savage that 'we hadn't, we spent the rest of the night trying to find a band' (in Savage 2009: 341). 'We' was Siouxsie and Steve Severin, who had never played a musical instrument before but fancied trying bass. Knowing Sid Vicious from Pistols' gigs, and on McLaren's recommendation, they approached him to play drums. Billy Idol, an old school friend of Severin, agreed to play guitar but dropped out the day before the festival on account of his commitments to Chelsea. He was hastily replaced by SEX habitué, Marco Pirroni. Bernard Rhodes agreed to let them practise in the Clash's rehearsal space but they only managed one, 20-minute rehearsal. Vicious felt this was enough. Rhodes later refused to let them use the Clash's equipment for the gig, however, when he spotted their swastikas. Subway Sect, whom Rhodes poached from McLaren around this time, were happy to lend them *their* equipment, however, so they were sorted. Siouxsie and the Banshees were born.

It was also at this time that things began to take shape in the squats around Maida Hill (Figure 6.4). In one, Palmolive and Kate Korus had now hooked up with Suzy Gutsy, almost completing the Slits first line-up. In another, Viv Albertine, Steve Walsh, Keith Levine and Sid Vicious were rehearsing as the Flowers of Romance. The bridge between the two camps, which brought Albertine and Palmolive into contact, cementing the basis of both bands, seems to have been Joe Strummer's recruitment to the Clash. Strummer was dating Palmolive and Mick Jones was dating Albertine.

Though fluid, the line-up of the Flowers was drawn exclusively from the two squatting communities: Palmolive, Albertine, Walsh, Vicious, Levine and two others, Jo Faull and Sarah Hall (who were in relationships with Steve Jones and Paul Cook at the time). The Slits were Palmolive, Korus (later replaced by Albertine), Gutsy and Ari Up, the

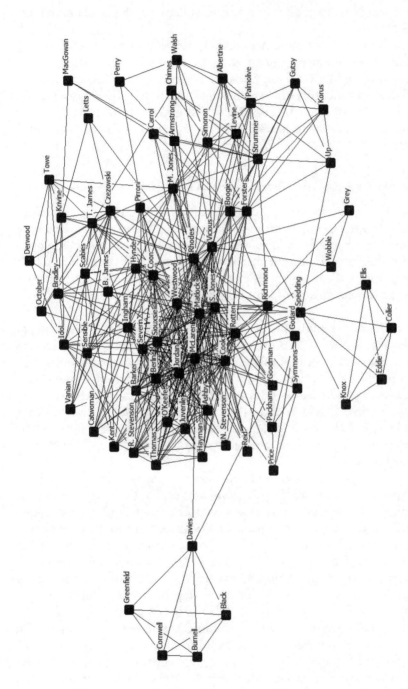

Figure 6.4 The London network (December 1976)

latter having met Palmolive and Korus at Patti Smith's first London gig on 16 May.

Up, who was 14 at the time, came to the attention of Palmolive and Korus because she was arguing with her mum, Norah Forster, a SEX habitué who was dating Chris Spedding. Forster was to become a mover and shaker in the early punk world herself, moreover, opening her house to various members of the Slits, the Clash and the Pistols. After a brief relationship with Steve Jones she became (and remains) Mrs Johnny Rotten.

From narratives to numbers: mechanisms of network formation

The above narrative gives a detailed qualitative account of the various events and meetings that brought different people in punk's emerging network together. It would be useful, however, before concluding, to identify the most important mechanisms of network formation which occur in this account and reflect briefly upon their relative importance. Three basic mechanisms of network formation are referred to:

1 *Foci*. As noted in Chapter 2, actors who share common interests, at least when they live within a circumscribed geographical area, tend to form networks because their shared interest leads them to converge upon what Feld (1981, 1982) calls network foci, where they meet and form bonds. Music lovers, for example, are more likely to know fellow music lovers because they will meet at gigs, in record shops and so on. Key foci in the above account are McLaren's shop and the King's Road area more generally, various arts schools, Sex Pistols' gigs and other gigs.

2 *Transitivity*. In a groundbreaking paper discussed further in Chapter 10, Mark Granovetter (1973, 1982) argues that ties within a network tend to cluster, such that actors who are tied to one another often share further contacts: a phenomenon termed 'transitivity'. We tend, for example, to be friends with our friends' friends. There are various explanations as to why this is and various qualifications regarding the scope of its application. However, the impact of this mechanism can be dramatic since a chance meeting of two previously unconnected actors can generate new ties between everybody in each of their circles. Joe Strummer's first contact with Mick Jones and Paul Simonon not only generated the bonds that would become the Clash, for example, but also brought others from Strummer's squat into the punk world, sparking other historically important working relations, such as those between Palmolive and Viv Albertine.

3 *Strategic attachment.* Tie formation can be a deliberate goal. Others may have something that we want and this may motivate us to seek them out. Examples of such strategic behaviour in our case are: *targeting*, which involves one actor pursuing another, whom they do not personally know, for a tie; and *advertising* in the music press.

In an effort to find out how important these mechanisms were in relation to the London network I surveyed all of the ties in it, looking at how participants met. Disentangling mechanisms was not always easy. Actors sometimes crossed paths several times within a short period and it was not always easy to discern the occasion on which they actually registered one another and 'met'. Similarly, it is not always easy to discern who met independently and who met via the mediation of a shared contact. Furthermore, strategic elements are difficult to identify because they imply intent, which I can't prove: some people were clearly star struck by McLaren, for example, and their 'bumping into him' at a gig may have been more contrived than 'bumping' suggests but I have no data to explore that. However, my results, as presented in Table 6.1, suggest that the most important mechanism of tie formation was the Sex Pistols' gig, closely followed by transitivity.

It might be argued that this challenges my argument, in Chapter 4, regarding the importance of the network for the formation of the punk world. It seems rather, a critic might argue, that it was the music which generated the network. We must move beyond linear models, however,

Table 6.1 Mechanisms of network formation

Mechanism		Ties generated (rounded percentage)
Foci	King's Road/SEX	64 (13)
	art school	9 (2)
	Sex Pistols' gigs	157 (32)
	other gigs	27 (5)
	squats	18 (3)
Total		*284 (59)*
Transitivity		152 (31)
Strategic attachment	targeted	5 (1)
	broadcast (advertising)	23 (4)
Total		28 (6)
Other		25 (5)

Table 6.2 Mechanisms of network formation by time

Mechanism		T1	T2	T3	T4	T5	T6
Foci	King's Road/SEX	28	3	7	8	2	15
	art school	8	0	0	1	0	0
	Sex Pistols' gigs	0	0	0	114	13	32
	other gigs	7	0	1	6	3	10
	squats	6	0	0	5	1	6
Transitivity		20	9	7	41	36	39
Strategic attachment	targeted	1	1	0	0	3	1
	advertising	3	0	3	14	3	0
Other		21	0	2	1	0	1
% of total ties (rounded)		20	3	4	39	13	22
Cumulative %		20	23	27	66	79	100

and recognise both that the network-facilitated events, such as gigs, and that gigs facilitated the growth of the network. A feedback process was in play.

As a first step in elaborating this argument, consider Table 6.2, which breaks the process of tie formation down by both mechanism and time. Notice that 27 per cent of ties are in place before the Sex Pistols played their first gig. The band, their gigs and their effect did not come out of nowhere. They emerged within a network. We know from the narrative above, moreover, that many of the participants within this 27 per cent were support personnel, comprising movers–shakers with resources, musos with know-how, artist-agitators and image makers, all of whom contributed to punk style in various ways.

Developing this further I returned to the blockmodel described in Chapter 5 and examined which within and between block ties were formed at Pistols' gigs. This analysis revealed that 45 per cent of all ties formed at Pistols' gigs were internal to block one ('Faces and Face Makers'), a further 29 per cent were ties linking block one to the block comprising the Sex Pistols (block two), and a further 8 per cent were linking block one to block three, comprising McLaren and Rhodes (82 per cent in total). In other words, Pistols gigs generated important ties within the Pistols' fan base and between that fan base and both the band and its manager but they were much less important in relation to other blocks within the network. They generated a localised neighbourhood within the wider network of the punk world but that wider network involved other neighbourhoods whose origins cannot be explained by reference to Pistols' gigs. Those other neighbourhoods were important sources of other bands whose existence was crucial to the generation of a wider punk world.

Concluding remarks: why London?

This chapter has covered a lot of ground. As a way if wrapping it up I want to return to the question raised in the previous chapter: why London and not, for example, Manchester or Liverpool? I suggested in the previous chapter that there are several factors which might explain the geography of punk's origin but my main concern was the network which linked London's critical mass of proto-punks, a network which, I suggested, was largely absent in Manchester. In this chapter I have considered how that network formed but are there any hints here as to why London might have got its network before other cities? I have suggested that the Sex Pistols' gigs played a big part in the growth of London's punk network but that is not a satisfactory answer to the question because punk was already taking shape by this point. There is perhaps a partial answer, however, in the form of the network generated around McLaren and his shop. This involved various well-resourced figures who helped to nurture and shape the Sex Pistols. It involved many young enthusiasts who were, to some degree, turned onto the Pistols because of the involvement of McLaren and Westwood (whose boutique enjoyed high status among 'alternatively inclined youths'. And it involved competition between McLaren and Rhodes in particular, which fuelled the process of punk's emergence.

I have suggested at various points in this book that what the Pistols were trying to do in London was not unique. Others in London, such as Mick Jones and Tony James in London SS, and outside of London, such as T. V. Smith and Gaye Advert in Devon and Pete Shelley and Howard Devoto in Manchester, were trying to do something similar. Their efforts came to nothing, however, at least prior to the breakthrough of the Pistols, because they were operating in a vacuum. Their projects and gestures had nowhere to go. The Pistols, by contrast, were operating in a context where they were surrounded by an, albeit initially quite small, circle of similarly minded others, who supported and shaped them in various ways. McLaren's Kings Rd network provided the launch pad from which they could perform and advertise their performances. It was the means through which they acquired a following and also imitators and competitors who, playing alongside them, would generate a punk world. McLaren and Westwood's shop served as a magnet, drawing likeminded individuals into a common space, servicing their (fashion)

needs and facilitating the formation of a network which, in turn, cultivated the collective effervescence that gave birth to punk.

Of course McLaren's wasn't the only alternative clothing shop in
the UK. I will show in Chapter 8 that Liverpool's punk and post-punk
worlds emerged in the context of a pre-existing bohemian enclave akin
to that occupied by McLaren and his associates. And innovative bands,
such as Deaf School and Albert Dock, were beginning to generate something of a music world within the Liverpool context. Perhaps Liverpool
could have nurtured the next big thing? We will never know, however,
because events in December 1976 took the development traced in this
chapter into a whole new dimension. It is to those events which I now
turn.

Note

1 Joe Strummer speaking on Don Letts's film, *Westway to the World*.

7

Punk goes national: broadcast networks, media and moral panics

For the first half of 1976 the UK's punk world, as described in Chapter 6, was a network of interactivity involving no more than 100 people and a handful of focal places in central London. By the beginning of 1977, by contrast, every major city and certain larger towns had their own local punk worlds, and these local worlds were connected, forming a national punk world. I discuss three of these new worlds in Chapters 8 and 9 and I discuss the shape and characteristics of the national network in Chapter 10. In this chapter I set the scene by asking how punk grew and diffused in the way that it did.

The short answer to this question is 'the media' or perhaps rather 'mediated and broadcast networks'. This short answer compresses two distinct processes which I want to tease apart, however, and raises further questions and complications which I need to address.

Mediated ties, broadcast networks

The social networks that I have discussed hitherto in this book involve face-to-face interaction. And the diffusion of punk through these networks occurred in a targeted manner. For example, when Steve Severin spread the word about the Sex Pistols, encouraging attendance at gigs, as described in Chapter 5, he approached those among his contacts whom he imagined would like the band, such as Siouxsie and Berlin. He may have mentioned the band to other contacts, such as his parents, but not with any expectation of recruiting them. And he didn't proselytise to strangers. Furthermore, he approached different people separately, in discrete interactions; a chat here, a phone call there and so on.

Diffusion through networks doesn't always work in this way, however. In some cases transmission is indiscriminate and a single broadcast simultaneously reaches a large number of people. When a flu-ridden commuter sneezes on a crowded bus, for example, they spread their virus simultaneously to a large number of unknown others. The expression 'broadcast network', which has been coined by network theorists to capture such situations, is unfortunate for our purposes because it can seem to suggest that such networks necessarily involve television and radio 'broadcasts'. They do not. A broadcast network exists wherever something is transmitted from one node to a large number of others, simultaneously and indiscriminately, as in my flu example. However, television, radio and other organs of the mass media are key elements in those broadcast networks responsible for diffusing culture during the punk era and they are my key example in this chapter.

The vast 'ganglia' of the mass media, as Raymond Williams (1970) calls it, reaches into almost every household in the land, and in the late 1970s exposure to it was much more uniform than today. There were only three TV channels and there were no videos, so programmes could not be recorded by audiences to watch in their own time. There was no internet. Access to news and entertainment, beyond one's immediate sphere of interaction, was restricted to a limited number of newspapers and magazines, and an equally restricted range of radio and TV programmes. Moreover, the communicative traffic in these broadcast networks, as in broadcast networks more generally, was largely unidirectional. Readers might have written to newspapers and audiences to radio and television stations, and journalists drew upon members of the world to which they reported for the stories which they reported. For the most part, however, the media coughed its content out onto audiences like the above-mentioned flu-ridden commuter.

Media messages are not infectious diseases, of course, and the metaphor, which has been used by several academics seeking to explain cultural diffusion (e.g. Sperber 1996), is a poor one. Cultural elements do not, as Richard Dawkins (1976: 192) says of 'memes', 'propagate themselves in the meme pool by leaping from brain to brain via a process which, in the broad sense, can be called imitation'. Audiences choose what media they expose themselves to and their interpretation and memory of broadcasts is shaped by their own interests and identities. Many youth fashions, for example, fail to 'leap' to adult 'brains', in spite of the close physical proximity between youths and adults (in families and schools) because adults understand youth fashions as 'for youths' and do not identify themselves in this way. Elements of culture carry a meaning which can be as offputting to some as it is attractive to others. Furthermore, decisions regarding appropriation are seldom purely individual. Actors discuss fashion and culture, likes and dislikes, with their friends, deciding jointly upon tastes and appropriations, and where they do decide alone their actions are informed by an anticipatory awareness of the likely responses of others.

However, culture does diffuse, radiating out from concentrated social and geographical pockets of innovation. Culture is, by definition, a property of collectives rather than individuals, and in order to have become such it must have spread through network ties from a small circle of pioneers to a wider group (Crossley 2014). This may be possible through face-to-face interaction, and certainly face-to-face contacts will play a role. As noted above, adoption is often subject to collective debate and reflections upon the likely responses of others. Indeed, Fine and Kleinman (1979) suggest that subcultures often diffuse between cities through informal ties between their residents (see Chapter 10). But broadcast and more especially media networks are an important part of this story too. Culture can move far and fast through the channels of the mass media (Thornton 1994). And punk is an example of this.

I begin my discussion of this by focusing upon the very early punk press, considering the way in which media coverage contributed to the naming and thereby the shaping of punk as a cultural phenomenon, and also the role of early media coverage in sparking the process which was to lead to Manchester becoming punk's 'second city'. After this I consider the 'moral panic' which brought punk into the mainstream cultural arena, massively increasing rates of adoption and adherence among the youth population (on the concept of moral panics, see Cohen 2002; Critcher 2003; Goode and Ben-Yehuda 1994; McRobbie 1994; Thornton 1994).

Early punk press

The very first mention of the Sex Pistols in any published form, according to Paul Gorman,[1] was an *NME* gig review on 7 December 1975. The gig was an all-night Christmas Ball at Queen Elizabeth College in London and the review is far from glowing. One audience member is quoted as saying that the band were playing for expenses and the writer, Kate Phillips, having speculated that the group were all 12 years old, 'or perhaps 19', notes that they are managed by Malcolm McLaren, who runs a shop called SEX, on the King's Road. She concludes, with more than a hint of sarcasm, that they may be the next big thing, 'Or maybe the Next Big Thing After That'.[2] Switching focus, she then notes that she and her fellow Christmas revellers drank a lot. Not a very auspicious beginning.

By August 1976 the situation had changed. Caroline Coon was writing with great enthusiasm, in *Melody Maker*, and not only about the Sex Pistols. Her piece talks about punk in general, referring to the Clash, the Damned, Buzzcocks, various US punk bands and also certain lower-profile UK punk bands, such as (Manchester's) Slaughter and the Dogs. Although it would only have been read by a small minority of young, UK-based music enthusiasts, and though only a fraction of them would have been interested, the Coon article was a turning point in the history of punk.

This is partly because the tiny fraction of the UK population who read and were interested in the article were still very much larger than the audience for punk gigs at that time and helped to swell that audience considerably. Punk did not exist outside of London and, to a lesser extent, Manchester (see below) before this point. This was the first that many music enthusiasts had heard of it. Furthermore, when punk bands, and the Sex Pistols in particular, began to cause controversy a few months later (see below), mainstream newspaper and television journalists looked at back issues of the music press for information. Coon's article, which was an A to Z of punk at the time, would have been a key source.

More importantly, although this was not the first time a music journalist had used the (US) term, 'punk', to label what was happening, this seems to have been the moment at which punk was christened, acquiring an identity and, given Coon's credentials as a cutting-edge music journalist, legitimacy. Individuals, bands, songs and items of clothing could all now be judged 'punk' or 'not punk'. The label was a lens through which to render musical interactivities in London, Manchester and elsewhere intelligible. The label framed the perception of these interactivities, as Danto (1964) suggests that art theory frames art (see Chapter 2), lending them a meaning, identity and status.

By naming punk and identifying its bands and artists Coon gave it symbolic reality. Punk now existed, officially. In some eyes this was the beginning of the end, a step towards the regimentation and stereotyping that would be punk's downfall (see Chapter 8). However, many of those involved appropriated the punk tag for themselves, not least Malcolm McLaren, when naming his first punk festival. And Coon was only doing what others had been doing for some time: reflecting upon the indeterminate something in which they were involved and seeking to make reflective sense of it. Moreover, as noted, she was not the first journalist to use the label 'punk' in this connection. Hers was the attempt that caught on, however, both within and outside of the punk world that it canonised.

Another, equally important and earlier article on the Pistols, which referred to them as 'punks', was Neil Spencer's *NME* review of a gig at the Marquee, discussed in Chapter 6. This review, which quotes Steve

Jones claiming that the Pistols were into chaos rather than music, resonated widely among a small but dispersed mass of discontented musical
enthusiasts, both within and outside of London, boosting attendance at
gigs. It even persuaded some, notably T. V. Smith and Gaye Advert, who
were living in Devon, to relocate to the capital – they would very quickly
form one of the most exciting of the early punk bands, the Adverts. In
attracting new audiences to London, moreover, the review helped to
create channels through which punk could flow out of the city and new
local punk worlds could be created further afield. The first of these new
worlds was in Manchester, which was to become, in the eyes of some,
punk's second city. This claim requires elaboration.

Punk heads north

Among those who read the Marquee review were two students at Bolton
College of Technology: Howard Trafford and Peter McNeish. McNeish
had played in a number of bands and the two were in the process of
putting together a new band, influenced by the Stooges and the Velvet
Underground. Spencer's review resonated strongly and excited them.
Having temporary use of a car they decided to travel to London the
following weekend, to find out more. They arranged to stay with
Trafford's old friend, Richard Boon, and rang the *NME* office to ask for
more details of the band. A slight misunderstanding led them to look for
a sex shop on the King's Road but they eventually found SEX and met
McLaren, who informed them that the Pistols were playing both that
and the following night.

They attended both gigs and, like a growing number of acolytes, were
transformed. Trafford became Howard Devoto, McNeish became Pete
Shelley and they set about putting their band, which they now called
Buzzcocks, together with fresh enthusiasm, with Boon as their manager.
Speaking further with McLaren, moreover, they decided to organise a
gig for the Pistols back up north.

The venue was to have been their Bolton College and Buzzcocks were
going to play support. In the event, however, a disastrous first gig at
the college on 1 April persuaded them that Buzzcocks weren't ready
for live performance and the college's social committee turned down
the option of the Pistols' gig. Not dissuaded, however, Devoto and Shelley
found both a local rock band to occupy the now vacant support slot and
a better venue in central Manchester. The Lesser Free Trade Hall was
a small upstairs room in a building which had hosted early Suffragette
meetings, Chartist rallies and Bob Dylan's infamous 'Judas' gig.[3] On 4
June 1976 it became the venue for the Sex Pistols' first Manchester gig.

The gig was every bit as historic as Dylan's. It is the focus of a book, *The Gig That Changed the World* (Nolan 2006), features in the opening sequence to the film, *24 Hour Party People*, and was deemed number one in *NME*'s listing '100 Gigs You Should Have Been At'[4] as recently as 2012. Furthermore, it is widely regarded as the catalyst for a chain reaction which gave birth to the successive punk, post-punk and dance worlds for which the Manchester is now famed:

> I've often done it for practice: join the line from the Sex Pistols all the way up to Mr Scruff and Badly Drawn Boy. Everything that happens is still a fall out of the Sex Pistols coming to the Lesser Free Trade Hall. There's no doubt about it – all the way through Joy Division to the Stone Roses, from the Fall to the Happy Mondays, all the way through the dance stuff, anything mad that happened at the Haçienda, you can draw it all back to that little explosion at the Lesser Free Trade Hall. It's not hard at all. (Paul Morley, cited in Nolan 2006: 15)

It is often joked that if everybody who claims to have been at the gig actually had then the Pistols would have filled a football stadium when, in fact, only twenty-eight advance tickets were sold (Nolan 2007: 32) and attendance probably didn't exceed sixty. Moreover, exactly who *was* there is a source of both contention and confusion, a state of affairs not helped by the fact that the Pistols played Manchester four times in relatively close succession during 1976: twice at the Lesser Free Trade Hall (4 June and 20 July), at the instigation of Devoto, Shelley and Boon, and then twice in December, at the Electric Circus, as part of the ill-fated Anarchy Tour (see below). It is widely agreed, however, that many of those in attendance went on to become central players in Manchester's punk and post-punk worlds, from the formative members of the Fall and Joy Division, through Morrissey and Jon the Postman, to Tony Wilson and celebrated producer, Martin Hannett. It is also clear, as discussed in Chapter 3, that most who attended did so because the Pistols had been likened to the Stooges in the Marquee review and had a known association, via McLaren, with the New York Dolls (a 17-year-old Morrissey was chair of the Dolls' UK fan club).

As in London, many of these attendees report an immediate conversion. Peter Hook went out the next day and bought a bass guitar, for example. Furthermore, again mirroring the process in London, enthusiasm was transmitted through personal networks, swelling the ranks for subsequent gigs:

> I've no idea of the time difference between the first and the second show but I just get the feeling that we'd all run around and said 'You've got to come, you've got to come'. (Paul Morley, cited in Nolan 2006: 72)

I was evangelical about it, honestly. I told everybody about that band, everybody I encountered, about the Sex Pistols. (Ian Moss, cited *ibid.*)

Maybe it's only in a small city that you can have that kind of communication, that can take you from thirty-five people on June 4th to several hundred on July 20th. The word goes out, the word spreads. (Tony Wilson, cited *ibid.*: 71)

And it wasn't just an audience that was created. Manchester very quickly acquired a roster of punk bands. Buzzcocks felt sufficiently well rehearsed by the time of the Pistols' second Manchester gig to play support and they were joined by Slaughter and the Dogs. Slaughter were a glam rock band who, like many others, jumped ship to punk when its star began to rise. Other bands in Manchester who did something similar include V2 and Wild Ram, who roadied for Slaughter on the night of their support slot with the Pistols, changing their name to Ed Banger and the Nosebleeds after the gig, following a fight which bloodied the nose of their lead singer and saw him christened a 'right head banger'.

Many new bands formed in the wake of the Pistols' early visits to the city too, however. As noted above, Peter Hook bought a bass the next day and, with Bernard Sumner, began rehearsing the band that would become Warsaw and later Joy Division. Similarly, Mark Smith and the friends with whom he had attended the June gig formed the Fall, who were gigging within six months. Another example, even though the balance of opinion now is that his first was the Sex Pistols' second Manchester gig, was Mick Hucknall, who formed the Frantic Elevators.

Furthermore, others began to look to other roles. In addition to band (and label) management, for example, Richard Boon looked to promotion; organising gigs and punk discos across the city. Paul Morley and his friend, Kevin Cummins, launched their respective careers in music journalism and photography via a punk zine, *Girl Trouble*. They also played in a band, the Negatives, with Boon, Dave Bent (who also ran indie label, Bent Records, and briefly managed the Drones) and Steve Shy, whose cleverly entitled, *Shy Talk*,[5] was another important early zine. Similarly, Linder Sterling, Malcolm Garrett and Peter Saville each turned their respective art-school educations to the task of poster and record sleeve design. And Tony Wilson, who had been at the first Free Trade Hall gig, having been personally invited by Devoto, who also sent him a cassette of the Pistols, used the music slot on his regional teatime TV programme, *So It Goes*, to publicise punk bands. He squeezed the Sex Pistols into the last programme of the first series, in August 1976, giving them their first ever television appearance, and the music in the second series was mostly punk.

These were not discrete individual actions. They were interactions. As in London, protagonists were responding to and influencing one another: inspiring, provoking, cooperating, coordinating and competing within an emerging network. New bands encouraged would-be promoters to step forward, while new promoters encouraged new and different bands to form; events enticed new audiences and growing audiences gave promoters the leverage to arrange further events. Zines fed off all of these activities, while at the same time encouraging them by publicising them. And all of this activity created foci which brought people together, creating a network and thereby a Manchester punk world.

The process of network formation is highlighted if we contrast the Manchester network presented in Chapter 5 (page 103), which includes a sample of Manchester's movers and shakers from June 1976, linked either by friendship or collaboration on a music project, with Figure 7.1, which maps relations between the same set of actors, on the same basis, as of April 1980. Having been fragmented into 29 separate components in June 1976, 17 of which were isolates, they now form a single component. Density has risen from 0.04 to 0.18, and average degree has risen from 3 (SD=4) to 10.9 (SD=6). Moreover, a further 41 per cent of pairs are linked by only one intermediary and a further 32 per cent by two intermediaries. Fragmentation and disconnection have given way to a compact network, and though my snapshots are separated by four years much of this transformation was achieved within a matter of months.

Moral panic

What was happening in Manchester in the summer of 1976 would soon begin in other UK cities, including Liverpool and Sheffield (see Chapter 8). Even many smaller towns generated clusters of bands who were active in the national punk world that was beginning to take shape (Glasper 2004; Ogg 2006). However, in many cases this was triggered and encouraged by a sequence of events which took punk and the Pistols from occasional coverage in the specialist weekly music press onto the front pages of the national dailies, making them household names.

On 8 October 1976 the Sex Pistols signed a contract with EMI. They released their first single, 'Anarchy in the UK', on 26 November, and McLaren and Rhodes were planning an accompanying promotional tour, the Anarchy Tour, for December and January. It was to feature the Pistols, the Clash, the Damned and (ex- New York Dolls) Johnny Thunder and the Heartbreakers. A few days before the tour was due to begin, however, on 1 December 1976, events took an unpredicted turn.

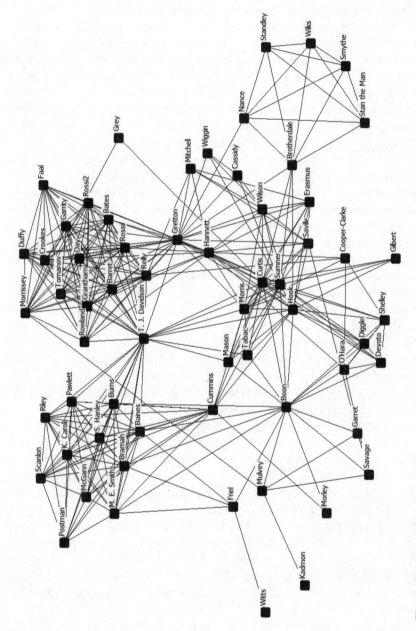

Figure 7.1 Manchester revisited

One of EMI's other acts, the celebrated rock band, Queen, pulled out of an interview on *Today*, a regional (London area) news programme and the company decided to replace them with the Pistols. Nobody got what they bargained for. The Pistols, who had taken their friends in the Bromley Contingent along with them, took full advantage of the green room, drinking heavily before going on. And so too, by most accounts, did their host, Bill Grundy. The interview, which only lasted a couple of minutes, started badly and then deteriorated. The downturn could have started when Steve Jones, responding to a question about the money the band had earned, replied: 'We fuckin' spent it, ain't we?' Given the programme's teatime slot such language was potentially scandalous but Grundy appears not to have heard it. Minutes later, however, he did hear a 'shit' from John Lydon and asked him to repeat the word. The already tense atmosphere worsened and Grundy, perhaps attempting to ease it, turned to the 'girls' of the Bromley Contingent. This strategy backfired, however, as he was perceived to be flirting with Siouxsie, prompting Jones to call him a 'dirty old man'. Grundy responded by inviting Jones to carry on and 'say something outrageous'. A couple of eff words later and Grundy's career was in tatters. He was suspended from the show and, shortly afterwards, the show itself was axed.

Initially McLaren believed that the Pistols were finished too. He rushed them out of the studio, furious that they had blown their big chance. In some respects he was right. Life did become difficult. In other respects, however, he couldn't have been further from the truth. The moral panic which followed made the Pistols a household name and swelled the ranks of the punk world out of all proportion.

Many viewers were outraged, jamming the Thames Television switchboard with complaints. One father allegedly smashed his TV in order to protect his children from this malign influence. And the shock quickly spread beyond the London area, when several national newspapers ran the story on their front pages. The *Daily Mirror*'s condemnation of 'the Filth and the Fury' and the *Daily Express*' 'Filthy Lucre' headline both achieved iconic status in Pistols' mythology, especially when the band and their entourage appropriated these phrases for their own purposes.

More problematically, the BBC (radio as well as television) refused to play 'Anarchy in the UK', denying the Pistols access to what is still the main means of selling records and achieving chart success in the UK. And several EMI workers refused to handle the record, slowing down production and distribution. That is, before production was halted altogether. Within weeks EMI decided to end their contract with the Pistols, making the EMI pressing of Anarchy a collectors' item.

These problems were exacerbated when venues and councils began to pull out of the Anarchy Tour. In some cases the band were asked to perform before councillors (they didn't). In other cases they were banned without even being given this opportunity. It is difficult to summarise the proportion of projected shows actually played because what was 'projected' changed as tour organisers tried to rearrange cancelled shows but of the nineteen shows advertised in an *NME* poster from 27 November 1976, sixteen were cancelled.

The Pistols' team did what they could to retrieve the situation. They managed to secure an extra gig at two of the places where they were allowed to play, Manchester and Plymouth, and they added a gig in Cleethorpes. Furthermore, they made a very famous shift of venue in Wales, from Cardiff Top Rank to the Castle Cinema in Caerphilly. However, the bands only played seven gigs in total, in five different locations (Gildart 2013).

The Caerphilly gig is famous because many locals were horrified and protested outside of the venue: singing hymns, lighting candles and trying to persuade people not to go in. As the protest was televised it added another iconic image to the many which the Pistols and punk were accumulating in December 1976. However, the reaction in Caerphilly is just one high-profile and theatrical example of a pattern common to most of the towns and cities scheduled for a Sex Pistols visit, and it was a less successful protest. The band played.

Even in towns where the Pistols were not scheduled to play there was a similar outcry on behalf of self-appointed 'moral entrepreneurs' (Becker 1963) intent on stopping punk in its tracks. Church groups, moral campaigners and tabloid journalists were among the most vocal opponents of punk. However, as Gildart (2013) shows, they were not alone. The Sex Pistols met with opposition from certain trade unions, students' unions and communist groups. Punks became 'folk devils' (Cohen 2002): symbols of all that was wrong with the UK, albeit among groups whose sense of what was wrong differed markedly, and a focus for the anger and anxiety which these problems and stresses were causing.

Attempts to stop the punks from playing inevitably provoked counter-fire. Some came from within the ranks of punk's apologists. Letters to the press by one Steven Morrissey were to be expected. Not all protestors were fans of the Pistols, however. Some hated the band as much as the censors did but they opposed the principle of censorship and supported the right of young people to make whatever racket and say whatever they wanted to. Others still felt that their own rights were being impeded. Even though the students' union at the University of East Anglia had voiced opposition to a planned Pistols' gig on campus, for example, they resented the vice chancellor's decision to cancel it, complaining to the local newspaper that this undermined their autonomy. Indeed fifty students mounted a brief occupation of the university's administration block (Gildart 2013).

Furthermore, as Stan Cohen's (2002) classic account of moral panics might have allowed punk's opponents to foresee, their attempts to quash it backfired, feeding it the oxygen of publicity and bestowing the excitement and allure of the forbidden upon it. They made life difficult for the Sex Pistols, who lost their recording contract and could not find UK venues in which to play. And this affected other punk bands too, prompting some to opt for a 'new wave' rather than a 'punk' tag (see Chapter 1). But their protests and outrage made punk very exciting and allowed it to jump from the relatively limited transmission networks of interpersonal contact, punk fanzines and the specialist music press to the national press, generating adherence within constituencies who might otherwise have remained oblivious to this previously underground musical phenomenon – as they had to the New York Dolls, Velvet Underground and Stooges. Everybody knew about punk now and huge numbers of young people wanted to find out more and become involved. They wanted to buy punk records, dress like punks and both see and form their own punk bands, generating a demand which prompted local cultural entrepreneurs across the UK to organise punk events. And all of this generated local punk networks and worlds.

As portrayed in the media, punks transgressed norms of bourgeois respectability. They challenged authority and symbolised the threat of chaos in an otherwise very ordered society. Much as this frightened some young people (not to mention the older generation) it mobilised many. The punks were breaking taboos, and breaking taboos, even if only vicariously, through identification with a heroic rebel figure, is exciting. In a fascinating and important study of US 'freedom summer' volunteers, Doug McAdam (1988) refers to it as the 'freedom high', suggesting that it has a huge impact upon all who experience it.

Moreover, punk, again particularly as constructed in media discourse, offered a sense of collective identity and belonging at a time when many young people were in need of it. The CCCS are wrong, in this respect, to suggest that the media only disarm youth subcultures. As Sarah Thornton (1994) suggests, they are often integral to subcultural formation – at least as a mass phenomenon. But the CCCS are right about the role of subcultures, or music worlds, in affording their participants a sense of meaning and belonging. Punks were a tribe, a home for the homeless.

And of course the controversy surrounding punk was a marketing opportunity which many were happy to exploit. We see an interesting example of this in Manchester. The Free Trade Hall would not have the Pistols back in December, for the Anarchy Tour, on account of the moral panic. There had been no trouble at the two previous gigs that year but the venue's managers trusted media portrayals over their own experience. The Palace followed suit. The Electric Circus was keen for the gig, however, and the promoters, anticipating what would become a standard trick in the punk repertoire, used the fact that the band had been banned by other venues to make their pitch: the Pistols and their fellow acts were billed as having been 'Banned From the Palace, Banned From the Free Trade Hall' (cited in Gildart 2013). Furthermore, they took the opportunity created by so many other cancellations to book the Pistols for an extra date on the tour. Their decision was endorsed by prolific letter writer, Steven Morrissey, who wrote to the *Manchester Evening News* that the Sex Pistols were speaking for the youth of the day. The gamble paid off. For the next ten months, after which it was closed on health and safety grounds, the Electric Circus became the centre of Manchester's punk world and a major focus for punks in the north more generally, hosting all of the major acts of the era.

Furthermore, while certain groups on both the left and the right wings of the political spectrum were keen to criticise punk and stop it in its tracks, others saw it as a recruitment opportunity and sought both to align themselves with it and co-opt it. It would be some years before a mainstream politician would confess to a passion for the Clash and expect to win political capital by doing so but the International Socialists and the National Front, notwithstanding reservations among some in their ranks, were both on the case in 1977. Each framed punk as an expression of underlying tensions and conflicts which they, as a political party, were seeking to address, shaping public perceptions of punk and indeed punk itself in the process.

It was in this context that ethnicity became a salient element in the punk mix. The National Front sought to recruit at punk gigs and to stir up racial hatred within the punk constituency, capitalising upon the politically innocent but naive flirtation with Nazi and fascist imagery by early punks, and giving it a more literal meaning. The Socialist Workers, by contrast, were key players in the alliance that gave rise to Rock Against Racism, a huge series of gigs, mostly by punk and reggae bands in the early stages, seeking to make a public stance against racism (Gilroy 1992; Goodyer 2009; Street 2012: 79–97).

Counterfactuals are difficult to decide and impossible to prove but it seems unlikely that the Pistols and the punk world more widely would have grown to the extent that they did in the absence of the moral panic triggered by the Grundy interview. The panic may have happened without Grundy. Britain was in crisis. The press, on the look-out for scandal at the best of times, were waiting for something like punk to demonise and blame. And the Pistols were an accident waiting to happen. The potential for scandal had been there on their first television appearance, on Tony Wilson's *So It Goes* programme. Jordan was sporting a swastika armband, which officials scarcely managed to conceal, and the band caused chaos as the cameras panned out and the show finished. It is very unlikely that punk would have spread as extensively as it did, however, without the mainstream media interest generated in the moral panic. And it may never have moved beyond London without the mediated networks represented by the specialised music press.

Conclusion

The aim of this chapter was to consider how London's punk world began to spread out, generating a national punk world. My answer, in brief, has been: the mass media. Media networks broadcast information regarding punk to individuals living both within and beyond London, stimulating many to become involved and sparking a process which led to the emergence of local punk worlds in cities across the UK.

In Chapter 10 I revisit the national context, considering the links between local worlds that allowed them, collectively, to form an integrated network and national world. Before I do, however, I want to look at three of these local worlds in more detail, and also to consider the transformation of punk into post-punk.

Notes

1 www.paulgormanis.com/?p=2550
2 *Ibid.*
3 In the mid 1960s Dylan began to play electric guitar on some songs and to move in a 'rock' direction, breaking with the pure folk orientation of his earlier music. Folk purists among his early audience were horrified and spoke out. When playing in Manchester, at the Free Trade Hall in 1966, he was heckled with the cry of 'Judas'. The altercation became famous because it was captured on a popular bootleg. The bootleg purports to be at the Royal Albert Hall in London but its true location has subsequently been discovered.
4 *NME* 12/03/12.
5 Correctly pronounced, Shy Talk sounds suspiciously like both Shite Talk and Shite Hawk – a widely used northern insult.

8

From punk to post-punk: a tale of three cities

Following the moral panic described in Chapter 7 punk became part of Britain's national consciousness. Everybody knew about it and every city had its own local punk world. Over time, however, the diffusion of punk gave way to opposition and adaptation, in Tarde's (2000) sense (Crossley 2014). Significant numbers of those who had been mobilised by the energy and DIY ethos of punk began to feel that it was ossifying; becoming uniform, limited and limiting. They wanted to do something different. Les Pattinson of Echo and the Bunnymen, for example, notes that: 'After six months of punk, everybody got bored with it and started getting into weirder things' (in Cooper 1982: 14). Julian Cope, whose band, the Teardrop Explodes, were the Bunnymen's main competitors in Liverpool's post-punk world, concurs:

> the punk thing had this kind of built-in obsolescence. When I first got into the idea, in November 1976, I thought I was way too late. But new people were finding the scene all the time. Now we figured punk would be over in a couple of months. We wanted something new. (Cope 1994: 43)

Likewise Linder Sterling, whose artwork, as well as her music, shaped Manchester's punk/post-punk identity:

> The original punk thing ran out very quickly ... in its initial purity punk was probably just six months or so ... with Howard [Devoto] being so articulate it happened early – this sense of 'It's not right, it's not right'. (in Reynolds 2009: 219)

Still inspired by its energy and DIY ethos, and still working within the networks of people, places and resources they had created around it, however, punk's early risers set about creating something new. Most were unsure where their musical experiments were headed but by playing with the punk format and introducing elements and influences from elsewhere they began to move beyond it.

They were joined by others who had only ever been inspired by punk's DIY ethos and the opportunities it created, never its style. Despite the existence of a lively punk world (Beesley 2009, 2010a, 2010b), many of Sheffield's post-punk bands exemplify this second relation to punk. Cabaret Voltaire, for example, pre-date the Sex Pistols and, notwithstanding the more up-tempo and aggressive feel of their classic single, 'Nag, Nag, Nag', were not obviously influenced, musically, by punk, but they rose to prominence in a nexus of DIY musical activism inspired and triggered by punk. Likewise the Human League. They were not impressed by punk music but they were excited by the possibilities it suggested:

> During the punk revolution everything became possible. All the things that had seemed completely unattainable were in reach, however unlikely. (Martin Ware, in Lilleker 2005: 43)

Musically, both the Human League and Cabaret Voltaire were influenced by Krautrock (Kraftwerk in particular) and other early synthesiser pioneers, such as Delia Derbyshire,[1] whose theme tune for the *Dr Who* television series was an early Human League cover, and Walter/Wendy Carlos, who composed the soundtrack for the film adaptation of *A Clockwork Orange* – a novel whose influence pervades Sheffield's early post-punk world.[2] In this respect they exemplify an interesting and widespread pattern. Their 'post-punk' music was influenced by pre-punk musical currents and experiments. As noted in Chapter 3, although the musical environment prior to punk was experienced as stultifying by many proto-punks there were various alternatives which they found inspiring. Punk drew upon one of these: the garage-glam of the Stooges, the New York Dolls, etc. When it kicked down the doors of popular music, however, many of the bands who came through drew upon the others.

Though mainstream, the importance of David Bowie and Roxy Music, combined with the Krautrock that was influencing both in the mid 1970s, is difficult to overestimate in this respect, particularly in the case of the 'futurists' and new romantics but also in relation to Manchester's Joy Division, who were the epitome of post-punk for some (they were originally called Warsaw, after 'Warszawa', a track on Bowie's 1977 *Low* LP). Reggae and ska were also very important, however, particularly in Coventry's Two-Tone world, and the US psychedelia popularised by Lenny Kaye's *Nuggets* compilation was equally influential, not least in Liverpool. In addition, various other musical forms, from folk to funk and rockabilly were all rediscovered and reworked, creating a diverse patchwork of DIY musical experimentation.

The formation of post-punk worlds, like the formation of London's original punk world, required a critical and networked mass of participants. In the case of post-punk, however, punk had largely done the work of assembling this infrastructure; mobilising young enthusiasts and bringing them into contact at gigs, venues, record shops and punk discos. The achievement of post-punk's pioneers was to 'coherently deform' (Giddens 1984; Merleau-Ponty 1962) the style produced within these worlds, transforming it from punk into a variety of post-punk formats.

Not everyone tired of punk. Punk worlds continued to form and grow even in those cities where vibrant post-punk worlds were emerging (Glasper 2004). If anything, however, the form which punk assumed in these worlds further motivated the move away from punk by post-punks who felt that it was becoming a parody of itself, devoid of the edge and possibilities it had once promised.

In this chapter and the next I discuss this transition as it played out in three of the major geographical centres of post-punk innovation: Liverpool, Manchester and Sheffield. I discuss each in turn, beginning with Manchester, whose story I pick up from Chapter 7. In each case I structure my discussion around a set of common academic themes, exploring differences but more especially similarities between these three local worlds which were particularly striking when I was examining the secondary and archival material regarding them. Four themes in particular are important:

1 *Focal places.* As suggested earlier in the book, local music worlds tend to form around particular places within a city. These places serve as 'foci' (Feld 1981, 1982), generating networks by attracting likeminded individuals and concentrating them within time–space. Equally, however, networks generate foci: places acquire reputations (within networks) and this contributes to their power of attraction. Moreover, it is not bricks and mortar as such which make a world's key places (although building design and construction can make a difference). Places take on their character and allure in virtue of the interactivities (and thus networks) of their habitués. World participants 'make' their music places through the ways in which they use building, objects and spaces. One of my aims in this chapter is to identify these places for each of the city-based worlds considered.

2 *Local culture, taste makers and the primacy of the network.* As the introduction to this chapter has already indicated, local punk and

post-punk worlds did not passively reproduce a punk culture transmitted from London. They selected, reworked and played with elements of punk, adding further influences and generating their own
version of punk and ultimately post-punk (London's punk culture too
was always in-process and gave rise to various forms of post-punk).
This happened in various ways, which I discuss, but I give special
attention to two factors which, I believe, contributed significantly
to the dominance of particular and different styles in each city (e.g.
electronic music in Sheffield and psychedelia in Liverpool): (a) the
influence of dominant *taste makers* within each world, who contributed disproportionately to shaping the style of other key participants;
(b) the high level of mobility of musicians between different bands in
the early stages of the world's development, which facilitated mutual
influence between a relatively high proportion of participants. The
closure suggested by established band line-ups can be misleading with
respect to emerging local worlds, I suggest, because of this movement
and because of the short-lived nature of many bands. Musicians are,
for some purposes, better through of as belonging to a network, out
of which temporary bands forms and into which they dissolve again,
than to a self-contained band.

3 *Support personnel.* As in the London world considered in earlier
   chapters, support personnel are central.
4 *Cooperation, conflict and elites.* Again like London, the interaction constituting the network in each of the three worlds involves a
   mixture of cooperation and conflict, and both are important. This
   manifests at the individual level but also at the level of factions and
   cores which are discernible in the network (see also Chapter 9).
   Furthermore, these clusters are not always equal but different. Some
   are dominant, others subordinate.

These latter two themes are taken up, by way of a formal network analysis, in the next chapter, and much of the discussion in this chapter serves
a contextual precursor for that analysis. The chapter stands in own
right, however, as a detailed qualitative analysis of some of the common
and key features of these music worlds.

Manchester

Manchester's critical mass of proto-punks were ready for the Pistols
when they arrived in the city for the first time on 4 June 1976 and, as
noted in Chapter 7, they spread the word quickly through their personal
networks, generating a local punk audience. With the addition of local

punk bands, some starting from scratch, others switching from a glam or 'pubby' style, a local punk world quickly took shape.

The Worst took punk at its word with respect to amateurism. Their drummer used a child's toy drum kit. However, first prize for DIY goes to Jon the Postman. Post Office employee by day, his music career began when, in a flash of drunken inspiration, he rushed a stage recently vacated by Buzzcocks and offered an a cappella rendition of 'Louie Louie'. Encouraged by the experience he repeated it on subsequent occasions to a point where his unannounced and uninvited performances became a welcome and expected ritual in the Manchester punk world. Eventually bands began to invite him to perform, adding him to the bill. He went on to release several records and, according to one Manchester-based music journalist, had an integrating effect on the city's punk world. He was a symbol around which the in-crowd bonded:

> Those not accustomed to the strange vision of him, straddling the stage, beer bottle clutched tightly in one hand, microphone in the other, would simply stare, aghast. Those 'in the know' whooped and clapped joyously. It was an 'in joke'. (Middles, cited in Ogg 2006: 310–11)

Linking bands and audiences were venues, pubs and hangouts which served as network foci, drawing the likeminded into a common space, at a common time, where they would form ties, hatch plans and exchange gossip, generating a distinctly Mancunian punk culture. Punk might have originated in London but a combination of local creativity, regional pride, opposition to the presumptions of the capital and poor channels of communication meant that it was reinvented in Manchester rather than merely emulated:

> you could be forgiven for thinking that the punk look was universal and compulsory. The punk clichés – swastika armbands, spiky hair, bondage trousers – were less evident in Manchester. Certainly out went kipper ties, billowing flares and Oxford bags, but in Manchester punk attitudes and ideas took precedence over concern with wearing the right clothes ... The fact that punk in Manchester wasn't so uniform was its great strength. (Haslam 2000: 119–20)

> You didn't need bondage trousers and spikey hair to be a Punk in Manchester, it was more a question of your attitude. Everybody got their clothes from the Salvation Army or antique clothing markets. Coming to London to see the Ramones in June I was astounded at how fashion oriented it was. (Malcolm Garrett, in Savage 1991: 405)

Some pictures of the time contradict these claims but the image of such bands as the Fall and Joy Division (notwithstanding Peter Hook's early flirtation with biker gear), generally bears them out and the notion that

Manchester did punk in its own way is frequently repeated. The role of geographical distance and sparseness of ties to London in bringing this about is nicely captured, in an evolutionary analogy, by Buzzcocks' Pete Shelley:

> It was a bit like Australia, you know, the animals had a chance to develop in their own peculiar ways, untainted by what was happening in the rest of the world. (cited in Lee 2002: 137)

The Electric Circus, which had hosted the two Anarchy Tour gigs, was the first of Manchester's 'punk places' and remained its focal point until it closed in October of 1977. In addition to the Pistols and many of the home-grown bands who managed to get their act together during its short life as a punk venue, it hosted many of punk's great and good, including: the Slits, Clash, Adverts, Damned, Jam, Stranglers and Vibrators. When it closed, local luminaries, including Buzzcocks, the Fall, John Cooper Clarke, Warsaw, Magazine and Jon the Postman, came together to give it a proper, two-night send-off, the highlights of which were captured on a 10-inch, colour vinyl mini album: *Short Circuit: Live at the Electric Circus*.

By this time, however, the transition from punk to post-punk was under way, pioneered by Magazine in particular. Howard Devoto had left Buzzcocks shortly after the release of *Spiral Scratch*, ostensibly to finish his studies at Bolton College. However, he had kept working on the independent label that he had founded to release the EP (*New Hormones*), with Richard Boon, and more or less immediately began putting together his new band. He was already finding punk limiting, and at least some of the audience at the last night of the Electric Circus, where Magazine made their debut, felt the same:

> That night showed the way forward ... There was a sense of shock, and then relief that some of the pre-punk strands some of us actually still liked – glam, avant-garde electronics, canonical quotation – were okay again. (Peter Saville, cited in Nice 2010: 20)

The demise of the Electric Circus coincided with the birth of many other venues in Manchester as various would-be promoters stepped up to the mark. Among them, those who would achieve greatest celebrity within Manchester's post-punk worlds were Richard Boon, who had promoted the Pistols' gigs at the Free Trade Hall with Devoto and Shelley; Martin Hannett, who already worked in a promotion cooperative, Music Force, prior to punk; and Rob Gretton, who promoted a series of gigs at a local pub with his friend, Vini Faal, who also managed Ed Banger and the Nosebleeds.

The presence of actors willing to take on such support roles was crucial to the formation and thriving of Manchester's post-punk world. Important though they are, artists are not the whole story. Without anybody in the support roles artists would have no opportunity to either perform or record. Promotion was only one string on the bow of the above-mentioned mover–shakers, moreover. Boon managed bands, including Buzzcocks; occasionally played in a band, the Negatives; and ran a record label (New Hormones). Hannett played in bands (e.g. the Invisible Girls and Jilted John); managed artists (e.g. John Cooper Clarke); was involved with record labels (firstly Rabid and later Factory); and is best known as a producer. Gretton was best known as the manager of a number of bands, particularly Joy Division, and as a partner in Factory Records, but he was also a DJ at punk haunt, Rafters, and an early champion of both Slaughter and the Dogs and Ed Banger and the Nosebleeds, occasionally taking on managerial duties for them, providing financial support and running a Slaughter-focused zine: *Manchester Rains* (a riposte to the Clash's 'London's Burning', according to James Nice (2010)).

The main venues booked by these and other rising punk promoters included: the Squat, the Oaks and local gay bar, the Ranch. As noted in Chapter 3 and also in my discussion of Louise's lesbian bar, in Chapter 6, gay bars were important because their owners and clientele were more accepting of the punks' sartorial experimentation. Pete Shelley, for example, comments: 'gay bars were the places where you could go and be outlandish with your dress and [not] be beaten up' (cited in Lee 2002: 138). Similarly, Jayne Casey, writing about Liverpool, observes:

> Obviously like all our mates we'd come from gay clubs. Before Eric's opened, gay clubs were the only ones that would let us in, because of the way we looked. We'd kind of been into dance music in gay clubs, so we brought that with us. (1993)

The shift to post-punk is most closely associated with another venue, however, and with the record label and mover–shaker most closely associated with it: that is, the Factory, Factory Records and Tony Wilson. Wilson had been at the Pistols' first Manchester gig, with his friend, Alan Erasmus, and he had subsequently used his (regional) television programme, *So It Goes*, to bring punk to the north-west. The ten editions of the second series included twenty-seven punk-related features, including at least one live performance by a punk or 'new wave' band per programme: sometimes in the studio, sometimes at a venue in Manchester, sometimes at Eric's in Liverpool. This publicity helped to swell the audience for punk in the north-west, attracting bands from further afield and giving the region a reputation for punk music.

Wilson loved the transgressive nature of punk, he loved the north-west of England and he cherished the opportunity to bring the two together through *So It Goes*. When the show was axed, therefore, following bad language in an Iggy Pop interview, he set about looking for an alternative: a club. He sought advice from his friend, Roger Eagle, who had managed Manchester's famous Northern Soul club, the Twisted Wheel, and was now running the key venue for punk in Liverpool: Eric's. Eagle advised him and the two decided that, where possible, they would synchronise the activities of their respective clubs. His partners in the club, however, were Erasmus and design student, Peter Saville. Saville was anxious to become involved in the punk world. His friend and fellow student at Manchester Polytechnic, Malcolm Garrett, had designed Buzzcocks' first post-Devoto record sleeve (*Orgasm Addict*), along with another student, Linder Sterling, who was romantically attached to Devoto and was acquiring a strong reputation for her challenging feminist and punk-inspired designs. Linder (she was and is known by her first name), who later formed Ludus, had designed for both Buzzcocks and Magazine. When he spotted Wilson at a Patti Smith gig, therefore, Saville made contact and pitched for work. He got more than he bargained for.

The Factory was named, according to local legend, when Erasmus spotted a sign announcing one of many factory closures in Manchester at the time and wished that just once a factory would open. Based primarily in the Russell Club, a West Indian centre in Hume, but also briefly at the New Osborne Club[3] in Miles Platting, the Factory ran regular gigs between 19 May 1978 and 21 June 1980. Punk bands, including Crass, the Damned and Slaughter and the Dogs, played there but from the very start line-ups reflected the 'coherent deformation' of punk into post-punk. The first gig at the Factory, for example, was headlined by Durutti Column, whom Wilson and Erasmus managed and who would become club regulars. Durutti Column would soon become a vehicle for the solo work of their figurehead, Vini Reilly (often accompanied by Bruce Mitchell on drums and with added sound effects by Martin Hannett), whose compositions were atmospheric, ambient, often instrumental and bore the hallmarks of his classical (piano) training. They were still a band when opening the Factory, with a more conventional style, but Reilly had shed the punk trappings of his previous band, Ed Banger and the Nosebleeds, and Durutti Column were moving into post-punk territory. Moreover, when they played the club a second time, in June 1978, they were supported by Sheffield's avant-garde electronic experimentalists, Cabaret Voltaire, who would also become regulars at the Factory and close friends with the band most closely associated it: Joy Division. When Wilson *et al.* decided to expand their venture, forming an independent record label, Factory Records, their first release, a 2 x 7 inch sampler, featured each of these three seminal post-punk bands (Cabaret Voltaire, Durutti Column and Joy Division), with the somewhat incongruous addition of comedian, John Dowie.

Independent record labels flourished during the post-punk era (see Chapter 10) and this process had already begun when Factory Records was launched. In Manchester, alongside New Hormones and Bent Records, Tosh Ryan and Martin Hannett had released a number of punk records on their Rabid label, and they had worked with local cultural entrepreneur, T. J. Davidson, who also had a label, TJM, and had released records by Mick Hucknall's punk-inspired band: the Frantic Elevators. Furthermore, Wilson was aware that his friend, Roger Eagle, was launching a label in Liverpool, to accompany his club (Eric's), while Rough Trade were thriving in London, Fast Product were thriving in Edinburgh and similar things were happening elsewhere. Records were the next logical step for Wilson *et al.* but the achievements of their competitors suggested that they needed to act quickly.

Taking advice from other indie pioneers and drawing in Martin Hannett, Factory Records was launched in 1978 (Rob Gretton would later complete the management line up). Erasmus's flat in Didsbury became the label's base. Many of the early sleeves were assembled and filled there, usually by the artists themselves, alongside others in the network who needed to earn a few pounds. The independent sector was largely a cottage industry and Factory, whatever its apparent grandeur and reputation, was no exception.

Of all of the bands to sign to Factory, Joy Division are the best known and most celebrated. They were one of the Manchester bands directly inspired by the Pistols' first visit. Peter Hook and Bernard Sumner were both there and began practising immediately afterwards. They became acquainted with Ian Curtis, who would become their singer, from gigs and from his distinctive jacket, which had the word 'Hate' painted on the back. He joined, however, after responding to an advert placed in a local record shop. They met their permanent drummer, Steven Morris, similarly, via an ad which Curtis placed in a Macclesfield music shop (Curtis and Morris both lived in Macclesfield and had gone to the same school). Rob Gretton, who would become their manager and also a Factory partner, was initially known to them as the DJ at Rafters, a key punk venue. He famously met any requests for songs with a forthright 'fuck off!'. However, he had managerial experience with Slaughter and the Dogs, Ed Banger and the Nosebleeds, and a short-lived band called the Panik, featuring Joy Division's original drummer, Steve Brotherdale, and when he saw their now legendary performance at a battle of the bands competition at Rafters he offered to manage them – cornering Sumner in a phone box the next day. Another member of the audience that night was Tony Wilson, who was equally impressed and struck up a lifelong association with the band from that point.

Joy Division's first record, *An Ideal for Living* (EP), was released on their own Enigma label just a month before their inclusion on the Factory Sampler, and a 12-inch version of the EP was later released in their own Anonymous label. All subsequent releases were on Factory, however, and their decision to stay with Factory, even after enjoying national success, releasing two celebrated studio albums (*Unknown Pleasures* and *Closer*) and three classic singles ('Transmission', 'Atmosphere' and 'Love will Tear Us Apart') played a crucial role in bolstering the 'indie revolution' associated with post-punk (see Chapter 10). Joy Division showed that independent labels could be more than just launch pads for bands en route to a major label; that cult and even mainstream success was possible on an indie. Furthermore, through the excitement which their music and image generated they lent an aura of authenticity and cool to the independent sector, reinforcing the belief, common among post-punks at the time, that independents allowed their artists a creative freedom that major labels did not.

That Manchester is sometimes said to have had a distinct post-punk style is in some part due to the impact of Factory and the creative team who worked with many artists on the label. Like the agitators in the London punk world, Wilson would introduce those bands he was interested in to the various philosophical and political ideas which inspired him. Saville would create a distinctive visual image for them through their record sleeves and promotional posters, unique to them but distinct from much else in the post-punk world and always Factory-esque in virtue of its artistic references and style. And Hannett would produce the music, putting his distinctive stamp upon it. He imposed a very strict regime on Joy Division, for example, insisting that Steven Morris record his drum parts one drum at a time – in a freezing toilet on one occasion. And he employed various strategies, including secret late-night sessions and freezing studio temperatures, to keep the band out of the studio when he was mixing. Though they later grew to like it, Peter Hook and Bernard Sumner hated *Unknown Pleasures* initially. Hannett had taken the punky sound that they aspired to and taken it somewhere different altogether. Likewise Durutti Column: Vini Reilly found the finished version of *Return of the*

Durutti Column (his first album) very different to the tracks that he had laid down in the studio.

Later in the chapter I will be considering 'taste makers' in Liverpool and Sheffield; that is, figures who exerted a disproportionate influence on the tastes of others, contributing to the generation of distinct stylistic clusters within their local world. The Factory team do not qualify as taste makers because they did not so much influence artists' tastes as contribute directly to their output (sometimes bypassing their tastes), but they clearly played a huge role in shaping Manchester's post-punk sound and style, as commonly perceived, and in branding the city's post-punk world.

The story of Manchester's post-punk world is not only the story of Factory, however. As Factory partner, Peter Saville, himself puts it:

> There were different factions, and antagonisms between different factions … In Manchester at that time Factory and Tony were just another clique. (Nice 2010: 58)

Liz Naylor, a contributor to the *City Fun* fanzine who enjoyed some involvement with Factory, is more forthright:

> We used to call them Fat Tory Records. The way they dominated the city felt very elitist, and so lots of factions developed. It felt like it really mattered, like a war in which you took sides. I don't know what for, though. (Liz Naylor, cited *ibid.*: 97)

There are two points to note here. First, and most obviously, the Manchester post-punk world involved different factions, who were to varying degrees aware of themselves as such and opposed to other factions. There is also a suggestion here, however, second, that the Factory faction were, for a time, dominant within the city's post-punk world. They were in a position to exert a disproportionate influence, which affected others in ways which those others were unable to do very much about.

One obvious band, if not faction, that fell outside of the Factory camp were the Fall. They too had been at the first Free Trade Hall gig, or at least the members of the original line-up had.[4] And they too responded almost immediately to the challenge which it issued, forming a band whose sound remains highly distinctive to this day. Furthermore, though they played at The Factory on various occasions, they took advantage of another emergent element in Manchester's punk/post-punk world, the Manchester Musician's Collective; a loose collection of artists and bands who pooled certain of their talents and other resources in an effort to create opportunities for performance.

Whatever the factions and conflicts, however, the ties of cooperation (on a musical project) between the central figures of the Manchester world for the period 1976–80 form a single network component (see Figure 8.1). Everybody has a path to everybody else.

Liverpool

Liverpool was slower off the mark with respect to punk than Manchester and its better-known punk bands, such the Spitfire Boys, Big in Japan (to whom the punk tag only loosely applies) and the Accelerators, failed to achieve the success enjoyed by the likes of Buzzcocks, John Cooper Clarke and Slaughter and the Dogs. The Sex Pistols had played in Liverpool on 15 October 1976, at the club which was to become the focal point of Liverpool's punk and post-punk worlds, Eric's, but this gig does not appear to have had the same mobilising effect as the Lesser Free Trade Hall gigs in Manchester and a planned second appearance on 11 December, at Liverpool Stadium, was cancelled following the Grundy incident.

However, Liverpool had its own Free Trade Hall moment on 5 May 1977, when the Clash played at Eric's. This was the moment when a group of Eric's regulars, some of whom roadied for local art-school pub rockers, Deaf School, decided to form their own band. Big in Japan may never have achieved commercial success but, along with Deaf School, they loomed large in Liverpool during the late 1970s, assembling a cast of movers and shakers who would be central to much that was to follow in the city's post-punk world, and beyond. The (soon to be) better known of its members were:

- Bill Drummond, who later achieved mainstream success with the KLF and its offshoots, and who, with Dave Balfe, managed Echo and the Bunnymen and the Teardrop Explodes. Drummond and Balfe also enjoyed some success, with Lori Lartey, as Lori and the Chameleons, and founded the Zoo record label.
- Dave Balfe, who, in addition to the above, played with the Teardrop Explodes, Dalek I Love You and the Turquoise Swimming Pools. He went on to become a successful band and label manager.
- Ian Broudie, who has enjoyed success both as a producer and as the founder member (singer, songwriter and guitarist) of the Lightning Seeds.
- Jayne Casey, who went on to form both Pink Military and Pink Industry, and later became involved in Liverpool's internationally successful dance club: Cream.

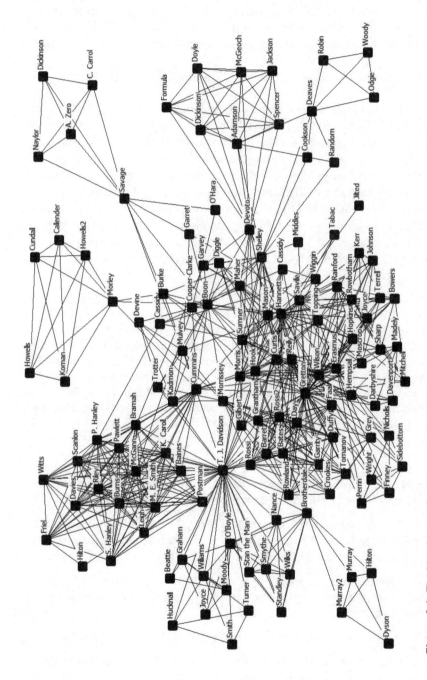

Figure 8.1 The Manchester network

- Peter Clarke (Budgie), who had played in the Spitfire Boys, with Paul Rutherford (later in the Opium Eaters and Frankie Goes to Hollywood), Holly Johnson and Pete Wylie (of Wah!) and who later moved to London, playing in both the Slits and Siouxsie and the Banshees.
- Holly Johnson, who later fronted Frankie Goes to Hollywood.

In addition to these personal successes, Big in Japan were important, again like Deaf School, whom they were inspired by, because they were a catalyst, inspiring others to form bands. Even those who didn't like them were mobilised by them. Julian Cope, for example, famously started a petition, posted in Probe Records, another key focal point of the Liverpool punk world, alongside Eric's, calling for them to disband. The petition was signed by, among others, members of Big in Japan.

This well-humoured response by the band shouldn't detract from the fact that, as in Manchester, there were factions in the Liverpool world. And relations between these factions were sometimes tense. Big in Japan singer, Jayne Casey, remembers:

> People like Ian McCulloch and Julian Cope ... they all really hated us and they formed an anti-Big in Japan society. They got a petition together, and when they had 2,000 names on it we had to split up. Then they got t-shirts with my face printed on them, so they'd all walk around in t-shirts with my face on them, getting everyone to sign these petitions, which we all signed because we were into it you know. 'He's got my face on his chest, he fuckin' hates me, I love it!' (laughs) So it was very antagonistic. They were into things like Jack Kerouac, quite dry things. We were just into 'camping out' and having a laugh. It was two separate scenes, and then they started to play instruments and wanted to be in bands, which is why they hated us so much to begin with, because we were doing it and they were sort of just coming up ... In later years we became friends, but it was very antagonistic in the beginning ... It was the most competitive I've ever seen in the Liverpool music scene at that time. (Jayne Casey 1993)

As with 'Fat Tory Records' in Manchester this was not only a matter of factions but also of a dominant faction who exerted a disproportionate influence. Casey herself, for example, notes that:

> we were the Eric's ... band and everyone hated us because we were dead cocky and dead mouthy. If you walked into Eric's, there was a little platform, and that was our table. (*ibid.*)

Julian Cope, an outsider at first, also spotted the spatial politics:

> At the bottom of the stairs, Peter Burns and Paul Rutherford were ensconced on their thrones, the territory of floor just before the main

doors. They would sit there, sometimes with Lyn [Burns] and their young acolytes, and slag people off as they entered the club.

[...] to a girl behind me who was wearing a leopard-skin pill-box hat, 'Ay gairl, worrav yer gorra dead cat on yer 'ed for?' (1994: 32)

With time, however, Cope himself was absorbed into the elite:

Eric's became a snobby snotty little scene. And I was as snotty as anybody else. You always are when you are on the inside. (*ibid.*: 73)

As Cope's 'promotion' shows, however, elite status was not fixed. Moreover, the movement of musicians between bands, in different combinations, which I discuss below, suggests that boundaries between factions were fluid and context dependent.

Beyond factions and elites these descriptions of Eric's illustrate how focal places, which generate networks, are also generated by those networks. They become places where interested parties meet because they acquire a reputation within certain networks, which draws particular people to them. Julian Cope notes in his autobiography, for example, that Eric's had loomed large in his imagination before he had ever been there because of the ways in which others talked about it:

See, Hilary had been to Eric's. It was *the* Liverpool club. Brian and I had twice been into Liverpool but failed to find it. We'd already missed the Sex Pistols when they played. The second time, we missed the Stranglers. Now we knew somebody who could take us there. (Cope 1994: 15, emphasis in original)

In addition, however, the place itself is 'made' by the uses to which its inhabitants put it. Physically Eric's was just a cellar in a building that had once serviced the docks. It enjoyed the distinction of being a stone's throw from where the Cavern had been but the Cavern too was just a dank cellar. What distinguished the Cavern was the fact that the Beatles regularly played there but it isn't just bands who transform places. Audiences 'make' clubs too by investing them with rituals, symbols and meanings. The Eric's experience was the experience of a club dominated by a particular in-crowd and their characteristic props and practices. The nature of the experience was no doubt very different for those within and outside of the in-crowd, respectively, but in either case Eric's was more than bricks and mortar. It was bricks and mortar invested by a network of interaction and the culture it generated.

The Clash gig that saw the birth of Big in Japan also marked a crucial turning point in Cope's own music career. On that night he met Pete Wylie and, through Wylie, Ian McCulloch. Between them they would be responsible for Liverpool's three best-known post-punk bands: Echo and the Bunnymen (McCulloch), the Teardrop Explodes (Cope) and Wah! (Wylie). Before that, however, they would play together, in different combinations and with many other future luminaries of Liverpool's post-punk world, in innumerable short-lived bands, beginning with the Crucial Three: a bedroom band in which Wylie played guitar, Cope played bass and McCulloch sang.

The movement of musicians between bands and the formation and demise of bands themselves was so rapid in Liverpool at this time that the network of musicians must be deemed more fundamental to what was going on than particular bands. Eventually certain line-ups became more fixed and enduring but for a time bands were temporary vehicles enabling different combinations of players to try one another out and play with musical ideas, moving on if the arrangement didn't suit. To many observers this had a comical side:

> In Probe, Geoff Davies and John Athey would sarcastically ask the name and line up of each group that we put together. There were so many combinations, it seemed like I'd played with everyone in Liverpool. (Cope 1994: 79)

It was an important formative process, however: for individuals, for the more enduring bands that eventually came out of it and for the post-punk world itself. And it was a process at once facilitated by and generative of a network of musicians. By working with new people musicians forged new ties but they often made contact with new people and heard about opportunities through existing contacts.

Interestingly, moreover, the above-mentioned factions do not seem to have posed a barrier to this fluidity. In addition to such future notables as Pete Burns, who would later form Dead or Alive, for example, the many short-lived bands that Wylie, Cope and McCulloch became involved in often included ex-members of Big in Japan. I have already noted that Bill Drummond and Dave Balfe managed the Bunnymen and the Teardrops (with Balfe playing keyboards in the latter). To this we might add that Wylie and Cope played in the Nova Mob with Budgie, while Wylie played in the Opium Eaters with Ian Broudie and (again) Budgie.

The network which these various short-lived bands and musical associations gave rise to, across 1976–1980 period, is visualised in Figure 8.2. Note that, as in Manchester, it forms a single component. The existence of factions and elites did not prevent everybody from being at least indirectly connected to everybody else.

Eric's and Probe were the key focal points for punks and post-punks in Liverpool: places where ties were made, bands formed, plans hatched

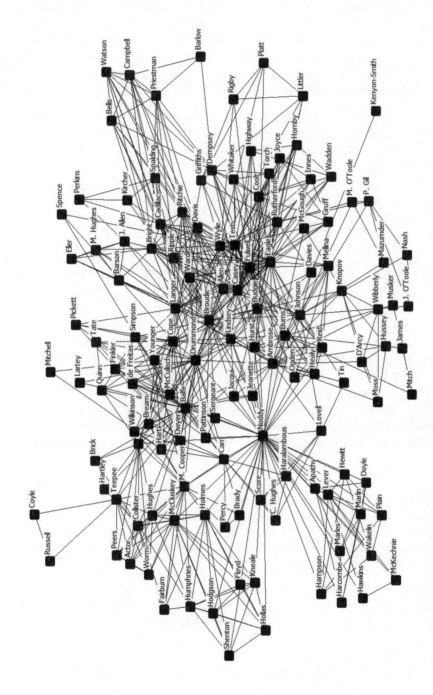

Figure 8.2 The Liverpool network

and the distinctive post-punk culture of Liverpool generated. Everybody who was anybody went to Eric's and Probe, with many future luminaries working at the latter at one time and the rest hanging out there, eagerly seeking out the opinions and recommendations of shop owner, Geoff Davies. Along with Eric's owner, Roger Eagle, and other Probe staff, Davies was a 'taste maker' in local post-punk circles:

> A lot of people's musical tastes were encapsulated by Probe; they would come in and find out about people they didn't know about ... If you knew somebody and they came in, you'd say 'Have you heard this?' (Norman Killon (Eric's DJ and Probe worker), in Strachan 2010: 136)

> Probe records was becoming more a scene focal point ... Geoff Davies was the coolest. Another person I had to know. And Probe Records began its reputation for not suffering fools gladly ... Roger Eagle had played a compilation ... (Cope 1994: 25)

Cope (*ibid.*) claims that Davies's passion for what he perceived to be good music was such that, on one occasion, when a customer asked if he could have the new Rush album, he replied: 'No you fucking can't ... where do you think you are, Virgin Records?' Davies disputes this account –'I wouldn't lose a sale! (in Ogg 2009, 492) – but he concedes more than enough to support the claim that promotion of 'good taste' was central to Probe's culture.

It is significant in this respect that Davies's musical loves centred upon the late 1960s psychedelic bands that the 'Liverpool sound' is often compared to. If there was a cluster of bands in the Liverpool post-punk world who betrayed a psychedelic influence then Davies, qua tastemaker, is part of the reason why, as ex-Probe worker Bernie Connor explains:

> Every weirdo and no-gooder in the city would gravitate there on Saturday. Geoff ... is the second most important man in the history of Liverpool music. That's after Brian Epstein. He loved the album Forever Changes by Love and he never stopped playing it to people. All the young kids who would come into the shop looking for punk or the Velvet Underground – he would never miss the opportunity to play them that record. That or Captain Beefheart. (2013: 25)

Given my earlier observation regarding the rapid movement of musicians between bands, however, we should add that certain bands may have shared a sound because their members had often played together in previous bands, influencing one another and undergoing formative musical experiences together. If the Bunnymen, Teardrop Explodes and Wah! sound similar, for example, this is because of the close association of their respective singers, socially and musically. Indeed, the Bunnymen and Teardrops both included the same song, 'Read It in Books' (entitled 'Books' when the Teardrop Explodes recorded it), in their early sets. Arguments persist about who wrote it.

Furthermore, the psychedelic leanings of these particular bands are also attributable, in some part, to Manchester's, the Fall. McCulloch and Cope loved the Fall and become very friendly with the band. Referring to the band's singer (Mark Smith) and keyboard player (Una Baines), Julian Cope claims that:

> Mark Smith's a genius. Did you see the Fall the other night? Sod Mo Tucker [drummer with the Velvet Underground], Una Baines is the new heroine.
>
> The Fall shot through us all. But not like they hit McCull, Dave Picket and myself ... I saw them 28 times in 1978...
>
> ...the main reason anything started to happen was because of Mark. (1994: 73)

The point is echoed by Ian McCulloch:

> The Fall were the first band I saw that had something a bit different ... I liked the Pistols and the Clash but they never struck that chord. (in Fletcher 1987: 17)

I return to links between Liverpool and Manchester in Chapter 10.

In contrast with both Manchester and Sheffield, Liverpool's two key foci seem to have had little competition for the patronage of the punks and post-punks, and they were situated very close to one another in the city centre, combining to form a small bohemian enclave which, as Strachan (2010) observes, also contained the Liverpool School of Language, Music, Dream and Pun: a converted warehouse which hosted various avant-garde art and theatre events, provided studio and rehearsal space for artists and musicians, and housed a small indoor bazaar (Aunt Twackies). The bazaar comprised clothing and other stalls, including one run by Jayne Casey, and one of two tearooms (O'Halligan's) which were also key foci for Liverpool's post-punks.

The attachment of Deaf School and another local band, Albert Dock and the Cod Warriors, to this enclave, in the years immediately prior to punk, contributed to its bohemian allure and its identity as a musical space. Furthermore, having been formed at the Liverpool College of Art (involving staff as well as students) and defying many of the dominant rock conventions of the day, both bands brought an element of arty experimentation and even DIY spirit to this musical space, prior to punk. Like the pub rockers who inspired and influenced the London punks, Deaf School and Albert Dock showed the way to other Liverpool wannabies.

Liverpool's boho enclave compares in important respects with the World's End area of Chelsea, where Malcolm McLaren and Vivienne Westwood set up their boutique and where many of London's pioneer punks, including the formative members of the Sex Pistols, first met and forged ties (see Chapter 6). The comparison is important because it points to the more general significance of such enclaves (see also Cohen 2007). If, as I have suggested, networks are crucial to the formation of new music worlds, then so too are the foci which generate those networks. Individual gigs, venues and record shops might suffice for this but where they cluster, geographically, creating a wider enclave in which the likeminded hang out over extended periods, thereby increasing the likelihood that they will meet, form ties and act collectively in pursuit of their shared interests, the effect is greater.

The appropriation of warehouse space at the Liverpool School is also important and finds an echo in both Manchester, where T. J. Davidson turned an old warehouse into a celebrated rehearsal space, used by almost everybody who was anybody in the city and immortalised in the video to Joy Division's 'Love Will Tear Us Apart', and Sheffield, where Cabaret Voltaire transformed a similar space into their Western Works studio, a resource used by many local bands. The industrial base of all three local economies was in terminal decline during this period, with devastating consequences for local people. One positive outcome, however, was the availability of big spaces close to the city centre where the artistically inclined could congregate and pursue their projects. Writing about Liverpool between the mid 1980s and the turn of the century, for example, Sara Cohen observes that:

> De-industrialisation had left an abundance of vacant industrial and commercial buildings, providing spaces that were relatively cheap and thus accessible for music businesses. Some parts of Liverpool city centre subsequently became known for their musical vibrancy. (2007, 111)

Adding:

> the appropriation of disused city buildings (often for limited periods of time) by music-makers, and particularly by those involved with alternative or bohemian cultures, has been a common and long-established tradition in Europe and North America. (*ibid.*)

And as Fish puts it:

> Unlike London, where rehearsal space was expensive and difficult to find, Sheffield's industrial decline offered no end of disused factory space ideal for up and coming bands to vent their musical spleens. (2002: 88)

Without wishing to detract from its devastating effects, we might argue on this basis that Britain's economic decline and crisis during the late 1970s was not only a provocation and inspiration for artists, as discussed in Chapter 3, but also a source of opportunities. It freed up important resources (i.e. buildings) for musicians' use.

The most obvious comparison to Factory Records, in Liverpool, though it operated on a smaller scale, was Zoo. Founded and run by Bill Drummond and Dave Balfe, the label served initially as a vehicle for releasing material by Big in Japan. It released singles by a number of other local bands, however, including the Bunnymen, Teardrop Explodes, Wild Swans, Those Naughty Lumps, and Drummond's and Balfe's own later band, Lori and the Chameleons. In addition, they released a compilation album, *From the Shores of Lake Placid*, profiling these and other Liverpool bands, including Dalek I Love You, whom Balfe had also been involved with (along with Andy McCluskey, later of Orchestral Manoeuvres in the Dark), and another of his projects, the Turquoise Swimming Pools.

Zoo was not the only indie label in Liverpool, however. Roger Eagle had a label (Eric's) and Geoff Davies, though his label (Probe Plus) only launched in 1981, was centrally involved in the emergent indie distribution networks of this period (Chapter 10). Furthermore, Balfe and Drummond were by no means the only ones seeking to promote Liverpool's post-punk music. Noddy Knowler, a producer and engineer who worked at the Open Eye Studios, working with many bands of the era, released a compilation in 1979 (on Open Eye Records): *Street to Street: A Liverpool Album*. It featured some familiar names, including Big in Japan and the Bunnymen but also lesser-known names such as the ID (a forerunner of Orchestral Manoeuvres in the Dark involving Andy McCluskey and Paul Humphries) and early Liverpool punk band, the Accelerators.

Sheffield

As elsewhere in the UK, a thriving punk world grew up in Sheffield and its surrounding towns through 1977 (Beesley 2009, 2010a, 2010b). There does not appear to have been a 'Free Trade Hall' moment, however, even though the Pistols and Clash played an early date there in July 1976 (the Clash's first gig). By all accounts the crowd steadily diminished as the night went on. However, Sheffield was ahead of the game in relation to post-punk. Cabaret Voltaire had begun experimenting with tape loops and synthesisers in 1973, producing their own distinctive form of post-punk before punk itself had surfaced. And when it did they took advantage of the opportunities for performance and recording this afforded. Punk stimulated them to play live, moving out of the loft at Chris Watson's parents' house, where they put together various demos, and it generated opportunities for them to do so. They had played a few slots around Sheffield prior to punk and sometimes drove around the city, playing their music out of the back of a van, but punk, ironically, facilitated their move into more conventional forms of musicking. Following the success of Buzzcocks' *Spiral Scratch*, furthermore, they sent a tape to Richard Boon in the hope of securing a deal with New Hormones. Boon liked it and passed it on to Tony Wilson:

> Word got around with a few people in Manchester and that led to us being asked to play the first Factory club (Richard Kirk, in Fish 2002: 210)

Likewise in Sheffield itself:

> By the end of 1976 the punk explosion had started and there was a very early fanzine in Sheffield called Gunrubber, it appeared about the same time as London's Sniffin Glue. Gunrubber was formed by Adi Newton (later to form Clock DVA) but it was mainly his sidekick, Paul Bower, who picked up on us, he thought the whole idea of us was hilarious. He knew of us from years back ... our mystique was larger than ourselves ... it was that whole mystique that Gunrubber picked up on – and so they did an article about us. We played a couple of times with this reputation built up around ourselves, so even though people thought we were absolutely crap, there was still this air of mystique. (Stephen Mallinder, *ibid*.: 209–10)

Paul Bower, whose own band, 2.3, were one of Sheffield's early punk bands, and Adi Newton had been involved in their own pre-punk experimentation, moreover, at a curiously named arts project for young people, funded by Sheffield City Council: Meatwhistle. There they had met other future protagonists of Sheffield's post-punk world, including: Glenn Gregory, later of Heaven 17; Ian Craig Marsh and Martyn Ware, who played in the Future with Newton, later founding both the Human League and Heaven 17; Howard Willey, who would have a longstanding association with the Human League; and Nick Dawson, later of the Extras, who were hugely popular in Sheffield but never released a record and so never achieved success outside of the city.

As in Liverpool, but more literally, the Meatwhistle crowd formed a different band every week. One of the more enduring of these bands, Musical Vomit, were deemed the original punks by Polystyrene of X-Ray-Spex, who saw them play at the Bath Arts Festival in 1974. We should treat this lightly. As with Slaughter and the Dogs in Manchester and Deaf School in Liverpool, however, Musical Vomit indicate that

London's proto-punks weren't the only ones looking for a way out of the mid-1970s musical desert and that the lead may have come from elsewhere had circumstances been different.

Musical Vomit were less important as a band, however, than as a catalyst, spurring both their own members and their friends at Meatwhistle on to further and better things. After a brief period as the Dead Daughters, for example, Ian Craig Marsh and Martin Ware teamed up with Adi Newton to form the Future; and the Future, a synthesiser based outfit, themselves teamed up on one occasion with Cabaret Voltaire to play as the Studs. After the Future, Newton formed Clock DVA and Ware and Marsh formed the Human League with Phil Oakey, who had been at school with Ware (their old mate, Glenn Gregory, turned them down). Though always more poppy and accessible than Cabaret Voltaire, the (early) Human League released a series of singles and two albums in which they, along with Cabaret Voltaire, Vice Versa (who would later achieve success as ABC) and Clock DVA formed a significant wing of the synthesiser-based 'futurism' which, in turn, comprised an important strand of post-punk.

Although by no means all of the Sheffield post-punk bands were synthesiser based the clustering of synthesiser-based bands in the city and the early use of synths by other key Sheffield post-punk bands, such as Artery, I'm So Hollow and They Must Be Russians, is question begging: why so many synthesisers? As with Liverpool's psychedelic slant the answer lies with taste makers, social networks and social influence.

Cabaret Voltaire deserve special mention in this context. They were prominent 'early risers' in Sheffield's post-punk world; a key reference point for others and an example of local success. As in the classic model of the taste maker, they were quick to pick up on innovations occurring elsewhere, subsequently disseminating that innovation among their contacts. Martin Ware (of the Human League), for example, describes the formative effect of first hearing Kraftwerk, on a tape put together by (Cabaret Voltaire's) Richard Kirk at a birthday party at Chris Watson's (of Cabaret Voltaire) girlfriend's house:

> The speakers were pumping out Trans-Europe Express by Kraftwerk. It was a formative night of my life. It was the first time I'd heard them ... as exciting as any live gig that I'd ever been to and it really made me want to write actual tunes. All thanks to Chris and Richard and Mal. (in Lilleker 2005: 41)

Ware had experimented with tape effects, computers and synthesisers before this time. This was not a complete conversion. But the impact was significant.

In addition, Cabaret Voltaire had resources which they shared with others, not least a studio (Western Works) and the expertise to use it. In addition to being musicians they were support personnel for others, and in a context, as I discuss below, where support was thin on the ground, making their resources all the more important. This put them in a position of influence whether they intended it or not.

The 'futurist' influence was further reinforced, however, as the psychedelic influence in Liverpool was reinforced, through mutual influence in a network which encouraged fluid collaborations between musicians, in temporary bands, before those musicians settled into more enduring line-ups. As in Liverpool, bands pursued similar ideas and styles because their members had previously worked and hatched plans and ideas together. Whatever similarities we might perceive between the early Human League and Clock DVA should not surprise us, for example, as Newton, Marsh and Ware had all played together in the Future.

The synthesiser bands were only one camp within Sheffield's post-punk world, however. Although they used synthesisers, bands like Artery, I'm So Hollow and They Must Be Russians were not synth bands, and other bands, such as the Extras, 2.3, the Negatives, Comsat Angels and Stunt Kites showed no obvious electronic influence. While Sheffield's electronic pioneers were an important part of its post-punk world, therefore, their sound was not the only sound in that world, let alone the city (there had been a strong folk world in the city since the late 1960s, for example (Hield 2010; Hield and Crossley 2014)).

Sheffield's equivalent to the Factory and Eric's was the Limit, which opened in March 1978 (Anderson 2009). Many of the key post-punk bands of the era, local and national, played there in the final two years of the 1970s and early 1980s (it closed in 1991). It was preceded by other clubs, however, such as the Crazy Daisy (where, in 1980, with only days to go before a major tour, Phil Oakey would recruit Joanne Catherall and Susan Sulley for the commercially successful line-up of the Human League) and the Now Society (NowSoc) at the University. It was unusual at this time for university bars to allow access to non-students, and this fuelled antagonism towards students in each of the three post-punk worlds examined in this chapter (even if, as Julian Cope admits, some of those who were most antagonistic towards students were students themselves). NowSoc found a way around this ruling, however, such that they could put on gigs which anybody could attend. Most early pioneers did:

> It was a really good way of getting people together. We went to all of the shows there and everyone who was up and coming went and played. (Phil Oakey (Human League), in Lilleker 2005: 49)

When the Limit opened, however, it assumed the role of central focus, alongside the Beehive pub (just across the road). The Beehive was a central focus for Sheffield's post-punks:

> The place positively buzzed with musical gossip ... Everyone you talked to seemed to be in a group: Artery, I'm So Hollow, Graph, 2.3, Clock DVA, the Stunt Kites, Hula –oh yes, and Pulp. The list was endless. All these people so busy with their musical projects, their trendy clothes and hanging around looking cool. (Fish 2002: 84)

Furthermore, when the pubs shut a select few would accompany Cabaret Voltaire back to Western Works, to carry on drinking and chatting.

This suggests a level of camaraderie between bands and perhaps also cooperation and mutual support. Cabaret Voltaire were particularly generous:

> I'd noticed that they'd recorded some of the other Sheffield bands at Western Works, so I approached Mal one night at a Now Society gig and asked him if we could have a day in their studio for free. He just said, 'Yeah, come on down.' We went in the following Sunday. We recorded two tracks which later came out as a split single. (Tony Perrin (TV Product), in Lilleker 2005: 47)

And they often stepped in to engineer and produce on such occasions. However, as in Manchester and Liverpool, this *esprit de corps* was balanced by competition and factions:

> Sheffield was full of bitching and rivalry. I had contempt for all other bands in Sheffield. Except Cabaret Voltaire ... A good show from the Cabs was just amazing. We only cared about the Human League. (Phil Oakey, *ibid.*: 46)

Oakey's claims are contradicted by his band mate, Martyn Ware: 'We didn't want to be kings of the Sheffield scene. We had friends in it' (*ibid.*). There is enough evidence of back biting and competition, however, to suggest that, as in Manchester and Liverpool, relations were an ambivalent mix of jealous competition on one side, friendship and cooperation on the other.

Also mirroring Manchester and Liverpool, moreover, there was a hierarchy; permeable and fluid over time but spatially embedded. If the Beehive was where the 'in-crowd' met:

> The Hallamshire, a hundred yards down the road, was more for the second stream. There was a definite pecking order. (Lilleker 2005: 47)

One very striking feature of Sheffield is the relative absence of dedicated support personnel such as Manchester had in Rob Gretton, Tony

Wilson, Martin Hannett, Tony Davidson and others, and Liverpool had in Bill Drummond, Dave Balfe, Geoff Davies, Peter Fulwell and Roger Eagle. Much of the moving and shaking seems to have been done by one man: the mysterious[5] Marcus Featherby. He managed various bands, promoted gigs and punk nights, ran various record labels (consecutively) and compiled an LP showcasing Sheffield's main punk and post-punk bands: *A Bouquet of Steel*. He appears to have been the only dedicated mover–shaker, however. Some of the bands played a support role. I have already noted Cabaret Voltaire's willingness to support others in various ways and Vice Versa showed similar generosity and insight when they financed and compiled an EP featuring themselves, Clock DVA, I'm So Hollow and Stunt Kites: *1980: The First Fifteen Minutes*. Even allowing for this, however, there were very few organisers supporting Sheffield's post-punks. A number of bands used Ken Patten's studio, set up in his semi in a quiet Sheffield suburb. And Patten was certainly a local musical entrepreneur who helped post-punk along its way. But beyond hiring his studio and engineering skills out to a number of bands, Patten, who was in his fifties, had no identification with or involvement in Sheffield's post-punk world. Likewise George Webster and Kevan Johnson, who ran the Limit. They managed the club and sometimes mixed with punters but took no further active interest in post-punk. The unnamed students who ran NowSoc were arguably important early support personnel. They combined enthusiasm for music with a willingness to become involved in an organisational role. However, the fact that they remain unnamed in the archives suggests that they didn't achieve great prominence, personally, in Sheffield's post-punk world.

The network of key participants in this world, linked where they either had a longstanding close friendship pre-dating their musical involvement or cooperated directly together on a musical project between 1976 and 1980, is visualised in Figure 8.3.

A tale of three cities

In the next chapter I compare the networks of Manchester, Liverpool and Sheffield, using the formal techniques of social network analysis. I want to conclude this chapter, however, by drawing out some of the qualitative similarities which have emerged in it.

That these worlds were constituted by the interactions of their members is obvious. Each of the worlds forms a single network component. Competition and the dominance of certain factions were important elements in each of these networks. Contact put some on an antagonistic footing and large densely connected network neighbourhoods became

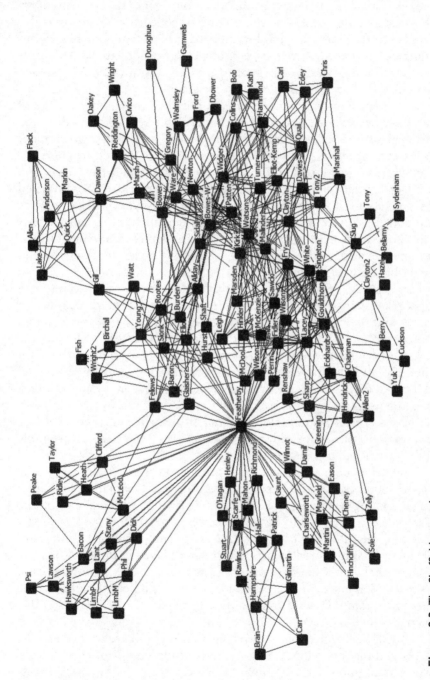

Figure 8.3 The Sheffield network

both dominant and relatively closed to outsiders, at least temporarily, whether their members realised and intended this or not (see also Crossley 2008c; Crossley and Ibrahim 2012; Hield and Crossley 2014). Competition had a positive aspect, however. It motivated participants to strive and innovate in an effort to get and stay ahead. Furthermore, factions and elites all proved fluid in the medium term.

More importantly, competition was not the whole story in any of the worlds examined. Relations are better described as ambivalent and variable; sometimes competitive, antagonistic and elitist; other times cooperative, friendly, supportive, generous and mobilised by collective identification. Resources and favours were shared and exchanged, and this was crucial to the flourishing of both the world as a whole and the artists within it. Artists cannot go it alone – music doesn't work like that – and they know it. Whatever their differences, other artists and bands are useful contacts and allies, and their common interests and involvement in shared activities inevitably generates empathy and friendship between them.

That artists cannot go it alone is also underlined by the crucial role of support personnel. From Rob Gretton and Tony Wilson, through Geoff Davies and Bill Drummond, to Marcus Featherby and Cabaret Voltaire, support personnel, whether or not they are also musicians, loom large in each of the three worlds I have looked at and play an important role. They have or at least use skills which musicians don't, taking on responsibilities and accessing resources on behalf of artists in a manner which frees the artist to focus more directly upon their art. Support personnel play a crucial role in taking bands out of their bedrooms and into rehearsal spaces, venues and studios. In this sense they play a crucial role in the formation and functioning of music worlds.

Connection between artists also goes some way to explaining the shared sound or style of some. In Liverpool and Sheffield in particular we see a lot of movement between bands, a process which allowed those involved to influence and be influenced by one another and to jointly negotiate the influence of established artists and traditions. Formative experiences were shared by artists who later played in different bands.

Influential taste makers within a world can be important too, however, shaping a number of bands within it and contributing to the impression that the world or even the city to which it belongs has a distinctive 'sound'.

Many of the connections which constitute a world are formed in focal places and place too looms large in each of the worlds discussed. Each was centred upon a small number of places where its key participants would cross paths. The network building significance of such foci is evident. The post-punk pioneers of Manchester, Liverpool and Sheffield tended to know others in their city because their love of alternative music drew them to the same places and relations were sustained, in some part, because they returned repeatedly to those same places. However, I have also suggested that networks 'make' foci, by which I mean, first, that places only serve as network foci when they acquire a reputation for good music within pre-existing networks, attracting likeminded individuals to them, and, second, that what makes the place is its use and investment by participants in their interactions, from the venue owners and promoters who decide that 'this' is the place where post-punk bands will play through to the local in-crowds who generate the practices which give the place its 'vibe'.

For all of the differences between them Manchester, Liverpool and Sheffield seem to have shared these key elements of 'worldness'. In the next chapter I will compare them further, focusing specifically upon their network structures.

Notes

1 Electronic and musique concrète composer most famous for her work with the BBC Radiophonic Workshop.
2 Both Heaven 17 and Clock DVA take their names from the novel, for example.
3 Where it was referred to as Factory 2.
4 Changes in the line-up were frequent and have become an integral part of the band's infamy (Simpson 2008).
5 Mysterious because: he appeared 'from nowhere' in Sheffield in the late 1970s, with a number of conflicting and exotic back stories; disappeared again, no less mysteriously, during the 1980s; and appears to have gone under different aliases both before and after his time in Sheffield.

9

Joining the dots: post-punk worlds as networks

In the previous chapter I introduced the post-punk worlds of Manchester, Liverpool and Sheffield, as they were in the final years of the 1970s, and I offered a preliminary analysis of them. In the present chapter I develop this analysis by way of an examination of their formal network properties (most of whose definitions were introduced in earlier chapters, especially Chapters 1 and 5). The analysis is motivated by a number of key concerns.

First, I want to see how well my earlier arguments regarding the importance of certain network properties stand up in relation to these new cases. Specifically, I hypothesise that each of the three networks will:

1 *Form a single component* (enabling communication and coordination).
2 *Manifest low mean geodesics*[1] (enabling fast and efficient communication/coordination).
3 *Manifest relatively high cohesion at the local level, as indicated by average degree and clustering*[2] (providing a conducive environment for the emergence of distinctive stylistic conventions and enforceable norms of cooperation and support).

In the absence of agreed benchmarks for geodesics and cohesion I have no straightforward criteria for testing these hypotheses but each will be critically discussed in light of the evidence.

Second, drawing on the discussion in Chapters 6 and 8, I want to test the claim that:

4 *Support personnel will be more central in each network for each of the three main measures of network centrality* (degree, closeness and betweenness).

And also to look for evidence of:

5   *Core–periphery structures.*
6   *Cohesive sub-groups.*

Finally, I want to compare the networks, teasing out similarities and differences, and identifying plausible explanations of both. In doing this I pay particular attention to the role of other key elements of music worlds: i.e. resources, places and conventions. I have argued in previous chapters that networks shape these other elements but this effect is reciprocal and I want to explore this. I begin with a discussion of basic network parameters.

Basic network parameters

The basic properties of each of the networks are presented in Table 9.1. Although there is some interesting variation, the similarity between the three networks is striking.

Table 9.1 Basic network properties

	Manchester	Liverpool	Sheffield
Number of nodes ('order')	129	131	130
Geodesics			
Components	1	1	1
Dyads at 2 degrees (%)	33	34	41
Dyads at 3 degrees (%)	37	48	33
Longest geodesic ('diameter')	6	5	6
Average geodesic	2.75	2.62	2.65
Cohesion			
Density	0.08	0.08	0.07
Average degree (SD)	10.85 (7.9)	9.82 (8.1)	9.45 (7.9)
Nodes with degree < 4 (%)	10 (8)	17 (13)	10 (8)
Clustering			
Clustering coefficient	0.79	0.79	0.77
Weighted clustering coefficient	0.56	0.45	0.39
Centralisation			
Degree centralisation	32.65	27.48	46.10
Betweenness centralisation	26.27	32.67	57.55
Closeness centralisation	33.13	38.62	42.22

Order

Note first that the order of each of the networks (i.e. the number of nodes) is roughly the same. We must be careful interpreting this figure because it does not capture the total number of participants in the world. It only captures those who were sufficiently prominent to merit mention in archives and secondary sources. For each network we can hypothesise that there is a shadow population of nodes who were not sufficiently prominent to make it onto public record, who are not included in my data. However, it is reasonable to assume that such nodes did not play a very significant role in the network, individually,[3] because this would have brought them into prominence. Furthermore, even if those whom I have captured in my survey are only the better-known participants it is still significant that we find roughly the same number in each world. I made no attempt to keep the networks at a similar size when gathering data and included every named participant in each world for whom I could find sufficient data.

What can we infer from this similarity of orders? Although I am interested in critical mass and believe that each of these cities would have had to reach a critical mass of interested potential participants before a world could develop I do not believe that the figures represent a critical mass threshold because that threshold is a minimum and we might expect variation above it.

Adding a further element to the theory of critical mass, however, we might infer that city-based worlds have an upper limit to the number of participants who can achieve prominence within them. Some social network analysts have argued that there is an upper limit to the number of alters that any one actor can maintain meaningful contact with (Dunbar 1992). Both cognitive capacities and resources (e.g. time and energy) become strained beyond a certain point. What we have here is more complex than this because music worlds are just one of several circles in which their participants are involved, and because we are hypothesising limits at the level of the network rather than the individual, but something similar may be at work. Sheffield's Beehive pub, where the 'premier league' of its post-punk world hung out, had a maximum capacity, for example, and may have become forbidding or unattractive to outsiders before it reached that capacity. If 'becoming involved' required hanging out at the Beehive, then there would have been definite limits as to how many people could become involved. Similarly, all participants would have had fixed limits to the number of others with whom they would be able to chat, form meaningful ties and cooperate on musical projects.

In addition, I have found in other studies (Crossley 2008c; Crossley and Ibrahim 2012), including work on music worlds (Hield and Crossley

2014), that strong ties between existing participants can make networks seem closed and unwelcoming to wannabe participants, irrespective of the intentions of insiders, and can dissuade them away from involvement. A network which is initially very open and recruits widely may become closed as identities, ties and conventions solidify, discouraging further recruitment by inducing a sense of alienation and non-belonging in newcomers akin to that which Schutz (1944) and Simmel (1971) each attribute to 'the stranger'.

This argument assumes that music worlds start small and grow but only to a point. As population size within a music world rises it reaches a threshold beyond which would-be participants are discouraged from becoming involved. Given that the constraints within each of our cities and city-based worlds (e.g. pub sizes, capacity of participants to form meaningful and cooperative ties) would have been similar it is likely that their thresholds would have been similar and it is no surprise, therefore, that their network orders are very similar.

This is just a hypothesis. It requires further analysis and testing. Furthermore, the mechanisms I have identified could only explain rough approximations between orders (the exactness of the comparison is partly due to chance). However, the finding is both interesting and puzzling and my explanation is at least a plausible starting point.

Components

That each network forms a single component is significant too. It confirms the hypothesis that I made in the introduction to the chapter. I expected to find a single component in each case because the three worlds we are analysing were each very successful and the likelihood of success is greatly enhanced when participants belong to a single communicative 'loop'.

Can we explain how each network became a single component? The concept of foci which I have used throughout the study is certainly part of the story because actors will not form ties if they do not meet. Ours are networks of musical cooperation, however, and we need therefore to explain how such ties arose and became so extensive. I have two suggestions.

One is that emerging music worlds, as noted in the previous chapter, are often characterised by a high level of fluidity in band membership; bands come and go with great frequency and individuals move between them seeking out the right combination of alters (in terms of both artistic inclinations and personalities) to join up with. In this way each participant builds up a considerable history of musical cooperation, over time, and the network of cooperation becomes increasingly 'joined up'.

This process is constrained, however, by the conventions of rock and pop music. Most bands will tend to have between three and five members, for example, reducing the number of alters with whom each player cooperates at any one time. Furthermore, in contrast to jazz, most players will only belong to one band at any one time. In addition, in so far as bands only have one singer, one drummer, one bassist, etc. players are only likely to have ties with players of instruments other than their own.

My second suggestion centres upon support personnel. Every world needs support personnel who organise and promote gigs, arrange rehearsal space, book studios, etc. Support personnel are often in short supply compared to musicians, however, and work with numerous bands more or less simultaneously. This causes them to connect otherwise distinct chunks of the network, drawing these chunks into a single component. Later in the chapter I will develop and test a hypothesis based upon this argument.

Geodesics

In addition to hypothesising, at the outset of this chapter, that the three worlds would each form a single component, I also hypothesised that each would be characterised by short mean geodesics. There are no standard values against which this claim might be tested. However, I would suggest that, at between two and three in each case, average geodesics in each of the networks are short. At least 78 per cent of pairs of nodes in each network are linked by fewer than 4 degrees, and in Liverpool this figure is 90 per cent. Given the nature of the ties involved this indicates compactness.

The chief reason for this, again, is the existence of a small number of support personnel who service a high number of bands simultaneously. Since many bands and artists link to the same support personnel the paths between them are short. I test this claim later in the chapter.

Cohesion

My final prediction in the introduction to the chapter was that the networks would be cohesive, at least at the local level. It is difficult to assess the magnitude of cohesion scores because average degree varies with tie type and density varies both with tie type and order such that we have no benchmarks. However, given that we are focusing upon cooperation in music-related activity I suggest that the average degree in each of our networks (10.85, 9.82 and 9.45 respectively) is high. Averages can split the difference between widely discrepant scores, of course, and the relatively high degree centralisation of Sheffield suggests that in this case this may be so (see below). Nevertheless, given that only a very small proportion of the nodes, in each case, have a degree below 4, it is fair to infer that each is relatively well connected.

Furthermore, the clustering coefficient[4] suggests that each node's individual network neighbourhood is relatively dense. Their contacts are in contact with one another, creating a cohesive cluster around them. When this clustering coefficient is weighted by degree it drops, suggesting that nodes with a higher degree experience lower ego-net density but that is only to be expected, especially if nodes with a higher degree are spanning various (cohesive) sub-groups within the network and perhaps coordinating between them. Building upon my earlier hypotheses I suggest that this is an effect of support personnel who connect to a disproportionate number of others, often linking separate factions within the network, each of whose members requires access to their (relatively rare) resources. This is tested below.

The relatively high average degree that we find in the networks is, in my view, an effect of the above-mentioned tendency, in the early days of a world's formation, for musicians to move between bands in pursuit of the right combination of alters, accumulating ties along the way, and the ego-nets they form tend to be clustered because they are forming bands, whose multiple members all cooperate together. The chief exception, as just noted, will be support personnel. They link to many bands, which gives them a higher degree than most, but they work separately with those bands, such that a greater proportion of their 'partners' are not connected to (cooperating with) one another.

The importance of local cohesion, to reiterate an argument that has run through this book, is that it tends to both encourage cooperation/ mutual support and facilitate the emergence of stylistic conventions. This, in turn, creates a social environment in which bands can thrive and a music world take shape.

Centrality, centralisation and support personnel

Although the three networks are similar in most respects, Sheffield is higher with respect to degree and betweenness centralisation (defined below). One of my aims in this section is to consider why. As a first step I must return to my earlier claims regarding the special position of 'support personnel'. Support personnel link to various different bands in a network such that they have a higher degree within the network and play a significant role in linking its various clusters together into a single component. They are the most central players in the network. We can test this claim by comparing average centrality scores for support personnel with other participants. I begin by recapping the definitions of the key forms of node centrality, adding a brief definition of their corresponding forms of centralisation.

Definitions

A node's *degree centrality* is its number of ties. The more ties a node has, the higher its degree. A high degree may mean that a node has a lot of work to do within a network, maintaining ties with many alters and responding to their requests for help. However, degree central nodes also have many alters in the network whom they can call upon for support, and are therefore likely to be influential. *Degree centralisation* is a measure of the dispersal of degree scores within a network and thus of the extent to which ties are monopolised by a small number of nodes. It is sometimes claimed that high degree centralisation leads to more efficient organisation in a network (Marwell and Oliver 1993).

A node's *betweenness centrality* is a measure of the extent to which it falls within the shortest paths connecting other pairs of nodes within the network. If John and Jane are (only) connected via Michele, for example, then this contributes to Michele's betweenness score. The more a node 'mediates' between pairs of others, the higher its betweenness. Betweenness is important because falling between actors who are not otherwise connected allows a node to play a brokerage role. She may, for example, command a 'fee' (material or symbolic) for facilitating the flow of information and other resources between parties, and she may take credit (accumulating status) for innovations which, in fact, she is only passing on (Burt 1992, 2005). In addition, she may have access to more diverse sources of information and innovation, making her an important figure to the various alters whom she mediates between. High betweenness isn't always an advantage, however. A betweenness central node may find herself struggling to maintain the peace between warring factions and/or trying to reconcile disparate and competing demands (Crossley 2008c). *Betweenness centralisation* is a measure of the extent to which brokerage potential is monopolised by a small number of nodes.

A node's *closeness centrality* is a measure of the path lengths separating it from each of the other nodes in the network. These path lengths are added up then inverted and normalised so that a high score indicates that a node has less distance to travel to reach all of the others in the network. Closeness is particularly important for communication and coordination. Shorter path lengths mean that information has less distance travel, such that nodes with high closeness could be both better informed as to what is going on and also better positioned to communicate their ideas.

Closeness centralisation is a measure of the extent to which closeness score are skewed, with a small minority having particularly high scores.

Another measure that I will use to consider the position and effect of support personnel is *ego-net density*. This involves calculating, for each node, the level of connection between the other nodes to which it is connected. As for density more generally, the actual number of ties is expressed as a proportion of the potential number.

Support personnel

Given what I have said about support personnel we would expect them to enjoy higher degree and betweenness, and lower ego-net density; higher degree, because they work with many alters (many bands); higher betweenness, because, in doing so, they link bands who would not otherwise be connected. For this reason, however, we would also expect them to have lower ego-net density, as their alters are less likely to have ties with one another.

I suggested earlier that it is support personnel who drag down the clustering coefficient of the networks when that coefficient is weighted for degree. If we find that support personnel have both a higher degree and a lower ego-net density, then that hypothesis is supported. In addition, a combination of low ego-net density and high degree among support personnel would support my hypothesis that support personnel hold large sections of the network together, reducing the number of components.

High degree and betweenness do not necessarily entail high closeness. All three types of centrality vary independently of one another. However, in this case I suspect that working with a high number of otherwise unconnected bands will disproportionately elevate the closeness scores of support personnel and I will test for this too.

Identifying 'support personnel' is not straightforward. Roles in music worlds, especially small, local and emerging worlds, are not clear-cut and many people play more than one role. In Liverpool, for example, Bill Drummond and Dave Balfe played in various bands, including Big in Japan but they also managed bands and founded and ran Zoo Records. They were musicians and support personnel. In addition, it is common for members of one band to offer (low-level) support to certain other bands: e.g. lugging gear or sharing rehearsal space and equipment. I therefore had to make a judgement, based upon the secondary literature, as to who played a significant support role in their music world, over and beyond routine low-level favours and irrespective of other roles for which they may be better known for. For these purposes I did not include those whose sole role was journalist or zine writer among support personnel.[5]

Table 9.2 Differences in mean centralities and mean ego-net density between support personnel and others

	Manchester	Liverpool	Sheffield
Number of identified support personnel	14	9	9
Degree	13.75**	22.03**	19.47**
Betweenness	590**	736**	678**
Closeness	69.53**	80.83**	48**
Ego-net density	−39.86**	−53.58**	−51.05**

Note: ** = p < .000

As Table 9.2 shows, support personnel did enjoy a significantly higher level of each type of centrality in each of my networks and a much lower ego-net density, and Ucinet's network-friendly t-test indicated that all differences were statistically significant. My hypotheses were supported.

Sheffield's centralisation

Turning now to the above-mentioned question of Sheffield's higher degree and betweenness centralisation, my answer is 'Marcus Featherby'. Table 9.2 suggests that the number of support personnel in each of the three worlds was roughly the same. These figures are deceptive, however, because in Sheffield's case they include some very marginal organisers and also bands whose support role, while extensive and important, was strongly focused in certain areas. As I noted in Chapter 8, Sheffield had far fewer dedicated support personnel and the bulk of the work was taken on by Featherby. This gave him a hugely disproportionate degree and betweenness in the Sheffield network and configured that network in a highly centralised way, at least with respect to degree and betweenness.

Featherby's influence upon the Sheffield network can be shown by removing him from it. It fragments into eight components (although the biggest of these contains 73 per cent of all nodes), degree centralisation drops from 46.10 to 16.3, and betweenness centralisation drops from 57.55 to 4.49 (closeness centralisation cannot be measured when a network has more than one component). Featherby made a big difference.

Core and periphery

It is not only support personnel who are distinguished in music world networks. A number of the quotations discussed in the previous chapter suggest that, in each case, participants perceived a dominant in-crowd.

Table 9.3 Core–periphery density matrix

	Manchester		Liverpool		Sheffield	
	Core (22%)	Periphery	Core (28%)	Periphery	Core (28%)	Periphery
Core	0.5	0.07	0.52	0.08	0.35	0.07
Periphery	0.07	0.06	0.07	0.04	0.07	0.04

In order to see whether this was borne out in network structure I ran a core–periphery routine on each of the networks (see Chapter 6, for a brief description of this routine). As we can see in Table 9.3, there is a clear core–periphery structure in each of the worlds and, with only a few exceptions, these structures are very similar.

In Liverpool and Sheffield, for example, the core comprises 28 per cent of the node set. The figure is slightly lower in Manchester, at 22 per cent, but not that different. Moreover, the internal density of the periphery is equally low in each case, ranging between 0.06 and 0.04, with core to periphery densities being slightly higher than that, at between 0.07 and 0.08. Internal core density is slightly lower in Sheffield than in either Liverpool and Manchester, at 0.35, but it is still much higher than the internal periphery and core–periphery densities. And the internal core densities of Manchester and Liverpool, respectively, are very similar, at 0.5 and 0.52.

Every node in each of the networks was, to some extent, a key player in the music world to which they belonged. If they weren't, then they wouldn't have made it to the archives and secondary sources through which I have identified them. They were all, in this respect, important. What this core–periphery analysis suggests, however, is that even among the key players there was a distinction between a core, who were closely networked, and a periphery who were more marginal. Of course we do not know how closely our core–periphery partition agrees with the perceptions of those who were quoted referring to in-groups and pecking orders in the previous chapter but the fact that two different sources of evidence (personal testimony and network analysis) point to the same conclusion, namely, that there was an in crowd among the key players, adds weight to that observation.

Blockmodelling the networks

A core–periphery partition is a very basic – and for that reason very important – network structure. In order to add more nuance and push my exploration of structure further I elected to blockmodel each of my networks. As in the analysis in Chapter 6, and for the same reason, I decided to base my model on 'structural equivalence'. Furthermore, again mirroring the analysis in Chapter 6, I elected to proceed inductively, using a hierarchical clustering method to ascertain how many blocks there are in the network. My analysis until now suggests that there are distinct positions in the network and thus a structure which might be captured by a blockmodel, and this is further supported by the qualitative evidence regarding factions which was discussed in Chapter 8. However, these suggestions of structure are not sufficiently precise to motivate hypotheses regarding exact numbers of blocks and relations between them. This is why I have opted for an inductive approach.

Blockmodelling is not designed to identify factions or other cohesive sub-groups. However, where they exist it will identify them because their members will tend to be structurally equivalent. Given that blockmodelling will also identify other positions in the network, not defined by cohesion but structurally equivalent for others reasons, this makes it the best means of exploring structure within a network. I begin with Manchester.

Manchester

The first step in constructing the model was to cluster nodes. I wanted a fine-grained model which made sense in terms of my qualitative understanding of Manchester's music world. The best solution involved twelve blocks. The next step was to count the members in each of the blocks and measure the density of ties both within and between them (see Table 9.4). Most blocks are about the same size. However, block nine is an exception. With forty-three members it contains one-third (33 per cent) of all nodes in the network. Another exception is block twelve, which contains only one member. That member is T. J. Davidson, the mover–shaker who owned the rehearsal rooms that most of the bands used at one time or another. His very high degree gave him a very distinctive profile of ties, making him a distinct cluster.

Turning now to the diagonal, it is interesting that block nine is the only block with an internal density lower than 0.4 and one of only two blocks with an internal density below 0.9. Its ties to other blocks are very weak too. Its internal density might be explained by its size – density typically drops as order increases – but given both its more general paucity of ties and its membership I suggest that it is a block of marginal participants.

Block ten also has a relatively low internal density and no ties to any other block except block one. Its members comprise members of bands and artists involved in Factory (whose key mover–shakers are in block

Table 9.4 Interblock densities and block membership in Manchester

	N =	1	2	3	4	5	6	7	8	9	10	11	12
1	6	1	1	0.29	0	0.17	0	0.05	0.03	0.05	0.72	0.67	0.17
2	4		1	0	0	0.66	0	0.11	0.06	0.13	0	0	1
3	14			0.99	0	0.03	0	0	0	0.02	0	0	0.5
4	6				1	0.02	0	0	0.01	0.004	0	0	0
5	8					0.75	0.14	0.02	0.03	0.03	0	0	0
6	7						1	0	0	0.01	0	0	0
7	7							1	0	0.02	0	0	1
8	17								0.93	0.005	0	0	0.77
9	43									0.07	0	0	0.3
10	9										0.44	0	0
11	7											0.95	0
12	1												1

Block one: Tony Wilson, Rob Gretton, Peter Saville, Alan Erasmus, Martin Hannett, Simon Topping.

Block two: Ian Curtis, Peter Hook, Bernard Sumner, Steven Morris.

Block three: Morrissey, Vinni Faal, Ed Garrity, Toby Tomanov, Pete Crookes, Vini Reilly, Billy Duffy, Wayne Barrett, Brian Grantham, Howard Bates, Mick Rossi, Ray Rossi, Mike Day, Phil Rowland.

Block four: Paul Morley, Michael Howells, Gus Callender, Pete Howells, Steve Cundall, Mike Koman.

Block five: Richard Boon, Howard Devoto, Pete Shelley, Steve Diggle, John Maher, Steve Garvey, Terry Mason, John Cooper Clarke.

Block six: John McGeoch, Barry Adamson, Martin, Jackson, Bob Dickinson, Dave Formula, Paul Spencer, John Doyle.

Block seven: David Wilks, Mark Standley, Ian Nance, Rev. P. P. Smythe, Steve Brotherdale, Stan-the-Man, Hugh O'Boyle.

Block eight: Tony Friel, Dick Witts, Jon the Postman, Kevin Cummins, Mark Smith, Una Baines, Martin Bramah, Karl Burns, Kath Caroll, Eric McGann, Yvonne Pawlett, Marc Riley, Craig Scanlon, Paul Hanley, Steve Davies, Mike Leigh.

Block nine: Lorraine Hilton, Linder Mulvey, Arthur Kadmon, Willie Trotter, Ian Devine, Jon Savage, Larry Cassidy, Vini Cassidy, Paul Wiggin, Alan Hempsall, Keith Darbyshire, Gary Madely, Robert Davenport, Suzanne O'Hara, Andy Zero, Kath Carrol, Liz Naylor, Bob Dickinson, Malcolm Garrett, Ian Deaves, Odgie, Woody, Robin Simon, Francis Cookson, Eric Random, Tony Tabac, Gillian Gilbert, Steve Burke, Ian Grey, Steve Murray, Craig Hilton, Stuart Murray, Tony Dyson, Mick Middles, Mick Hucknall, Neil Smith, Brian Turner, Kev Williams, Wes Graham, Joe Moody, Jeff Beattie, Chris Joyce, Jilted John.

Block ten: Jez Kerr, Martin Moscrop, Donald Johnson, Peter Terrell, Mike Finney, Steve Perrin, Pip Nicholls, Adrian Wright, Alec Sidebottom.

Block eleven: Bruce Mitchell, Chris Joyce, Dave Rowbotham, Phil Rainford, Steve Hopkins, Tony Bowers, Colin Sharp.

Block twelve: Tony (T. J.) Davidson.

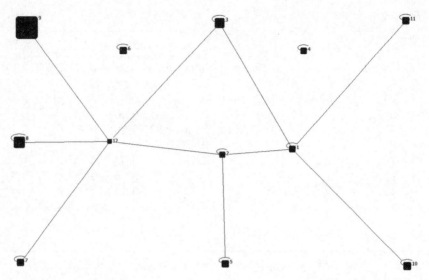

Figure 9.1 A blockmodel of the Manchester network

one). Its internal density is relatively low because several artists and bands are lumped together who have no direct tie to one another. What they have in common is their tie to Factory and lack of (measurable) involvement with anybody else.

The high internal density of the other blocks suggests that they are cohesive sub-groups within the network – 'factions' – and their existence supports the qualitative evidence regarding the existence of factions. An examination of the membership of the blocks suggests that they are mostly based around bands. As mentioned, for example, there is a Joy Division block (block two) and there are also Buzzcocks and Magazine clusters (blocks five and six), and a block including the combined membership of Slaughter and the Dogs and Ed Banger and the Nosebleeds (block three).

The structure of the network is best drawn out by way of a graph. For the visualisation in Figure 9.1 I have set the density threshold for connection at 0.25 (25 per cent). Nodes are sized in accordance with size of block membership. Those blocks with more members appear bigger.

The most striking feature of the visualisation is the centrality of blocks twelve (T. J. Davidson) and block one (Factory bosses). This is consistent with everything that I have said both in this and the previous chapter. The added value of the graph, however, is that it highlights the extent to which these two centres served different constituencies. Each is linked to blocks two and three, but where twelve is linked to seven, eight and nine, one is linked to ten and eleven. The Manchester world had two centres.

Liverpool

In the case of Liverpool I opted for an eleven-block solution. There were a number of notable similarities to Manchester (see Table 9.5). First, we have one block, block three, characterised by both a relatively large order (37 per cent of the nodes in the network as a whole) and a relatively low internal density (0.06). As in Manchester, this block comprises the marginal characters within Liverpool's post-punk world. Second, most other blocks have a relatively high internal density, suggesting that they are cohesive groups and might be interpreted as 'factions', particularly where the density of their (positive) ties to other blocks in the model is weak. Third, they are, for the most part, occupied by members of overlapping bands.

The graph of the model in Figure 9.2 (which again connects blocks where their density of ties is greater than 0.25 and sizes them in proportion to their order) shows that the Liverpool network is slightly less connected than the Manchester network: five of its blocks are isolates compared to only two in Manchester and these include its 'big' block of marginals (see Figure 9.2). However, as in Manchester we find two central nodes (four and five), each connected both to one another and to others in a 'double fork' configuration. These two central blocks comprise a block of (mostly) support personnel (block four) and a block comprising mostly members of Deaf School (block five).

Another interesting block in relation to Liverpool is block one. This block includes many of the better-known musicians in the world, including members of both Echo and the Bunnymen and the Teardrop Explodes, and also central organisers such as Bill Drummond and Dave Balfe. It is an internally cohesive block (density=0.36), although its internal density is low compared to many, and it is the second largest block (n=23) but it is only weakly tied to other blocks such that it appears in the graph as an isolate. Drawing upon a qualitative understanding of those involved, as well as these measures, I interpret this block to be a distinct and dominant faction within Liverpool's post-punk world: an in-crowd.

Sheffield

The best cluster solution for Sheffield involved fourteen blocks (see Table 9.6). As in Manchester, one of these was a solitary individual (Marcus Featherby, block ten). His pattern of ties, and particularly his high degree, was so distinctive that he constituted a separate block even

Table 9.5 Interblock densities and block membership in Liverpool

N =	1	2	3	4	5	6	7	8	9	10	11
1	23	0.36	0.09	0.05	0.14	0.15	0.02	0.03	0.08	0.04	0	0
2	6		1	0.02	0.75	0	0	0	0	0	0	0
3	48			0.06	0.02	0.02	0.002	0.008	0.03	0	0.01	0
4	4				1	0.95	1	0	0	0	0	0
5	10					0.96	0	0	0.01	0.03	0.5	0.3
6	10						0.4	0	0	0	0.1	0
7	8							1	0.19	0	0	0
8	8								1	0	0	0
9	6									0.73	0	0
10	4										1	0
11	4											1

Block one: Julian Cope, Ambrose Reynolds, Budgie, Bill Drummond, Holly Johnson, Dave Balfe, Ian McCulloch, Paul Simpson, Dave Pickett, Mick Finkler, Gary Dwyer, Ged Quinn, Troy Tate, Will Sergeant, Les Pattinson, Pete de Freitas, P. H. Mart, Kevin Wilkinson, Bream, Bobby Carr, Jacqui, Jeanette, Noddy Knowler.

Block two: Pete Burns, Phil Hurst, Martin Healy, Walter Ogden, Mike Reid, Francesco Mellina.

Block three: Pete Wylie, Sue James, Mitch, Joe Musker, Dave Littler, Pete Griffiths, Mike Rigby, Steve Platt, Paul Rutherford, Stephen Spence, Keith Hartley, Steven Brick, Chris Russell, Peter Coyle, Steve Lovell, B. F. Tin Peter Gill, Jed O'Toole, Brian Nash, Mark O'Toole, Sonia Mazumder, Phil Spalding, Peter Kircher, Jonathan Perkins, Geoff Davies, Andrew Kenyon-Smith, Lori Lartey, Paul Barlow, Tony Mitchell, Pete Younger, Dave Fairburn, Alex Plain, Bob Wakelin, Cliff Hewitt, Danny Hampson, Tim Lever, Joey McKechnie, John Hawkins, Chris Martin, Lee Marles, Kathy Apathy, Brian Harcombe, Tony Doyle, John Brady, Mike Percy, Hari Haralambous Heidi Cure, Chris Hughes.

Block four: Pete Fulwell, Jayne Casey, Roger Eagle, Ken Testi.

Block five: Ken Ward, Phil Allen, Ian Broudie, Clive Langer, Steve Lindsey, Bette Bright, Enrico Cadillac, John Davis, Ian Ritchie, Max Ripple.

Block six: John, Highway, Wayne Wadden, Paul Hornby, Nicky Cool, Steve Torch, Tim Whitaker, Martin Dempsey, Charlie Gruff, Chris Joyce, Neil Innes.

Block seven: Andy McCluskey, Julia Kneale, Neil Shenton, John Floyd, Malcolm Holmes, Steve Hollas, Gary Hodgson, Paul Humphries.

Block eight: Alan Gill, Dave Hughes, Chris Teepee, the Worm, Max the Actor, Kenny Peers, Martin Cooper, Paul Collister.

Block nine: David Knopov, Nathan McGough, Denyse D'Arcy, Dave Wibberly, Wayne Hussey, Jon Moss.

Block ten: Bob Bellis, J. J. Campbell, Henry Priestman, Martin Watson.

Block eleven: James Eller, Jo Allen, Martin Hughes, Ben Barson.

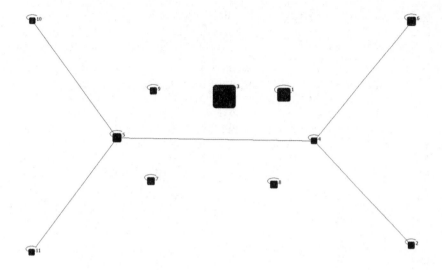

Figure 9.2 A blockmodel of the Liverpool network

when the network was partitioned into much fewer blocks, and we can see from Figure 9.3 that he was a very central figure in the network as a whole. The other most central block (block one) involves the members of Cabaret Voltaire. Interestingly, however, though these two blocks are very central, a number of other blocks, especially five (members of assorted bands, particularly Artery) and six (Vice Versa) are also fairly well connected. Indeed, for this density threshold (>0.25) Sheffield is the best connected of the three models.

The isolate in the model comprises members of the Extras, a popular band within the city but one who remained relatively self-contained, not engaging in the 'transfer market' that many of the other bands engaged in and not recording, so therefore not forming traceable ties of cooperation with others in the network. Importantly, as in each of the other worlds, Sheffield's largest block, block nine (n=39), is a non-cohesive block (density=0.07). Again I would interpret this block as a block of minor, more marginal participants.

Space restrictions prevent me from pushing this blockmodel analysis further. Briefly, however, what we see, particularly by looking at the graphs (Figures 9.1–9.3), is, first, the way in which each network can be composed into distinct camps, often cohesive but involving at least one camp of more marginal participants, which is neither internally cohesive nor strongly connected to other camps, and, second, conversely, the existence of two or three camps, usually containing a small number of

Table 9.6 Interblock densities and block membership in Sheffield

	N =	1	2	3	4	5	6	7	8	9	10	11	12	13	14
1	3	1	0.45	0.77	0.5	1	0	0	0	0	0	0	0	0	0
2	11		0.44	0.06	0.14	0	0.09	0.06	0.03	0	0	0	0	0	0
3	9			0.97	0.1	0.04	0.33	0	0.03	0	0	0	0.08	0	0
4	10				0.76	0.02	0.1	0.01	0.06	0.03	0	0	0.21	0	0
5	9					0.44	1	0	0.15	0.02	1	0	0	0	0
6	3						1	0	0	0.02	0	0.83	0	0	0
7	8							0.96	0	0	0	0	0.09	0	0
8	11								0.46	0.01	0.64	0	0.05	0	0
9	39									0.07	0.72	0	0.02	0	0
10	1										1	1	1	0.71	1
11	6											0.93	0	0	0
12	7												1	0	0
13	7													0.91	0
14	6														1

Block one: Richard Kirk, Stephen Mallinder, Chris Watson.
Block two: Martin Ware, Ian Craig Marsh, Phil Oakey, Adrian Wright, Glen Gregory, Mark Civico, David Bower, Dave Walmsley, Mick Ford, Ian Reddington, Ken Patten.
Block three: Adi Newton, Jud Turner, Charlie Collins, Roger Quail, Dave Hammond, Simon Elliot-Kemp, Rod Sidall, Bob Baker, Kath Baker.
Block four: Paul Bower, Haydn Bowes-Weston, Paul Widger, John Clayton, Russel Davies, Tony Russian, Lisa Marshall, Chris Russian, Carl Russian, Bob Edey.
Block five: Mark Gouldthorpe, Mick Fidler, Neil McKenzie, Garry Wilson, Simon Hinkler, Yosef Sawicki, Gary Marsden, Rod Leigh, Jane Wilson.
Block six: Stephen Singleton, Mark White, Martin Fry.
Block seven: Nick Dawson, John Lake, Simon Anderson, Robin Allen, Robin Markin, Andy Quick, Andy Gill, Steve Flack.
Block eight: Paul Shaft, Paul Le Slonk, Martin Lacey, Steve McDool, Joseph Hurst, John Baron, Tony Perrin, Garry Birchall, Alan Fish, Alan Watt, Ron Wright.
Block nine: Terry Gamwells, Kevin Donoghue, David Sydenham, Darren Berry, Chris Hendrick, Paul Bellamy, 'Tony', Hazel Member, Jah Slug, Pete Eason, Brad Martini, Fraser Charlesworth, Steve Wilmot, Jim Darnill, Steve Cheney, Graeme Gaunt, Andy Hinchcliffe, Kevin Bacon, Andy Peake, John Mayfield, Craig Zelly, Mark Sole, Gordon Yuk, Nigel Cuckson, Dave Clayton, Mick Limb, Paddy Limb, Dave Lant, Dave Lawson, 'Psi', 'Stany', Nick Hawksworth, 'Phil', Didi Dave, Elaine McLeod, Les Heath, Pete Ridley, Derek Taylor, Brian Clifford.
Block ten: Marcus Featherby.
Block eleven: John Allen, Steve Chapman, Nigel Renshaw, Mick Greening, Brent Sharp, Ashley Eckhardt.
Block twelve: Ian Elliott, Ian Burden, Martin Rootes, Nick Allday, Pam Young, Mik Glaisher, Steve Fellows.
Block thirteen: Paul Hampshire, David Patrick, James Carr, Steven Rawlins, Gavin Brain, Lyndon Scarfe, Paul Gilmartin.
Block fourteen: John Stuart, Bryan Hall, Steve Richmond, Andy Henley, Ade Mahon, Marcus O'Hagan.

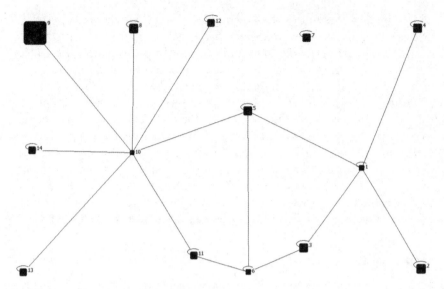

Figure 9.3 A blockmodel of the Sheffield network

participants, which enjoy a high level of connection to other camps. In this way the blockmodel takes up beyond our core–periphery analysis, suggesting a more differentiated hierarchy and greater likelihood of factional tensions between camps.

Conclusion

This chapter has covered a lot of ground. In concluding it I want to draw out a number of headlines which contribute to the central arguments of the book. First, the network structures analysed in the chapter support the argument that I made about networks, collective action and music worlds in Chapter 4 and are similar in all significant respects to the London network analysed in Chapters 5 and 6. They form a single component, with short average path lengths and manifest relatively high local cohesion. In addition, certain other properties of the London network were replicated here. Specifically, and echoing the qualitative analysis in Chapter 8, we find evidence of both core–periphery differentiation and of further, relatively distinct (potentially conflicting) factions or camps, and we find evidence that support personnel occupy central positions.

Network properties and structure are important because, as I argued in the earlier chapters of the book, they facilitate the collective action which, in turn, facilitates the emergence of a music world. They facilitate the organisation of events, the formation of bands, the emergence of distinctive conventions, the mobilisation of resources and the collective identification of 'places' for world building and hanging around. I also suggested in earlier chapters, however, that these other emergent elements of worlds (places, conventions, events, resources, etc.) play a role in shaping the networks which, in turn, shape them. I have begun to explore this in the current chapter by considering how such factors as the size of meeting places, conventions regarding the size and composition of bands and scarcity of resources might constrain a network to develop in particular ways. Further work is necessary if we are to be more confident in relation to such claims and achieve a more comprehensive understanding but I hope that I have at least made a start.

Notes

1 A geodesic is the shortest path length between any two nodes. The mean geodesic is calculated on the basis of every possible pair of nodes in the network.
2 Clustering is measured by ego-net density. For each ego we look at the proportion of their immediate contacts who are linked to one another. This figure, expressed as a number between 0 and 1 is then averaged. In some cases this average is weighted according to degree: i.e. the ego-net density of nodes with more contacts is accorded a greater weight in the averaging process.
3 They may have been important collectively if they contributed to audience size, making gigs, recordings and zines more viable.
4 See n. 2.
5 Zine writers and journalists complicate matters. If we tie them to all others with whom they 'work' and include interviewing as working then many have ties to a large number of artists, and are very central. As journalists it is their job to make contact and interview people. I did not have access to information on who my zine writers and journalists interviewed, however (most zines are not archived comprehensively anywhere). I therefore only included other ties which they had. For this reason their ties are drastically underestimated and it seemed inappropriate to include them as 'support personnel' for purposes of this test.

10

The small world of British post-punk

Music worlds exist on different scales: local, national, international and increasingly (since the turn of the century) virtual (Bennett and Peterson 2004). With the exception of Chapter 7, which examined the way in which punk 'went national' as an effect of broadcast media and moral panic, my focus in this book has been upon local worlds. The local was very important to both punk and post-punk in a number of ways. Musicking is always local in one respect: it happens somewhere, in a particular locality (although recordings and virtual spaces complicate that claim). Furthermore, local identities often figured strongly in punk and post-punk worlds. The identity of the Liverpool, Manchester and Sheffield worlds discussed in the previous two chapters was a regional identity and often bound up with local pride. The rivalry between Liverpool and Man chester carried over to their post-punk worlds (although, as we shall see, this didn't prevent considerable positive connection between them), for example, and a strong sense of opposition to the pretensions of London was evident in the archives of the Manchester world in particular. However, as Chapter 7 intimated, the punk and post-punk worlds also existed on a national level. In this chapter I consider how this came about.

In the previous chapter I argued that local worlds are possible by virtue of a network of connections between their participants. This chapter is premised on exactly the same claim. National music worlds are possible by virtue of a network of connections between their participants. Activities are coordinated, and tastes, identities and styles shared, to whatever extent they are, because participants are in contact: communicating, exchanging ideas and resources, and influencing one another.

This contention begs two questions. First, assuming that the participant population of a national music world is the sum of the participant populations of each of its constituent local worlds then it is much bigger than the local worlds we have been examining, raising the question of how its network is structured so as to facilitate coordination, fast and efficient diffusion of information, styles, ideas, etc. In the absence of such coordination and diffusion I would be reluctant to say that a national world existed but I believe that it did and, to reiterate, this raises the question of how. Second, how does contact happen given the greater geographical dispersal of participants as we move from the local to the national scale? In a city-based world participants converge upon the same small number of foci and thereby enjoy regular face-to-face contact but how is contact established and maintained when participants live miles apart?

The chapter is a response to these two questions. I begin by looking to complexity science, a branch of academic inquiry which precisely addresses the question of coordination in very large systems, from insect swarms to neural networks. Specifically, I discuss two theories of network structure which show how very large networks are sometimes characterised by relatively short average path lengths, a property which, in turn, makes effective, efficient coordination and diffusion possible. One of these theories, posited by Duncan Watts (1999, 2004), hypothesises a structure involving numerous dense clusters, connected by 'weak ties' (see Figure 10.1). The other, posited by Albert-László Barabási (2003), suggests a structure centred upon a small number of hubs, each with a huge number of connections to other nodes in the network (see Figure 10.2). I will be suggesting that the network of Britain's post-punk world between 1976 and 1980 involved elements of both of these structures.

Turning to the second of the above-mentioned questions, I will seek to identify the mechanisms which forged ties at the national level, simultaneously generating a network whose structure resembles the (different) models of Watts and Barabási. The early part of the chapter looks at the mechanisms which structured the post-punk world along the lines suggested by Watts. The latter, echoing Barabási, focuses upon hubs.

My empirical examples are still, to some extent, Liverpool, Manchester and Sheffield. Rather than taking them individually, however, I will be thinking about the relations between their various participants, and I will be using this as a means to think about the intercity connections which constituted the national post-punk world more generally. Furthermore, I will be looking beyond the three when the demands of answering my questions require this.

Coordination and diffusion in big networks: the 'small world' phenomenon

Both Watts and Barabási take their lead from the work of the social psychologist, Stanley Milgram (1967; Korte and Milgram 1970; Travers and Milgram 1969). Milgram's research suggested that the average path length between the tens of millions of citizens comprising the US population was a mere 6 degrees. That is, any two people selected at random from the US population are, on average, connected by a path of 6 degrees or, to paraphrase Milgram, every US citizen is, on average, at a mere 6 degrees of separation from the president.

This is the so-called 'small world' phenomenon and it has framed much of the above-mentioned work in complexity science. Coordination in complex systems comprising hundreds of millions of nodes is possible, it is argued, because average path lengths are still surprisingly short in such systems. Information only has relatively short distances to travel, which means that it can travel quickly and with minimal distortion. In addition to coordination, of course, this also means that it is plausible to explain whatever homogeneity we perceive in the behaviour (i.e. styles, tastes, identities) of nodes in terms of their diffusion through the network.

This begs a further question, however: what type of structure enables hundreds of millions of nodes to be connected by such short paths? This is the question that has exercised the complexity scientists and, as noted above, they have come up with two different theories, each equally plausible and each supported by empirical evidence on real-world complex systems.

Watts's (1999, 2004) model hinges upon the idea of 'weak ties' postulated by Mark Granovetter (1973, 1982). As a way into it consider the following. If I have a tie to twenty people, each of my alters has a tie to twenty people, each of their alters has a tie to twenty people and so on until we reach the 6 degrees of separation identified by Milgram, then I am linked (at 6 degrees or fewer of separation) to $20^6 = 64,000,000$ people. That is larger than the estimated size of the current British population. Furthermore, given that Milgram's definition of a tie, for purposes of this research, was 'being on first name terms with', and that most people are on first-name terms with many more than twenty others, that is a conservative estimate.

There is a problem however. The above calculation assumes that each of my twenty contacts have a different twenty contacts to me and to one another; likewise their contacts and so on. This is unlikely. If we were randomly connected to others, then my friends probably would have different friends to both me and one another. Any overlap would be coincidental and very unlikely in a large population And, as Watts (1999) shows, large simulated networks with randomly allocated ties do usually have the short average path lengths characteristic of 'small worlds' (on this point he draws from the seminal work of Erdös and Rényi 1960). However, real world social ties are not random. They are structured. More specifically, as Granovetter (1973) argues, transitivity is the norm in human social relations. We are usually friends with our friends' friends. There are various reasons why, not least that our friends tend to bring us into contact with their friends, who then become our friends and vice versa. The key point for our purposes, however, is that structure challenges one of the assumptions of our initial (mathematical) solution to the small world problem; namely, that ties within a network are independent of one another and random.

If Granovetter throws a spanner in the works of our first attempted solution, however, he offers a further, better solution of his own, according to Watts. Though actors' strong ties tend to be transitive, Granovetter argues, most also have weak ties which are intransitive; that is, most people have a number of acquaintances, whom they may not know very well and to whom they may only chat when they happen to meet by chance, who are unknown to the others in their friendship circle. To adapt one of the empirical cases discussed by Granovetter, I may very occasionally bump into old school friends who are completely unknown to others in my current social circle.

Granovetter is interested in such ties because, he claims, they are often a good source of information. Information gleaned from close friends, he claims, is often already familiar to us because we have the same sources as our friends. Transitivity in relations means that information tends to get endlessly regurgitated. Weak ties, however, because intransitive, reach about beyond our usual sources and potentially tell us something new.

The significance of such ties for Watts is that, in his view, they 'behave' like random ties, and his simulation studies show that the addition of a few random ties to otherwise highly clustered networks radically reduces average path lengths. Networks do not need to be completely random to induce the small world effect. A relatively small proportion of random ties in an otherwise clustered network is sufficient. Furthermore, Granovetter's work on weak ties, as interpreted by Watts, suggests that real-world social networks involve exactly this balance of structure (transitivity) and randomness (intransitivity). Thus, Watts argues that the networks which characterise the social world and 'small world networks' more generally comprise dense, transitive clusters, linked to one another by a proportionately small number of 'random' ties (see Figure 10.1).

According to Barabási (2003), by contrast, path lengths are shortened and the small world effect achieved in the large networks of complex systems by the existence of hubs to which a large proportion of nodes within the network are attached. Because a majority of actors link to these hubs they are linked to one another via the hub at a distance of only

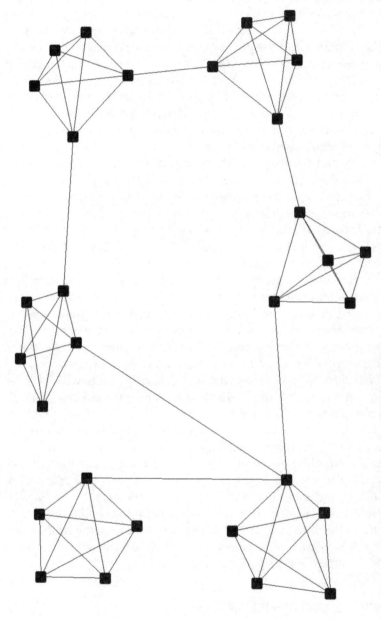

Figure 10.1 A simplified and idealised representation of Watts's model

2 degrees,[1] and path lengths, as a consequence, are short (Figure 10.2). My link to Amazon's website, for example, links me to many millions of others who also link to it, at a distance of only 2 degrees. Like Watts, Barabási offers empirical evidence from a variety of real-world complex systems, as well as simulation studies, to support this idea. The network structures of many large complex systems are characterised by hubs.

These hubs exist, Barabási continues, because of what he calls 'preferential attachment'. This entails that new nodes entering a network tend to attach to those nodes which they perceive to be the best connected. This increases the degree of these nodes, making them more attractive to other new nodes and so on in a process which eventually makes these nodes hubs in a hub-centred network.

Both Watts and Barabási are physicists and their ideas require sociological fine-tuning if they are to apply meaningfully to the social world (see Crossley 2008a, 2005; Scott 2011). Watts's invocation of randomness, for example, though it might only mean 'intransitive' in practice, is problematic because much of what we know about homophily in social relations suggests that even an actor's weak ties are likely to have a specific social profile and are not formed randomly. Similarly, Barabási's ideas of preferential attachment, though important, must be rethought in sociological terms. There are limits to the number of meaningful ties any one social actor can accumulate, for example, and well-connected people sometimes cease to attract new contacts because their 'popularity' either intimidates or provokes a backlash against them. Similarly, other properties of a node than their degree, such as their resources, may make them targets for 'preferential attachment'. The particular complexity of human reality often defies reduction to the relatively simple rules of physicists' models.

In addition, both writers posit models which apply to a wide range of complex systems, including neurological systems, food webs and insect swarms. This is only possible because they work at a very high level of abstraction, disregarding concrete details which are often essential to a substantive understanding of such systems. We need to bring these abstractions down to earth if we are to put them to sociological use. In what follows this is exactly what I do, demonstrating in the process that the network structure of Britain's national post-punk world involved elements of both models.

Connected clusters and intercity ties

Watts's model envisages small world networks as tightly integrated clusters, linked by weak ties. In the case of Britain's national post-punk

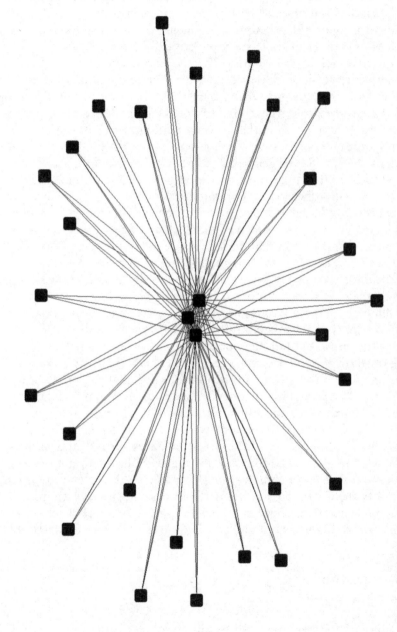

Figure 10.2 A simplified and idealised representation of Barabási's 'hub' model

world the obvious clusters are local, city-based worlds, such as we have considered in Liverpool, Manchester and Sheffield. Punk and post-punk didn't take root in 'Britain' as such but rather in specific towns and cities, including but not exclusively those just mentioned.

Cities are important, as I argued in Chapter 4, because the size of their populations is more likely to meet the critical mass necessary to enable the collective action that makes a viable music world, and because, knowing this, music enthusiasts from smaller towns and villages are likely to gravitate towards their nearest city, swelling the number of enthusiasts within it. Furthermore, networks tend to be spatially concentrated for the simple reason that travel is costly in terms of time, energy and money, thus constraining the time–space trajectories of most people (Giddens 1979, 1984; Hägerstrand 1975). Most music enthusiasts, most of the time, will travel to their nearest city in pursuit of their passion, hooking up with other locals, but not much further.

However, city-based worlds are not entirely cut off from one another. In an interesting paper on subcultures which pre-dates Watts's work but anticipates elements of it, making similar use of Granovetter, Garry Fine and Sherryl Kleinman (1979) argue that tight-knit subcultural groupings in different cities are often connected to one another by weak ties between their members. Within the city, ties are strong and transitive but members of these strong, transitive clusters often have friends or relatives with similar (subcultural) interests to them in other cities and these (intransitive) ties link the local worlds to which they belong, facilitating the flow of influence, information, etc. between them.

The image that this suggests is plausible and similar to that described by Watts. However, Fine and Kleinman focus upon subcultures, a concept which tends to limit their focus to consumers within music worlds (see Chapter 2). I would like to extend the idea to worlds more fully, including, in addition to audiences, artists and support personnel. More importantly, they are vague about the origin of inter-city ties and their argument is speculative. We need to elaborate upon and clarify their ideas as they apply in our case, identifying the mechanisms that generate intercity ties. I have identified five such mechanisms in the various accounts and archives I consulted when researching this book:

1 touring bands;
2 travelling audiences;
3 routine geographical mobility;
4 the lure of 'foreign' opportunities and resources; and
5 festivals.

Touring bands

Bands' early live performances often cluster in venues close to home. As they develop, however, they usually wish to play further afield. There are various reasons for this but for those bands who aspire to 'making it' a central reason is the need to build a national (and eventually international) following. This inclination is reinforced from the audience side. Although local bands may be enjoyed and celebrated there is a limit to the satisfaction they provide. Even the best local bands begin to sound stale if they are seen too frequently, or are the only band playing in a town. As audiences hear of other bands from other places (e.g. on the radio), they want to see those bands too, creating an incentive for local promoters and venue owners to book rising bands from out of town.

This generates intercity ties. Promoters forge ties with bands from other cities and the bands themselves influence and impact upon local audiences; an obvious example being the Sex Pistols' first Manchester gig (see Chapters 7 and 8). In addition, in the smaller venues associated with specialised music worlds, such as Eric's, the Factory and the Limit, where local as well as touring bands from out of town often play, bands are more likely to mix with audiences, including members of other local bands, sometimes building meaningful and durable interpersonal ties. The Sex Pistols did this when they played in Manchester, consolidating ties with Pete Shelley, Howard Devoto and Richard Boon, which were formed when the latter travelled to London to see two of their shows.

To give a further example, when the London-based Slits first played Manchester they made ties with various members of Liverpool's Spitfire Boys, who had travelled to Manchester to see them. This involved members of both bands offering to put one another up when playing in one another's cities. Slits' biographer, Zoe Street Howe, explains:

> Another soon-to-be bosom pal and honorary 'boy-Slit' [the Slits were originally an all-girl band] was future Frankie Goes to Hollywood star Paul Rutherford, who first saw the Slits when the [Clash's] White Riot tour [on which the Slits played support] hit Manchester's Electric Circus ... 'That was the first time they'd played up north, and I just fell completely in love with them. I thought they were amazing ...' says Paul.
>
> 'I was in the Spitfire Boys at that time, and when they later got their first gig just as themselves up north in Eric's in Liverpool, we got [the] support [slot]' (2009: 49)

Indeed, the Spitfire Boys' drummer, Budgie, briefly joined the Slits, playing on their celebrated *Cut* LP.

The flow of bands between towns and cities, as they tour, creates links between their music worlds. It generates an intercity or national network and world.

Travelling audiences

As the above examples illustrate, audiences travel too. This may be because of limitations of access. Early punks in both Liverpool and Sheffield sometimes went to Manchester's Electric Circus to see bands, for example, because the venue was one of the earliest outside of London to put on regular punk gigs. Alternatively, it may be because of commitment to a band. As noted in the previous chapter, Julian Cope, who was living in Liverpool, claims to have seen the Fall twenty-eight times in 1978, mostly in Manchester, and usually accompanied by Ian McCulloch and Dave Pickett (also from Liverpool). Similarly, from the other side of the M62, Paul Morley (2008) reports that he and others regularly ran buses from Manchester to see bands at Eric's in Liverpool.

As with touring bands, in the context of relatively small venues this tends to generate ties between participants (both musicians and audiences) from the cities involved. Cope, McCulloch and Pickett became friends with Mark Smith and other members of the Fall, for example, often staying at each others' flats when visiting:

> We used to have a right laugh … Mac used to write songs like, 'You Don't Notice Time on the New Bury Road'. I went up to stay at Mac's in Liverpool once and their idea of fun was him and Cope and about ten other guys walking around looking like David Bowie, talking about records, in the pouring rain. (Mark Smith, in Fletcher 1987: 17)

And they also got to know other people who were close to the Fall. Jon the Postman, for example, comments:

> There was a lot of cross-fertilisation between the Liverpool and Manchester scenes … I knew Julian Cope, Wylie, Ian McCulloch. They used to go and see the Fall; they were big Fall fans. (in Haslam 2000: 135)

The movement of audiences between city-based music worlds creates links between those worlds, again contributing to the formation of a national music world.

Geographical mobility

People who grow up in one city, establishing roots there, sometimes then move to other cities, laying down new roots but without completely abandoning their original contacts, such that they form a bridge between networks in different cities. Students moving to university typically do this but not only students.

Eric's owner, Roger Eagle, is a good example. He had previously run the Twisted Wheel, a celebrated Northern Soul club in Manchester and had retained Manchester links after moving to Liverpool. Indeed, he remained living in Manchester initially, commuting to Eric's and occasionally sleeping on Geoff Davies's (of Probe Records) couch. As a consequence Eagle served as a bridge between the post-punk worlds of the two cities. He had ties to Tony Wilson, for example, which informed Wilson's decision to film live punk performances from Eric's for his *So It Goes* TV programme and contributed to the 'twinning' of Eric's and the Factory, with bands passing between the venues when visiting the north-west. Furthermore, it allowed Eagle to recommend Liverpool's Orchestral Manoeuvres in the Dark to Wilson, who secured them several gigs at the Factory and arranged for them to release their first single, 'Electricity', on Factory Records.

Similarly, moving things back in the other direction, Eagle's ties to T. J. Davidson led to his introduction to (Manchester's) Mick Hucknall, who was playing with the Frantic Elevators at the time and whose love of Northern Soul resonated with that of Eagle. Eagle subsequently managed the Frantic Elevators and Hucknall DJd at Eric's for a while, becoming a part of Liverpool's post-punk world:

> we spent a lot of time rehearsing in that Mathew Street part of [Liverpool] ... then I'd stay on and DJ in the evenings ... There was a whole scene around Probe Records; everyone knew everyone. I was pleased to be in Liverpool ... We got to know a lot of the Liverpool bands. (Mick Hucknall, in Strachan 2010: 139)

Eagle's geographical mobility created a tie between the post-punk worlds of Liverpool and Manchester. He became a conduit through which information, ideas and influence could flow, and he brokered arrangements which allowed bands from one city to move in the social circles of the other, effecting further links.

Opportunities and resources

Another band who, like Liverpool's Orchestral Manoeuvres, were adopted by the Manchester post-punk world were Sheffield's Cabaret Voltaire. They were regulars at the Factory and very good friends with the members of Joy Division; so much so that when Joy Division singer, Ian Curtis, committed suicide, the Cabs' Stephen Mallinder was one of the first of a very small list of people who were approached to replace him.[2] This relationship began, as noted in the previous chapter, when

Cabaret Voltaire sent a demo to Richard Boon, who was impressed and passed the tape to Tony Wilson.

This is an example of ties being formed across cities, as they sometimes are within cities, when one party spots the opportunities or resources available from another and makes contact on that basis. Cabaret Voltaire approached Richard Boon because he had a record label (New Hormones) and appeared to be open to new forms of music. Orchestral Manoeuvres' approach to Tony Wilson, though brokered by Roger Eagle, is another example of the same thing.

Futurama: a festival hub

National worlds may not centre upon particular focal time–spaces in the way that local worlds do. However, they are not completely lacking in foci. As worlds take on a national identity it is common for cultural entrepreneurs to organise events which mobilise that identity and further shape the world, drawing its various dispersed participants together. Festivals are a good example. Malcolm McLaren and Bernard Rhodes attempted to consolidate early punk developments by organising the 100 Club punk festival in London, in September of 1976, for example, and Marc Zermati did something similar when he organised the first ever punk festival in Mont-de-Marsan in France in August 1976 (see Chapter 6).

The key post-punk festival of the late 1970s and early 1980s was the Futurama Festival, organised by John Keenan. Keenan had been a local promoter in Leeds, arranging punk and post-punk gigs at Leeds Polytechnic and then later at what he called the F Club. In 1979, however, he organised the first Futurama Festival, held over two days (8–9 September) at the Queens Hall in Leeds. Among the bands booked were many from the three local worlds examined in this book: Echo and the Bunnymen, Joy Division, Cabaret Voltaire, Orchestral Manoeuvres, the Fall, the Teardrop Explodes and A Certain Ratio. If Sheffield seems underrepresented it wasn't the following year, at Futurama 2. Alongside a repeat appearance by the Bunnymen and performances from Durutti Column and the Frantic Elevators were: Clock DVA, Artery, Y (who would later become Danse Society), Vice Versa and I'm So Hollow. The Beehive would have been virtually empty that weekend!

The festival, which continued annually throughout the early 1980s, had a city base in Leeds but in both conception and execution it reached beyond that city. It was a national event. It booked bands and drew audiences from around Britain, transcending the localism that most music events inevitably entail, contributing to the formation of both a national post-punk identity and concrete ties which lent that identity substance. It forged a link, both symbolic and practical, between the bands who played at it, bringing them before audiences whose members came from around the country, and bringing those audience members together too.

Mapping intercity ties

I have no information regarding ties formed at Futurama. However, as we see in Figure 10.3, which combines the network maps for Liverpool, Manchester and Sheffield analysed earlier in the book, adding the relatively few intercity ties identified earlier in this chapter (a considerable underestimate of the actual number of ties which existed), these few additional ties are sufficient to configure Britain's post-punk world along the lines suggested by Watts. We have three, relatively dense city-based clusters linked by a few ties. Interestingly this is enough to make the average path length for the whole network as small as 4.2 degrees (with 55 per cent of all pairs separated at 4 or fewer degrees). In this representation Manchester participants broker between those in Liverpool and Sheffield. I found no direct ties between Sheffield and Liverpool. Further work would be required to see if there were any. I am less concerned with the accuracy of this particular network map and the many ties I may have overlooked, however, more concerned with the fact that the map is good enough to illustrate how Britain's post-punk world resembled the model suggested by Watts.

This, in turn, is important, to return to the rationale for Watts' work, because this structure would have facilitated a level of effective coordination and diffusion within the national network. We should not be surprised by similarities that we spot between post-punks in Liverpool, Manchester and Sheffield, nor should we be surprised by whatever coordination we can identify between their various activities and events. Touring bands, touring audiences, routine geographical mobility, resource seeking and festival organisation created links between them, generating a network with relatively short average path lengths which, in turn, facilitated both coordination and diffusion. These were not the only links connecting the post-punk world, however.

The indies

It is not only people who move between and link cities. We should also consider the movement of recordings and zines; a process enhanced by the boom in independent record labels ('indies') associated with punk and post-punk (Hesmondhalgh 1998, 1999; King 2012; Ogg 2009; Taylor 2010; Young 2007).

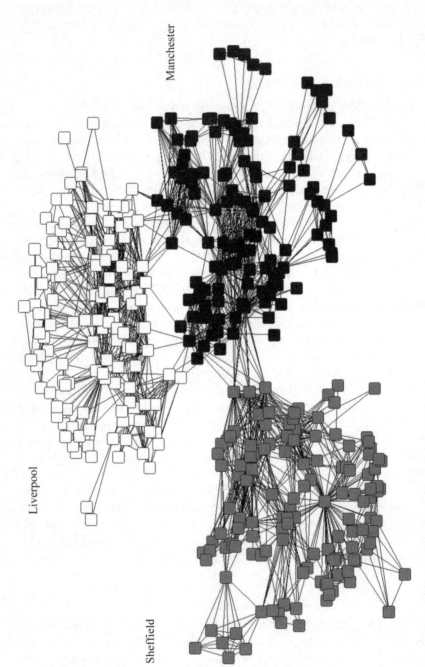

Figure 10.3 A preliminary specification of intercity ties

The definition of indies is contested. They are independent from the large established record companies ('majors') but there are different degrees and forms of independence. For example, many so-called indies rely upon the majors for distribution and, as noted in Chapter 3, the majors often encourage this, sometimes seeking to cultivate their own 'independent' wings. Furthermore, as the key difference between majors and indies is the scale of their operations some indies eventually become majors and we find medium-sized labels whose status is unclear. As Alex Ogg (2009) observes, for example, Virgin and Island Records each had a good claim to independent status for the period we are looking at but few people would think of them in this way because of the scale of their operations.

These definitional issues need not concern us here, however, because the labels I will focus upon, during the period under discussion (1976–80), represented a true cottage industry. They were based in bedrooms, flats and kitchens, and struck no deals with major labels. They may, on occasion, have paid to use pressing plants owned by a major, on a one off basis, but in many cases they did not even have this relationship. More importantly, and central to my argument, they worked within their own, independent distribution network.

Independent labels have existed for as long as records. And there have been periods, prior to punk and post-punk, when they were integral to innovations within popular music, supporting new forms and artists whom the majors, widely known for their conservatism and risk-aversion, ignored. As I noted in Chapter 3, for example, Richard Peterson (1990) makes a convincing case that indie labels were integral to rock 'n' roll's breakthrough into the mainstream. Similarly, Ogg (2009) points to Motown as an example of indie-based innovation.

These examples are both from the USA. Developments in Britain were slower before the 1970s. There had been important indie labels before this time, such as Topic, a folk-focused label established in 1939,[3] which played a key role in the folk revival of the late 1960s (and remains the leading folk label in Britain), and Dandelion, founded in 1969 by John Peel (see below) and Clive Selwood for the purposes of releasing left-field music which they liked and which would not otherwise be released. These examples are largely isolated, however. There is no evidence of a significant indie sector prior to punk.

Not that the vanguards of first-wave punk, or at least those in London, signed to indies. The Pistols signed to EMI, moving rapidly to A&M after the Bill Grundy episode and even more rapidly to Virgin when A&M lost their nerve (within weeks) and dropped them. Similarly, the Clash famously signed to CBS, prompting Mark P to proclaim in *Sniffin'*

Glue that punk was now dead, and the Banshees signed to Polydor. Only the Damned pursued an independent path, and even then only for their first single. 'New Rose' was released on 22 October 1976 on Stiff Records, a label founded that same year and one of two indie labels which emerged in the context of the pub rock boom (see Chapter 3). The other pub rock indie was Chiswick Records, formed by Ted Carroll and Roger Armstrong in 1975 (see Chapter 5, for an account of their link to McLaren and punk).

Carroll, Armstrong and Stiff founders, Jake Riviera and Dave Robinson, would prove an invaluable resource for other early pioneers in the indie boom of the late 1970s, generously sharing their know-how. However, the real impetus for the boom, as testified by many early pioneers in the now numerous accounts of it (e.g. Hesmondhalgh 1998, 1999; King 2012; Ogg 2009; Taylor 2010; Young 2007), came at the very end of 1976, when Manchester's Buzzcocks formed their own label, New Hormones, to release their first EP: *Spiral Scratch*.

Forming their own label involved approaching local music promoter, Martin Hannett, the only person in Manchester they knew of who knew anything about the music industry, and asking him what to do (Richard Boon also spoke to the Chiswick and Stiff founders). Hannett offered to produce them and knew of a studio and pressing plant they could use. All that remained was to borrow £500 from family and friends, to fund the release; take a photo for the cover (an amateur snapshot in Manchester's Piccadilly Gardens); find somewhere to print up the sleeves; stick 500 records into 500 sleeves; then distribute and sell the record. It worked. The first run of 500 copies quickly sold out, prompting further runs, with sales eventually reaching 16,000.[4]

Buzzcocks capitalised upon the EP's success by signing to a major label (United Artists). However, *Spiral Scratch* triggered a wave of both bands and would-be indie label owners seeking to follow its example. New labels sprung up every week during the late 1970s. The ZigZag Small Labels Catalogue for 1978 identifies 231 UK-based independent labels, rising to over 800 by 1980, before dipping to 322 in 1981 (cited in Ogg 2009).

These developments were informed by the DIY ethos of punk and post-punk. Early classic, 'Handlebars', by the Desperate Bicycles, for example, released on their own Refill label, ends with the rallying cry: 'it was easy, it was cheap – go and do it!'. Their second single, 'The Medium was Tedium', follows this up by explaining, on the sleeve, how the record was made and how much the process cost. The Desperate Bicycles acknowledged the influence of Buzzcocks on their decision to form a band and release a single, and they in turn were acknowledged by Scritti Politti, whose first single, 'Skank Bloc Bologna', released on their own St Pancras label, included a complete breakdown of all costs involved in making the record on the sleeve. Such information was intended to serve a number of purposes but one such purpose was to encourage others to follow suit by releasing their own record – which many did.

All of the early indie releases were seven inch singles or EPs. Over time, however, LPs were released, challenging the idea, still prevalent at that time, that independent labels were only a first step for bands who would later move onto a major label to fully establish their career. Indies weren't a first step. They were the real deal. Indeed, indie labels became part of the post-punk identity and ethos, an oppositional move against the dominance of the majors and their conservative and commercially driven practices. Independence was equated with artistic integrity and authenticity.

All early indies faced two key problems, however: distribution and promotion. Pressing 500 copies of a record and getting a group of friends to slip them into sleeves was one thing. Selling them was another. The labels needed a way of distributing their records, and publicising and airing them so as to cultivate a market. They needed a network linking the local music world in which they were situated to others around Britain.

One early means of distribution was for bands to sell their records at their gigs. Another was to persuade local independent record shops, whose owners were often music enthusiasts with a passion for local talent and left-field artists, to stock and sell it to members of the band's local following. Indeed, Buzzcocks managed to persuade the manager of their local Virgin record store to stock *Spiral Scratch*, and he persuaded a number of other Virgin branch managers to do the same.

Over time this practice evolved. Label owners and/or bands would pack a car with copies of the record(s) they wanted to distribute, look up the names and addresses of independent record shops around the country, and drive around them attempting to sell copies. Often a few copies would be sold and where record labels were run out of record shops and had a number of releases, reciprocal arrangements were often forged. A small network of independent record shops began to take shape:

> Everywhere I went, places like King's Lynn, Manchester, Liverpool, Birmingham, Newcastle – I found independent shops everywhere. They took my records. When I went round a second time, people were starting their own labels. They'd say, 'I've got a record as well' … There was a

movement, albeit a loose movement ... no formal association ... a loose friendship between shops up and down the country. And we all knew we were part of a revolution. (Bruce Findlay ('Bruce's Records'), cited in Ogg 2009: 351)

This 'revolution' was helped on its way by the fact, noted by David Hesmondhalgh (1998: 258), that specialist and independent record shops were on the increase in the late 1970s, following a dip in the late 1960s. In 1978 there were 1,750 such shops in Britain, accounting for 32 per cent of the country's total outlets. By 1981 the figure had risen to 2,370 (*ibid.*).

This practice further evolved when some labels and particularly record shops began to distribute by mail order. This was usually backed up, as in the case of *Spiral Scratch*, with adverts in fanzines and sometimes the national music press. This worked particularly well for record shops because, in addition to the cash flow necessary to advertise in one of the national weeklies, they had a large stock of records to sell, some of which might be sought after and difficult to obtain. Two London-based shops, Small Wonder and Rough Trade, both of which also ran their own labels, became particularly well known for their mail order services. Each published a small catalogue of records every week in the back pages of the national music press.

From clusters to hubs

The early links between independent record shops were relatively decentralised. There were no hubs. However, each shop might itself be regarded as something of a hub in the wider distribution network. Many towns had independent record shops, which punks and post-punks gravitated towards, making the shop one of the focal places of their local world. The shops, in turn, were linked by the reciprocal arrangements struck by their owners, as we have seen. Each local shop was therefore a link point between post-punks in one town and post-punks everywhere else. Furthermore, interaction between shop owners in different towns, whether in person or by phone, allowed for the circulation of gossip and rumour. The local record shop owner was a focal figure and good person to know because they had contacts in other towns and therefore knew what was going on.

This structure became more centralised and hub-cantered when Rough Trade began specialising in distribution: buying records in bulk from indie labels and selling them onto other independent record shops throughout the country. As its reputation grew, Rough Trade became the key means by which hundreds of independent labels distributed their wares and therefore an important hub in the national post-punk network. As Ogg explains, bands or record labels would trudge down to London, hoping to persuade Rough Trade to take copies of their record:

> Rough Trade could count on flocks of ... bands from all over the UK descending on them, usually on an away day ticket that would stretch to a visit to Small Wonder. The third leg ... would often be an attempt to sneak past BBC security in order to hand deliver a copy ... to John Peel. Who would, seemingly more often than not, play it. (Ogg 2009: 181)

I return to John Peel. Presently, however, note that, combined with Rough Trade's buying practices, which gave scant consideration to the likelihood of commercial success and involved paying up front for several hundred copies of a record by an unknown artist, this made the business of making and selling independent records viable for many who would not otherwise have been able to do so:

> The economics of releasing a single ... became tenable almost overnight. Rough Trade would customarily stock between 300 and 500 copies ... [with the artist] nearly recouping the initial outlay in one fell swoop. (*ibid.*)

Rough Trade wasn't the only hub in the distribution network. In the mid 1970s the majors, who managed their own national distribution, reduced supply to small independent shops and increased its cost. This created a gap in the market which was filled by so-called 'one stops'; that is, small firms who bought in bulk from the majors, capitalising upon the discount this entitled them to, and then distributed to smaller shops at a lower price than the majors themselves were prepared to offer. Key examples of one stops were Spartan and Pinnacle and both became involved in indie distribution (Hesmondhalgh 1998).

In addition, in the early 1980s, overwhelmed by the scale of independent distribution, Rough Trade teamed up with six other record shops, including Probe in Liverpool, to share the burden of the work, forming the Cartel. Each shop represented a particular area of the country and worked its area. Bands from the north-west of England wishing to have their record distributed were invited to work directly with Probe, for example, rather than travelling down to London to negotiate with Rough Trade. If a deal was struck, then Probe would both distribute the record within the north-west and ship it out to each of the other six regional hubs, who would distribute it within their own area.

This hub-centred distribution network resembles the model suggested by Barabási. This is important because, as Barabási intends, it allows us to explain both coordination and diffusion in the national punk world. Post-punk records were transported across the country, from bands eager to sell to audiences keen to buy, and each transaction in the chain was an opportunity for gossip and thus for the circulation of information, stories and ideas. This 'system' didn't operate in isolation, however.

Media networks

In addition to records, the independent record shops stocked a range of zines from around the country, sourcing them on a similar basis. Paul Bower, who founded Sheffield's first punk zine, the *Gun Rubber*, recalls:

> I used to hitch down to London with a bunch of fanzines, go to Rough Trade and they would buy the lot, cash upfront. (Paul Bower, in Lilleker 2005: 31)

And there is clear evidence that his zine was read outside of Sheffield:

> Rubber 6 included a plea from one Steve Morrissey of Manchester for people to sign a petition to get the film of the New York Dolls on the Old Grey Whistle test from 1972 repeated. Yes, that Morrissey. (*ibid.*)

There is no evidence to suggest that this call to arms was a success but the incident illustrates the way in which the indie distribution network linked up participants in post-punk music worlds across Britain, extending their conversations and the flow of information about bands and trends over bigger distances, generating a national post-punk world.

At a further level it illustrates the importance of mediated, broadcast networks, as discussed in Chapter 7, in linking up local network members in the context of a national music world. Different media outlets are hubs in the national network, providing a common link and reference point for all involved. This is why radio playlists often cause such a furore among music industry players; because inclusion on a playlist means instant connection with a huge, geographically dispersed population.

I do not have the space here to elaborate in detail upon the mediation and broadcast structure of the national post-punk network but I do want to make a few observations. First, the non-mainstream nature of post-punk meant that it was not well represented on most radio playlists or, indeed, in other mainstream media outlets. This meant that post-punk records generally failed to achieve exposure and publicity, by contrast with mainstream acts, resulting in records either failing to reach the Top 40 or reaching much lower positions than might otherwise have been expected. This, in turn, deprived the records and artists of opportunities for exposure and publicity in a vicious circle. I should also add that artists on independent labels were particularly disadvantaged in this respect because their labels lacked the influence over major media outlets that the majors enjoyed, influence which increased the likelihood of artists being included on playlists. They also lacked the finances necessary for independent publicity and promotional activities.

Having said this, however, it is widely acknowledged that the national music press, comprising *NME*, *Melody Maker*, *Sounds*, *Record Mirror* and to some extent even more mainstream-focused magazines, such as *Smash Hits*, took great interest in punk, post-punk and the indie boom. The music was taken very seriously and accorded great significance. Information about artists, events and recordings was broadcast, and certain journalists (e.g. Jon Savage and Paul Morley) became established as important authorities on these forms of music. 'The weeklies', as they were known, and/or certain of their writers, became important hubs in the national post-punk network.

The centralisation which this brought about within the network was further consolidated in 1980, moreover, with the formation, at the instigation of Iain McNay, of Cherry Red Records, of the independent single and LP charts: alternative 'hit parades' for records that 'didn't go through the major record distributors' (McNay 1997), based on sales at selected independent stores across the country. The purpose of the chart, which was published in most of the weeklies and even certain mainstream publications, such as *Smash Hits*, was clear for McNay:

> It helped shops order records, provided information for radio stations on what was really selling, and showed record companies abroad which companies were worth talking to regarding licensing releases for their territories. (*ibid.*)

In other words, it constituted a centralised information hub which facilitated both coordination and influence in the post-punk world. In addition, it established a common reference point for participants in local punk and post-punk worlds around the country, helping to create a national punk/post-punk world. It reflected national buying trends but also allowed trends to form at the national level by giving interested record buyers throughout Britain a signal as to what others elsewhere were buying and listening to. Furthermore, it helped to create an alternative 'star system'. Bands and artists who would not come within a mile of the official chart might remain in the indie charts for months, establishing certain of their works as classics. For example, Joy Division's 'Love Will Tear Us Apart', which (originally) spent six weeks in the official chart, peaking at number 13, spent a total of 195 weeks (nearly four years) in the indie charts, with ten weeks at number 1. Similarly Bauhaus's 'Bella Lugosi's Dead', which failed to make the mainstream chart at all, spent 131 weeks in the indie chart (Lazell 1997). Bands like Crass, the Dead Kennedys, the Men They Couldn't Hang, Vice Squad and Spizz Energi, who nobody outside of the punk/post-punk world had heard of, were 'household names' within the national punk/post-world world and the indie charts played a big role in this process. Again, the chart created an information hub to which all involved could refer.

The indie charts had an important symbolic significance. Although the criteria for inclusion were entirely based on distribution deals, rather than aesthetics, such that cheesy novelty records occasionally figured, the existence of an alternative chart suggested that the music in it, which was predominantly punk and post-punk, was indeed an alternative to the mainstream, with its own aesthetics and buying public. It wasn't, as some might otherwise have supposed, simply music that wasn't good enough to make the mainstream Top 40. The post-punk world was a source of alternative aesthetic standards.

Furthermore, there was an important exception to the above-mentioned radio silence: John Peel, a (BBC) Radio 1 DJ who was an institution of both the punk and post-punk worlds. As David Hesmondhalgh comments: 'most people interested in punk read the weekly music press ... and listened to John Peel's weekday evening radio show' (2008: 259). Peel was associated with new and challenging music throughout his career. This meant psychedelia, prog rock and folk music when he first began at the BBC in 1967, and hip hop and dance music at the time of his death in 2004. Through the late 1970s and early 1980s, however, it meant punk and post-punk, which he championed with unmatched enthusiasm.

Loved by his audience, he had a quirky style and idiosyncratic charisma. Chatter between records was notably less frequent and depressed in tone if Liverpool Football Club had lost a game, for example, and it was not uncommon, much to the delight of his listeners, for him to accidentally play the B-side of a record or play it at the wrong speed, not noticing until the song was almost over and jokingly passing the incident off when he did. If he liked an LP he might play it in its entirety over one or two shows, again to the delight of his audience: whether or not they liked the record, his disregard for 'good practice' was part of his allure and part of the fun. More importantly, the usual pluggers and playlists held no sway with him. Peel played what he liked and that usually meant records, punk and post-punk, which other DJs weren't playing and which audiences would never have heard were it not for him. Bands sent him tapes and self-released singles and he very often played them, sometimes inviting unsigned bands to record sessions for his programme and thereby bringing unknown artists before a national audience.

Every Christmas Peel would compile his 'Festive 50', a chart of listeners' all-time favourite tracks (switching to their favourite tracks of the year in 1982). The chart reflected the artists that Peel championed and bore no resemblance to the mainstream chart. Like the indie charts, and alongside his sessions and regular playlists, it created a sense that post-punk was a source of alternative aesthetic values. Peel affirmed and lent legitimacy to the view of many of his listeners that there were far more exciting things to listen to than the stuff of the mainstream Top 40.

Peel's chief importance, from our point of view, however, is his role in linking post-punk activities in different parts of the country. He was a major hub, through which much of the best music of the era passed, a link between the various city-based punk and post-punk worlds taking shape in Britain during the late 1970s, constituting them as nodes within a national, networked world. Many of the artists discussed in this book benefited from this hub. The Fall recorded twenty-four sessions for Peel altogether, for example, the Bunnymen recorded seven and Cabaret Voltaire recorded two, while Joy Division has seven entries in the Festive 50 for 1980 (the year Ian Curtis died), including five in the Top 20 (Garner 2007). These bands transcended their local origins and became national through Peel.

Conclusions

Each of the chapters before this one, with the exception of Chapter 7, has been focused upon the emergence of punk and/or post-punk networks and worlds within a particular city, whether Liverpool, London, Manchester or Sheffield. In this chapter, building upon Chapter 7 and extending the focus of that chapter, I have considered how these various local punk and post-punk worlds, along with others like them across Britain, became linked in a national post-punk network and world.

The network structure of this national world is a mixture of the architectures suggested by Watts and Barabási. The inevitable concentration of activities within specific cities and the tendency for participants, audiences in particular, to limit their participation to one city, creates clusters in the network, as Watts predicts, but as he also predicts these clusters do not remain completely closed off from one another. Touring bands, the music tourism of audiences, the search for resources, routine geographical mobility and festivals all forge ties across cities, generating a structure of interconnected clusters. On the other hand, however, as Barabási suggests, we observe the emergence of hubs which link geographically dispersed participants by serving as a common point of contact between them. This happened within the distribution networks which formed around the new indie labels, as Rough Trade and other Cartel members took on the lion's share of work in getting records from labels to shops. It also happened in mediated, broadcast networks as particular journalists and DJs became central reference points for a majority of post-punks, nationally, and took on the role of brokering between artists and audiences.

Watts and Barabási both introduce their model structures in the context of a discussion of coordination in large, complex structures. They want to know how coordination is possible in systems or networks involving millions of nodes and, assuming that this will only be happen where nodes tend to be connected by short paths, seek out the structures which best facilitate this. The fact that the national post-punk world can be viewed as combining elements of each of these systems does not necessarily mean that it was well coordinated, nor that diffusion worked effectively with it. However, in so far as we believe that it was relatively coordinated and that tastes, styles and identities diffused quickly and effectively through it, the proximity of its network structure to their models is part of the reason why.

Notes

1 Their tie to the hub and the hub's tie to the other person.
2 In fact Joy Division's guitarist, Bernard Sumner, took on the role as the band morphed into New Order.
3 As an offshoot of the Worker's Music Association.
4 http://en.wikipedia.org/wiki/Spiral_Scratch_(EP)

11

Conclusion

In this book, drawing upon Howard Becker's (1982) concept of 'art worlds', I have conceptualised punk and post-punk as 'music worlds' existing both on the local, city level and also spanning towns and cities, on a national level. Concentrating upon the 1975–80 period I have tried to explain:

1 The emergence of the first UK punk world, in London.
2 The process of diffusion which carried punk to other towns and cities, leading to the emergence of punk worlds in those cities too.
3 The transformation of punk, in several of these worlds, into something which became known as post-punk.
4 The intercity ties which linked the various local post-punk worlds, constituting a national post-punk world.

Addressing these issues has raised further issues which I have had to bracket or gloss over in order to make my project manageable. I want to end this book by briefly identifying some of these, and mapping out topics for further research. Before I do, however, I will briefly recap the central arguments of the book.

Many accounts of the birth of punk focus upon social strains and frustrations which its pioneers are said to have reacted against. Birmingham's Centre for Contemporary Cultural Studies explains punk as a response to the twofold alienation of working-class youth, for example, and to frustration at the co-optation of previous youth cultural responses to this alienation. Others have explained it as a response to the economic, political and social crises which beset British society in the mid 1970s. Alternatively, punk is explained as a response to the poor state of popular music, both mainstream and underground, during the mid 1970s, on behalf of a generation whose musical horizons and expectations had been shaped by the more excit-ing artists of earlier decades.

This latter story has been revised in recent years by authors who point to a variety of pockets of musical innovation, deep in the underground, which offered punk's pioneers some relief from this otherwise bleak aesthetic environment and encouraged them to become involved. Punk's pioneers were 'musos' inspired by underground and provocative innova-tions, on this account, and their early efforts were as much an attempt to emulate their underground heroes (e.g. the Stooges and New York Dolls) as rebel against prog rock and saccharine pop.

The merits of these different claims vary when checked against the avalanche of personal testimony and quality music journalism on punk which has been published in recent years but even if each of the claims were right about the motivations of punk's pioneers they would still be problematic as explanations of the emergence of London's punk world. Sociological analyses of collective action, including many studies of protest, social movements and revolution, stress that the strains, frus-trations and grievances which individuals collectively mobilise around cannot explain that mobilisation, at least not on their own (Crossley 2002). Grievances are far more common than mobilisation itself which begs the question of the difference between situations where grievances occasion collective action and those where they do not? Mobilisation evidently has preconditions other than the frustration which it vents and the key sociological question is as to what they are?

This criticism applies equally to the idea that punk emerged in response to the inspiration offered by earlier underground innovation. It is one thing to desire to spark a new wave of musical innovation, another to participate in collective action which actually brings it about. Collective desires rest upon important social mechanisms for their realisation and it is the job of the sociologist to identify and analyse those mechanisms.

These are not cavilling points. They are essential to an explanation of punk. Punk initially emerged among a very small population of young people in London but London was hardly the only city in the UK affected by the crises of the mid 1970s and there is no reason to suppose that these crises impacted upon London's proto-punks any differently to anybody else. If punk were an inevitable response to crisis, why didn't it take shape in all corners of the UK simultaneously? Likewise, even if London's proto-punks had all been working class (they weren't), they would only represent a tiny fraction of working class youth in the UK, begging the question of why and how they, specifically, mounted the resistance to working-class youth alienation that, in the view of some, punk represented.

Many and perhaps all proto-punks had been inspired by the pre-punk influences referred to above and there is strong evidence of dissatisfaction with prog rock and the musical mainstream among them. When John Lydon was discovered by Bernard Rhodes, for example, he was famously wearing a Pink Floyd T-shirt which he had modified with the words 'I Hate'. But again punk's London pioneers were by no means the only young people who were frustrated with contemporary music or who identified with and wished to emulate the garage-glam of such bands as the Stooges. Martin Hannett, who would become a key player in Manchester's punk and post-punk worlds, wrote a scathing attack on the state of pop music in early 1975, for example, while a few miles up the road, in Bolton, Howard Devoto and Pete Shelley were attempting to cover songs from Iggy and the Stooges' *Raw Power* LP in a band they were putting together. Again this begs the question: why did punk emerge in London? Why not Manchester, or Glasgow, Penzance, Belfast or Aberystwyth?

I suggested in Chapter 4 that we can narrow the likely 'point of origin' for punk to one of the UK's larger cities on account of the need for critical mass in collective action. The establishment of a new music world such as punk requires resources (skills, equipment, spaces to rehearse) and a big enough body of people willing both to put those resources at its disposal, where they have them, and to play the various roles required for a flourishing music world: e.g. artists, audiences, managers, promoters, roadies, etc. Over time a music world may recruit and convert neophytes for those roles, swelling its ranks, but only if it first has something to offer them in the form of gigs to attend, bands to follow, etc., and that necessitates a small but big enough group of people with the necessary resources and orientations at the outset: a critical mass.

A critical mass is not always easy to find, however, particularly where, as in the case of punk, the orientation which characterises its members is relatively rare: namely, a passion for particular underground musical worlds, a desire to belong to such worlds oneself, an attraction to similarly underground and outré fashions. Whatever its geographical dispersal, the aesthetic orientation of the proto-punks, their profile of likes and dislikes, was an underground orientation and relatively rare. Big cities are important in this context because the size of their population means that, all things being equal, orientations of any kind are found in greater numbers, increasing the likelihood that they will exist in sufficient numbers to constitute a critical mass and facilitate collective action. A fraction of a percent of a population of one million people is still quite a lot of people but a similar fraction of a small town population numbering in the thousands may be too small to mount any significant form of action. Furthermore, anticipation of critical mass in the city can trigger a self-fulfilling prophecy: individuals outside of a big city who have minority tastes and interests gravitate towards the city in expectation of finding larger numbers of likeminded others with whom to hook up, thereby swelling the ranks of 'likeminded others' in the city and depleting their numbers outside of it.

This argument may apply especially to London, the biggest of the UK's cities, but it does not apply only to London. It explains why punk was very unlikely to emerge first in one of the UK's smaller towns or cities but it only narrows the likely point of origin to one the bigger cities.

A further factor in London's favour is its cultural dominance and consequent concentration of opportunities for musical success. I suggested in Chapter 3 that the specific opportunity structures identified in Richard Peterson's (1990) account of the rise of rock 'n' roll do not appear to have played a role in relation to punk. However, I noted some evidence that both record labels and music journalists, especially those who shared in the punks' negative appraisal of prog rock, were on the look-out for 'the next big thing' in the mid 1970s, creating an opportunity for emerging worlds. As both were disproportionately based in London and inclined to the parochial view that nothing much of interest happens outside of the capital, bands and music worlds located there had a much greater chance of coming to their attention and enjoying these opportunities. Furthermore, awareness of these opportunities both increases the incentives for musical activity and innovation within the capital and encourages aspiring musicians to migrate there, further boosting the city's critical mass of musicians and depleting that of towns and cities elsewhere.

This still begs the question, however. Opportunities only exist for already emerging artists and worlds and therefore presuppose a prior process of emergence which must be explained. Punk went national and mainstream as a consequence of the publicity (including the moral panic (see Chapter 7)) which coverage in both the music press and mainstream media provided and of the distribution and promotion of their music by major record labels but the media and industry picked up on something that was already taking shape without their intervention and, important though the media and industry were in enlarging and mainstreaming this something we must ask how and why the something was happening in the first place.

My explanation centres upon networks. A critical mass will achieve nothing, indeed it is no more than a theoretical construct, in the absence of relationships between its members and those relations, which make it a network, generate emergent properties which are in turn central to the mobilisation of collective action and the generation of a music world. In a network whose members share particular tastes and interests and where those shared tastes and interests frame interaction, the likelihood of collective action centred upon those interests increases sharply. The combined effect of competition, mutual support and incitement draws network members into action, shifting their reference group and shielding them from external factors which might otherwise inhibit involvement. Participants are pressured to cooperate with and trust one another, generating an environment which supports and enables actions that would not otherwise be possible. And the excitement which this generates, loosening social controls (both internalised and interpersonal) and self-consciousness, coupled with mutual influence in interaction, is generative of new cultural forms and a sense of collective identity to which all involved are inclined to orient.

That different towns and cities around the UK have played midwife to celebrated music worlds both before and after punk, from the Merseybeat to heavy rock (in Birmingham and its surrounds), Northern Soul to Madchester, demonstrates that the cultural dominance of the capital is not a prerequisite for the formation of such networks. In the case of punk, however, a networked critical mass of proto-punks did assemble first in London, and that is why punk first emerged in the capital.

I have only been able to support this contention by comparing the network structure binding London's critical mass of punk pioneers, at the time when punk was beginning to take shape, with the critical mass in punk's second city, Manchester. Perhaps proto-punks elsewhere formed a tight-knit network which failed to generate an exciting music world for some other reason? Perhaps they generated an exciting music world but their distance from the cultural opportunities of the capital meant that nobody ever got to hear about it? Perhaps. However, the contrast between the network structures of London and Manchester is stark. The Sex Pistols' first gig in Manchester had a huge effect, pulling the city's proto-punks into a common orbit where they began to hook up, form bands and collectively organise the events and spaces that would constitute their punk world. Prior to this visit, however, any such collective action would have been virtually impossible because very few of them knew one another. There were small pockets of proto-punk activity but they were destined to remain small and lacked significance because they had no way of reaching out to likeminded others who would enjoy and spark off them. The situation in London could not have been more different. All of punk's key players were connected there in a dense and compact network. Everybody involved was linked to a high number of others who were also involved. London's proto-punks did reach out to and spark off one another, and the nexus of interaction and excitement this gave rise to also facilitated recruitment and 'conversion' of others who would not otherwise have belonged to the punk or proto-punk camp.

Competition was equal to cooperation in the process whereby this network cultivated a punk world, as it would be in the networks of Manchester, Liverpool, Sheffield and all other towns and cities which were to host punk and post-punk worlds. Learning through personal connections of other bands who were doing something similar to one's own and taking big steps forward added a sense of urgency to the proto-punk's projects, incentivising the hard work necessary to 'get it together' and encouraging the innovation and risk taking that gave punk its distinct and provocative style. But cooperation, albeit grudging in some cases, was important too, as was the 'social capital' constituted by the network. The existence of networks meant that, in addition to the resources they had directed access to, the post-punks enjoyed indirect access to a much wider pool of (others') resources. This is social capital as Nan Lin (2002) defines it. Corresponding to James Coleman's (1990) more structural definition of social capital, however, the tendency for dense and (relatively) closed networks to generate strong incentives for cooperation, trust and mutual support, if not also the *esprit de corps*, solidarity and morale identified by Blumer (1969), also generated an environment highly conducive to the collective action which generated punk. Furthermore, as various studies of 'cultural deviance' in dense networks (Bott 1957; Milroy 1987) and Coleman's (1988) reflections on the deviant incentive structures that such networks can cultivate, suggest, such networks also provide a good environment for the cultivation of the stylistic innovation and provocation which characterised punk. Going against the grain is much easier in an environment where others are doing the same and, in that context, can assume a sense of both normality and importance.

This all begs the question of how and why a network formed in London and not, for example, Manchester or Liverpool? Chance and contingency undoubtedly play a role here. As I argued above, the fact that Liverpool, Manchester and other cities have been the point of origin and geographical centre of different music worlds both before and after punk (e.g. heavy metal, Northern Soul, Merseybeat) indicates that networks focused upon particular musical tastes and interests might assemble first in any reasonably large city, further suggesting that what makes the difference in any particular case is not the city itself or any of its particular distinguishing features but rather localised, transient and contingent mechanisms whose effect is well understood by sociologists but whose appearance in any given time and place is quite unpredictable.

The London network came together as a consequence of what Scott Feld (1981, 1982) calls network foci – events and places where like-minded actors tend to converge and form ties. We can analyse these foci in some detail retrospectively (see Chapter 6). However, we could not have predicted their appearance in advance.

The main foci for the London punk world was a shop on the King's Road which became a magnet for young people with a taste for underground fashions and music, some of whom wanted to form bands and two of whom (Steve Jones and Paul Cook) asked the shop's co-owner, Malcolm McLaren, if he would manage their band. McLaren wasn't particularly interested in music at the time, having become disillusioned when the rock 'n' roll which had excited him during his youth began to fade but he agreed, apparently believing that the band might provide a vehicle for advertising and selling his clothes (the shop was called SEX for much of the early history of punk and it is no coincidence that the band were named the Sex Pistols). Along with one or two others in the World's End area of Chelsea, the shop began to pull a small group of these young people into the same orbit, linking them both with one another and with an assorted cast of small businesspeople, artists, musos and politicos whom McLaren had got to know over the years and who would invest money, time and their various skills and ideas into the musical projects of these young proto-punks. When the Sex Pistols first put a set together and began to gig the shop was their primary means of publicity and early Pistols' audiences were recruited in large part from the shop.

That McLaren happened to meet Sylvain Sylvain of the New York Dolls (a fellow rag trade entrepreneur) at a 'New York clothing trade show' in 1971 is also important (Sylvain 2010). McLaren became a clothing supplier for the Dolls and as he got to know them became a fan. Furthermore, his association with the band, which his friend, Nick Kent, wrote about in the NME early in 1975, increased his kudos among the proto-punks who frequented his shop. More important still, however, when the Dolls' fortunes began to wane early in 1975 McLaren spent a short period in the USA managing and attempting to help them. This proved to be the kiss of death for them but it introduced McLaren to the New York punk world which was emerging around CBGB and related clubs, and to such characters as Richard Hell. How much of the style of London's subsequent punk world can be explained by McLaren's brokering between the two cities remains a contentious issue but it is indisputable that he was inspired by what he saw and returned to London, in mid 1975, newly enthused about music, keen to see something comparable to New York in London, and eager to be involved in making it happen. Had there been no network of proto-punks for him to work with or had he not been connected to this network his desires would have found no means of expression but, as I have already indicated, his shop was generating the requisite network around him.

During the very early days of punk the shop was the key focus pulling proto-punks into orbit and generating a network between them. This was sufficient to give rise to the Sex Pistols and a small band of followers, and it also generated indirect ties between the Pistols and others who were groping in a similar direction, not least London SS, whose core membership would form the nucleus of a number of seminal punk bands, including the Clash, Chelsea, Generation X and the Damned. The Sex Pistols' gigs took things to the next level, however, proving to be a fertile ground for recruitment to the punk cause. It is significant in this respect that many early gigs were at art colleges. If anybody was likely to be attracted to the provocative and unconventional style that the early network had cultivated and which the Sex Pistols embodied it was art students. As the Pistols began to infiltrate to the pub rock circuit, however, they found another constituency there too, for somewhat different reasons. Pub rock was deliberately raw and raucous and, influenced by it to some extent, so too were the Pistols. When pub rock enthusiasts such as Joe Strummer, Shane MacGowan, Stuart Goddard (Adam Ant) and Vic Goddard (no relation) first saw the Pistols they were immediately seduced. Punk spoke to the tastes cultivated in the pub rock world but advanced them in a way which appealed, in particular, to younger pub rockers.

It is at this point that the media became important, extending punk's reach beyond these immediate constituencies and thereby growing its network. An early review of a Pistols' support slot for pub rockers, Eddie and the Hot Rods, at the Marquee, was particularly important. A quotation from Steve Jones claiming that the Pistols were into chaos rather than music excited the interest of many but a comparison with the Stooges and mention of a cover of the Stooges' 'No Fun' were equally important. As noted above, the Pistols' key musical influences were underground, the preserve of a minority, but members of this minority were not specifically concentrated in London. Concentrations were to be found in many cities. However, they were not connected, as London's proto-punks were and, as such, enjoyed little outlet for the development and expression of their tastes. When, during their routine scouring of the music press, they came across mention of these short-haired, UK-based Stooges imitators, they were therefore excited, intrigued and, in some cases, moved to check the Pistols out. Some, such as T. V. Smith and Gaye Advert, moved to London to be a part of what was going on. Others, specifically Howard Devoto and Pete Shelley, just visited but invited the Pistols back to Manchester, mobilising others in the city who had read about the Pistols, bringing them together and kick-starting a process of world formation akin to that in London in which the Pistols themselves had taken shape.

A feature article on punk in *Melody Maker* in August 1976, by Caroline Coon, further broadcast news of it, but again largely to those whose existing enthusiasm for the likes of the Dolls and Stooges in particular already disposed them towards such things. The real step change occurred when bad language during a local TV interview put the Pistols on the front page of several national tabloids and sparked a moral panic about punk. The panic closed down many of punk's opportunities for growth. The Pistols in particular were instantly barred from many venues and their projected Anarchy Tour was decimated. As sociologists might have predicted, however, demonisation of punks in the media and attempts to suppress it in local contexts spread the word far more quickly and extensively than would otherwise have been possible, exciting a great deal of interest and sympathy among many young people. Within a few weeks everybody in the UK had heard of punk and huge numbers of young people across the country were identifying as punks. The attempt to suppress punk catapulted it into the mainstream, making it exciting and alluring even to conventional youths, with chart-focused musical tastes, who would not otherwise have been remotely interested in it.

This undoubtedly contributed to the process whereby local punk worlds began to spring up in towns and cities across the UK. Young people changed the way in which they looked, began to buy punk records and, in some cases, looked to form their own bands. Record shops and venues, with varying degrees of effort on their own part, became identified as 'punk spaces'. And every major record label wanted, indeed needed their own punk band, if not a roster of such bands. Even within the early months of punk fever, however, some became quickly disillusioned. Punk had signalled a challenge to uniformity and had hinted at various musical possibilities but to the eyes and ears of certain early risers it had quickly abandoned these values, becoming uniform in both look and sound: just another fashion. However, it had, at least in some cases, created a local music world, a network of people, places and resources, which the disaffected could draw upon to do something different, often reaching behind punk to influences which the very early punks themselves has been inspired by but failed to pick up: e.g.

Krautrock, reggae, psychedelia and, closer to the mainstream, David Bowie and Roxy Music. In short, while punk still thrived in certain contexts multiple varieties of post-punk began to take shape within the organisational infrastructure which its pioneers had assembled.

Post-punk is often identified with locality and local pride. We associate it with Liverpool, Manchester and Sheffield, with Coventry's Two-Tone world, Bristol's funkier, jazz-inflected sounds, with the Leeds bands and with those ex-punks in London, associated with the Bromley Contingent in particular, whose return to Bowie and congregation at such clubs as the Blitz and Camden Palace gave rise to the new romantics. Local worlds were in many cases linked, however, giving rise to national punk and post-punk worlds. In some cases these links were face to face but they were also mediated through venues, the music media, the circulation of recordings and by a boom in independent record labels, with associated distribution networks. On one level this national network looks like the 'small world' networks described by Duncan Watts (1999, 2004), with assorted dense, city-based clusters linked by 'weak ties' (see Chapter 10). In other respects it looks like Albert-László Barabási's (2003) 'scale-free networks', with such hubs as John Peel and Rough Trade providing a crucial link point between huge numbers of widely dispersed post-punk enthusiasts. In both cases, however, the key point is that post-punk, like punk, happened because of connection and networks; because what one person did both affected and was affected by what others were doing. This was partly a matter of mutual influence and diffusion but also, as in punk, of competition on one side and cooperation, support and mutual facilitation on the other.

My account is agency based. Punk happened because enthusiastic, resourceful and creative young people made it happen. However, this was collective enthusiasm, resourcefulness and creativity. Nobody was acting in isolation and nobody's innovations arose in a vacuum. Punk took shape in a network of interaction. The proto-punks interacted in an indirect manner with their predecessors, variously borrowing from and rebelling against their musical predecessors, but no less importantly they interacted directly with one another, sparking off one another in a process to which all contributed but none could distinguish their own unique contribution. Innovations diffused and 'caught on', stimulating further innovations; resources were mobilised and exchanged; and both opportunities and constraints were created. Agency was attached to structure, in other words, in a single process.

Over the time that I have been writing this book numerous further questions and issues, not addressed directly in the book, have occurred to me, not least in the context of seminars and lectures where I have presented various bits of the story. I have been fortunate that punk, post-punk and even network diagrams all seem to provoke a positive reaction from students and colleagues, generating enthusiastic audiences and stimulating exciting conversations which have carried me far from where I thought I was headed. I don't have the space to mention, let alone address all of these issues here but I want to conclude the book by briefly outlining a few of them. Needless to say, my aim here is to pose questions rather than provide answers.

An obvious question concerns the wider applicability of these ideas. Could heavy metal, Merseybeat, Northern Soul, Riot Grrrl, reggae, Motown, jazz, rock 'n' roll and other music worlds be analysed in the same way? I believe that they could and preliminary work supports this (Crossley *et al.* 2014). The details will be different, of course, but the basic mechanisms (networks, critical mass, collective effervescence, etc.) will be the same. That is just a hypothesis, however, and it must be tested.

Mention of other music worlds begs two further questions. First, the question of boundaries: where does one music world end and another begin? Can a focus upon networks help us to answer this question? Boundaries are often contested and in some respects, therefore, it is impossible for the analyst to draw them in a way that is not at least partially arbitrary. However, we need to think about issues of inclusion and exclusion, and in particular to think about the most analytically useful ways of deciding them.

Second, there is the question of the distinction between mainstream and underground music worlds. Many questions abound here. Some, again, concern boundaries: how do we define the mainstream music world and what, conversely, constitutes a world being 'underground'? Some bear upon the peculiarity of the mainstream: is it a music world in the same way that smaller and more specialised (underground) worlds are worlds and can it be analysed on the same way? Is there one mainstream or several? I suspect that a modified form of the model I have developed here and a modified version of the analysis I have offered would provide an interesting and useful way of addressing these questions. Again, however, that is a hypothesis which must be explored in further, future work.

Moving on, and assuming for the moment that I am right about the way in which music worlds emerge, several people have asked about their demise: how and why do they fall apart or decline when they do? It is important when considering this issue to distinguish between death and evolution. The worlds I have examined in Manchester and Liverpool, for example, shifted their focus from punk and post-punk to dance, hosting two of the most celebrated dance clubs in the world (the Haçienda and Cream) and there was at least some continuity in their networks. Jayne Casey, the early Eric's face who fronted Big in Japan was involved in Cream, for example, while the Haçienda was jointly owned by members of the Factory collective and members of New Order, the latter of whom had generated their financial stake as Joy Division, the most celebrated of Manchester's post-punk bands. Sheffield, meanwhile, was a key site for the second, post post-punk wave of electronic music, and early releases on the Warp record label that spearheaded this second wave included work by Cabaret Voltaire's Richard Kirk.

When studying the early punk worlds I was struck by the rapid rise and fall of certain bands and sometimes equally rapid movement of players between bands. This suggested to me that the network of participants was in some ways more important than particular bands. Bands often seemed little more than convenient arrangements within the network which allowed participants to rehearse and/or experiment until better bands came along. The rise and fall of particular worlds (e.g. punk, post-punk, dance) within the context of the same network suggests something similar. There can be no doubt that participants were committed to punk or post-punk or dance at the time of their involvement in it, and of course the network itself evolved, drawing new people in and losing others, but in some ways the network and the various resources attaching to it is more enduring than the stylistic conventions and tastes that define it in any particular time, an observation which begs the question of why and how tastes and stylistic conventions shift change as they evidently do.

In so far as it is appropriate to talk of the decline and death of worlds and their networks, however, and in so far as this is not simply explained by the decline (burn-out, disillusionment, death, etc.) of their key participants, two key factors jump out from the literature, both related to success. First, success takes bands on tour, away from their local world and from one another, breaking up the network that once constituted their world. When asked by Jon Savage what happened to the 'close-knit network' that nurtured punk, for example, Viv Albertine replies:

> I suppose when everyone started going on tour and becoming a working band, really. ... it didn't last long, hanging around the clubs ... You don't see your mates any more, and suddenly you're in the career of it all, and it's a bloody bore. (in Savage 2009: 305)

Second, success can cause a sudden influx of new participants whose participation alters the network and world in a way which alienates early participants and prompts them to move on.

These are just suggestions. They need further exploration and they are certainly not the only factors contributing to the decline of worlds. We would also need to explore how tastes change: e.g. from punk, to post-punk to dance. Indeed, changing tastes are an important factor to consider more generally in research on music worlds. We might at least start by looking at these factors, however.

The final issue which I wish to flag for further consideration at this point is the relation of music worlds to wider social divisions: e.g. race, gender, age and social class. I have suggested in this book that punk had a mixed-class base but was largely white in its first incarnation and also a preserve of the young. I have explained this by reference to homophily in the networks which gave rise to punk. For a variety of reasons social actors are more likely to form ties with others who share a similar status position and identity (e.g. age and race) with them, and these ties will shape their tastes and aspirations. Consequently music worlds, which emerge out of such networks and recruit within them, will tend to have a distinct status profile – the profile of the network which gave rise to it. These ideas need further examination and testing.

Furthermore, we should be mindful of gender divisions, which work in different ways. Men and women do not segregate in their leisure in the way that age and racial groups often do, at least heterosexual men and women do not (sexuality is another divide we should consider), and music often brings them together: e.g. on the dance floor. Many music worlds remain male dominated, however. Punk and post-punk were better than some in this respect but far from equal. While relations between men often serve to recruit them to bands and other music projects relations between women and between women and men do not seem to have the same effect. Following Cohen (1997) I am inclined to think that networks and the gendered meaning of ties play an important role in explaining this; a male friend is a potential band mate, a girl-friend is not. Again, this needs further research.

References

(All texts used as sources for network data are marked with an *asterisk)

Abbott, A. (1997) 'Of Time and Space', *Social Forces*, 75(4): 1149–82.
Abbott, A. (2001) *Time Matters*, Chicago, IL: University of Chicago Press.
*Adams, C. (2002) *Turquoise Days*, New York: Soft Skull.
*Anderson, N. (2009) *Take It to the Limit*, Sheffield, UK: AcmRetro.
Andrews, K. and Biggs, M. (2006) 'The Dynamics of Protest Diffusion', *American Sociological Review*, 71: 752–77.
*Ant, A. (2006) *Stand and Deliver*, London: Pan.
Ball, P. (2011) *The Music Instinct*, New York: Vintage.
Bangs, L. (1987) *Psychotic Reactions and Carburetor Dung*, London: Serpent's Tail.
Barabási, A.-L. (2003) *Linked*, New York: Plume.
Bayton, M. (1998) *Frock Rock*, Oxford: Oxford University Press.
Becker, G. (1996) *Accounting for Tastes*, Cambridge, MA: Harvard University Press.
Becker, H. (1951) 'The Professional Dance Musician and His Audience', *American Journal of Sociology*, 57, 136–44.
Becker, H. (1963) *Outsiders*, New York: Free Press.
Becker, H. (1974) 'Art as Collective Action', *American Sociological Review*, 39(6): 767–76.
Becker, H. (1976) 'Art Worlds and Social Types', *American Behavioral Scientist*, 19: 703–15.
Becker, H. (1982) *Art Worlds*, Berkeley, CA: University of California Press.
Becker, H. (1995) 'The Power of Inertia', *Qualitative Sociology*, 18(3): 301–9.
Becker, H. (2004) 'Jazz Places', in Bennett, A. and Peterson, R. (eds), *Music Scenes*, Nashville, TN: Vanderbilt University Press, 17–30.
Becker, H. (2006a) 'A Dialogue on the Ideas of "World" and "Field" with Alain Pessin', *Sociological Forum*, 21: 275–86.
Becker, H. (2006b) 'The Work Itself', in Becker, H., Faulkner, R. and

Kirshenblatt-Gimlett, B. (eds), *Art from Start to Finish*, Chicago, IL: University of Chicago Press.

*Beesley, T. (2009) *Our Generation*, Peterborough, UK: Fastprint.

*Beesley, T. (2010a) *This Is Our Generation Calling*, Peterborough, UK: Fastprint.

*Beesley, T. (2010b) *Out of Control*, Peterborough, UK: Fastprint.

Bennett, A. (2006) 'Punk's Not Dead', *Sociology*, 40, 219–35.

Bennett, A. (2013) *Music, Style and Aging*, Philadelphia, PA: Temple University Press.

Bennett, A and Hodkinson, P. (eds) (2012) *Ageing and Youth Cultures*, London: Berg.

Bennett, A. and Peterson, R. (eds) (2004) *Music Scenes*, Nashville, TN: Vanderbilt University Press.

*Beverley, A. (1980) *The Sid Vicious Family Album*, London: Virgin.

*Birch, W. (2010) *Ian Dury*, London: Sidgwick & Jackson.

Blau, J. (1989) *The Shape of Culture*, Cambridge, UK: Cambridge University Press.

Blau, P. (1974) 'Parameters of Social Structure', *American Sociological Review*, 39(5): 615–35.

Blau, P. (1977) 'A Macrosociological Theory of Social Structure', *American Journal of Sociology*, 83(1): 26–54.

Blumer, H. (1969) 'Collective Behaviour', in McClung-Lee, A. (ed.) *Principles of Sociology*, New York: Barnes & Noble, 166–222.

Blumer, H. (1986) *Symbolic Interactionism*, Berkeley, CA: University of California Press.

Borgatti, S. P., Everett, M. and Freeman, L. (2002) *Ucinet for Windows: Software for Social Network Analysis*, Harvard, MA: Analytic Technologies.

Borgatti, S. P., Everett, M. G. and Johnson, J. (2012) *Analysing Social Networks*, London: Sage.

Bott, E. (1957) *Family and Social Network*, London: Tavistock.

Bottero, W. and Crossley, N. (2011) 'Worlds, Fields and Networks', *Cultural Sociology*, 5(1): 99–119.

Bourdieu, P. (1993) 'Social Space and the Genesis of Classes', in *Language and Symbolic Power*, Cambridge, UK: Polity, 229–51.

Breiger, R. (1974) 'The Duality of Persons and Groups', *Social Forces*, 53(2): 181–90.

Burnett, R. (1992) 'The Implications of Ownership Chances on Concentration and Diversity in the Phonogram Industry', *Communications Research*, 19: 749–69.

Burt, R. (1992) *Structural Holes*, Cambridge, MA: Harvard University Press.

Burt, R. (2005) *Brokerage and Closure*, Oxford: Oxford University Press.

Byrne, D. (2012) *How Music Works*, Edinburgh: Canongate.

*Casey, J. (1993) interview by Lin Sangster, www.appelstein.com/cif/jaynecasey.html (last accessed 28/06/13).

*Chase, H. (2009) *Magazine*, Newcastle upon Tyne, UK: Northumbria Press.

Christianen, M. (1995) Cycles in Symbol Production, *Popular Music*, 14: 55–93.

Clarke, G. (1990) 'Defending Ski-Jumpers', in Frith, S. and Goodwin, S. (eds), *On Record*, London: Routledge, 81–96.

*Clarke, J.-C. (1983) *Ten Years in an Open Neck Shirt*, London: Arena.

Clarke, J., Hall, S., Jefferson, T. and Roberts, B. (1993) 'Subcultures, Cultures and Class', in Hall, S. and Jefferson, T. (eds), *Resistance through Rituals*, London: Routledge, 9–79.

*Clerk, C. (1988) *The Damned*, London: Omnibus.

Cohen, S. (1991) *Rock Culture in Liverpool*, Oxford: Clarendon Press.

Cohen, S. (1997) 'Men Making a Scene', in Whiteley, S. (ed.) *Sexing the Groove*, London: Routledge, 17–36.

Cohen, S. (2002) *Folk Devils and Moral Panics*, London: Routledge.

Cohen, S. (2007) 'Decline, Renewal and the City in Popular Music Culture', Aldershot, UK: Ashgate.

Coleman, J. (1988) 'Free Riders and Zealots: the Role of Social Networks', *Sociological Theory*, 6(1): 52–7.

Coleman, J. (1990) *Foundations of Social Theory*, Harvard, MA: Belknap.

*Connor, B. (2013) untitled, the *Guide* (weekend arts supplement to the *Guardian* newspaper) 21/09/13, 25.

*Coon, C. (1982) *1988*, London: Omnibus.

*Cooper, M. (1982) *Liverpool Explodes*, London: Sidgwick & Jackson.

Cope, A. (2010) *Black Sabbath and the Rise of Heavy Metal Music*, Aldershot, UK: Ashgate.

*Cope, J. (1994) *Head-on/Repossessed*, London: Element.

Critcher, C. (2003) *Moral Panics and the Media*, Buckinghamshire, UK: Open University Press.

Crossley, N. (1996) *Intersubjectivity: The Fabric of Social Becoming*, London: Sage.

Crossley, N. (2002) *Making Sense of Social Movements*, Buckinghamshire, UK: Open University Press.

Crossley, N. (2005) 'The New Social Physics and the Science of Small World Networks', *Sociological Review*, 53(2): 351–8.

Crossley, N. (2007) 'Social Networks and Extra-Parliamentary Politics', *Sociology Compass*, 1(1): 222–36.

Crossley, N. (2008a) 'Small World Networks, Complex Systems and Sociology', *Sociology*, 42(2): 261–77.

Crossley, N. (2008b) 'Pretty Connected: the Social Network of the Early UK Punk Movement', *Theory, Culture and Society*, 25(6): 89–116.

Crossley, N. (2008c) '(Net)Working Out: Social Capital in a Private Health Club', *British Journal of Sociology*, 59(3): 475–500.

Crossley, N. (2009) 'The Man Whose Web Expanded: Network Dynamics in Manchester's Post-Punk Music Scene 1976–1980', *Poetics*, 37(1): 24–49.

Crossley, N. (2010a) 'Networks, Interactions and Complexity', *Symbolic Interaction*, 33(3): 341–63.

Crossley, N. (2010b) 'The Social World of the Network: Qualitative Aspects of Network Analysis', *Sociologica*, (1): www.sociologica.mulino.it/main

Crossley, N. (2011) *Towards Relational Sociology*, London: Routledge.

Crossley, N. (2013) 'Interactions, Juxtapositions and Tastes', in Depelteau, F. and Powell, C. (eds), *Conceptualising Relational Sociology*, Basingstoke, UK: Palgrave Macmillan, 123–44.

Crossley, N. (2014) 'Relational sociology and culture', working paper, University of Manchester.

Crossley, N. and Bottero, W. (2014) 'Music Worlds and Internal Goods', *Cultural Sociology* (forthcoming).

Crossley, N. and Ibrahim, J. (2012) 'Critical Mass, Social Networks and Collective Action: the Case of Student Political Worlds', *Sociology*, 46(4): 596–612.

Crossley, N., McAndrew, S. and Widdop, P. (eds) (2014) *Social Networks and Music Worlds*, London: Routledge.

*Cummins, K. (2009) *Manchester: Looking for Light through the Pouring Rain*, London: Faber and Faber.

*Curtis, D. (1995) *Touching from a Distance*, London: Faber and Faber.

Dancis, B. (1978) 'Safety Pins and Class Struggle', *Socialist Review*, 8(3): 58–83.

Danto, A. (1964) 'The Art World', *Journal of Philosophy*, 61: 571–84.

Davis, J. (2006) 'Growing up Punk', *Symbolic Interaction*, 29(1): 63–9.

Dawkins, R. (1976) *The Selfish Gene*, Oxford: Oxford University Press.

DeNora, T. (2000) *Music in Everyday Life*, Cambridge, UK: Cambridge University Press.

Depelteau, F. and Powell, C. (2013a) *Conceptualising Relational Sociology*, Basingstoke, UK: Palgrave Macmillan.

Depelteau, F. and Powell, C. (2013b) *Applying Relational Sociology*, Basingstoke, UK: Palgrave Macmillan.

Dewey, J. (1894) 'Theory of Emotion I', *Psychological Review*, 1: 553–69.

Dewey, J. (1895) 'Theory of Emotion II', *Psychological Review*, 2: 13–32.

Dewey, J. (2005) *Art as Experience*, New York: Perigree.

DiMaggio, P. (1987) 'Classification in Art', *American Sociological Review*, 52(4): 440–55.

DiMaggio, P. (2011) 'Cultural Networks', in Scott, J. and Carrington, P. (eds), *The Sage Handbook of Social Network Analysis*, London: Sage, 286–300.

Dowd, T. (2004) 'Concentration and Diversity Revisited', *Social Forces*, 82(4): 1411–55.

Dowd, T. (2007) 'Innovation and Diversity in Cultural Sociology', *Sociologica*, 1: www.sociologia.uniroma1.it

*Drummond, B. (2001) *45*, London: Abacus.

*Drummond, B. (2008) *17*, London: Penkiln Burn.

Dunbar, R. (1992) 'Neocortex Size as a Constraint upon Group Size in Primates', *Journal of Human Evolution*, 22(6): 469–93.

Durkheim, E. (1915) *Elementary Forms of the Religious Life*, New York: Free Press.

Durkheim, E. (1974) *Sociology and Philosophy*, New York: Free Press.

Edwards, G. (2009) 'Mixed methods approaches to social network analysis', National Centre for Research Methods (UK) review paper.

Edwards, G. (2014) 'Infectious Innovations?', *Social Movement Studies*, 13(1): 48–69.

Edwards, G. and Crossley, N. (2009) 'Measures and Meanings: Exploring the Ego-Net of Helen Kirkpatrick Watts, Militant Suffragette', *Methodological Innovations On-Line* 3(2).

Elias, N. and Dunning, E. (1993) 'The Quest for Excitement in Leisure', in Elias, N. and Dunning, E. (eds), *The Quest for Excitement*, Oxford, Blackwell, 63–90.

Emirbayer, M. (1997) 'Manifesto for a Relational Sociology', *American Journal of Sociology*, 99(6): 1411–54.

Emirbayer, M. and Goodwin, J. (1994) 'Network Analysis, Culture and the Problem of Agency', *American Journal of Sociology*, 99: 1411–54.

Erdös, P. and Rényi, A. (1960) 'The Evolution of Random Graphs', *Publications of the Mathematical Institute of the Hungarian Academy of Sciences*, 5: 17–61.

Erickson, B. (1996) 'Culture, Class and Connections', *American Journal of Sociology*, 102(1): 217–51.

Faulkner, R. and Becker, H. (2009) *Do You Know?*, Chicago, IL: University of Chicago Press.

Feld, S. (1981) 'The Focused Organisation of Social Ties', *American Journal of Sociology*, 86: 1015–35.

Feld, S. (1982) 'Social Structural Determinants of Similarity among Associates', *American Sociological Review*, 47: 797–801.

Fernandez, R. and McAdam, D. (1988) 'Social Networks and Social Movements', *Sociological Forum*, 3: 357–82.

Fine, G. and Kleinman, S. (1979) 'Rethinking Subculture', *American Journal of Sociology*, 85: 1–20.

Finnegan, R. (1989) *The Hidden Musicians*, Cambridge, UK: Cambridge University Press.

Fischer, C. (1975) 'Towards a Subcultural Theory of Urbanism', *American Journal of Sociology*, 80(6): 1319–41.

Fischer, C. (1982) *To Dwell amongst Friends*, Chicago, IL: University of Chicago.

Fischer, C. (1995) 'The Subcultural Theory of Urbanism: A Twentieth-Year Assessment', *American Journal of Sociology*, 101(3): 543–77.

*Fish, M. (2002) *Industrial Evolution*, London: SAF.

Fish, S. (1980) *Is There A Text in This Class?*, Cambridge, MA: Harvard University Press.

*Fletcher, T. (1987) *Never Stop*, London: Omnibus.

*Florek, J. and Whelan, P. (2009) *Liverpool, Eric's*, Runcorn, UK: Feedback.

Fonarow, W. (2006) *Empire of Dirt*, Connecticut, CT: Wesleyan University Press.

*Ford, S. (2003) *Hip Priest*, London: Quartet.

*Foxton, B. and Buckler, R. (1993) *The Jam*, Chessington, UK: Castle Communications.

Frith, S. and Horne, H. (1987) *Art into Pop*, London: Methuen.

*Garner, K. (2007) *The Peel Sessions*, London: BBC Books.

*Gatenby, P. and Gill, C. (2011) *The Manchester Music History Tour*, Manchester: Empire.

Geels, F. (2007) 'Analysing the Breakthrough of Rock 'n' Roll (1930–1970)', *Technological Forecasting and Social Change*, 74: 1411–31.

*George, B. (1995) *Take It Like a Man*, London: Pan.

Giddens, A. (1979) *Central Problems in Social Theory*, London: Macmillan.

Giddens, A. (1984) *The Constitution of Society*, Cambridge, Polity.

*Gilbert, P. (2005) *Passion Is a Fashion*, London: Aurum.

Gildart, K. (2013) 'The Antithesis of Humankind', *Cultural and Social History*, 10(1): 129–49.

Gilmore, S. (1987) 'Coordination and Convention', *Symbolic Interaction*, 10(2): 209–27.

Gilmore, S. (1988) 'Schools of Activity and Innovation', *Sociological Quarterly*, 29(2): 203–19.

Gilroy, P. (1992) *There Ain't No Black in the Union Jack*, London: Routledge.

Gilroy, P. (1993a) *Small Acts*, London: Serpent's Tail.

Gilroy, P. (1993b) *The Black Atlantic*, London: Verso.

*Gimarc, G. (2005) *Punk Diary, 1970–1982*, San Francisco, CA: Backbeat.

*Glasper, I. (2004) *Burning Britain*, London: Cherry Red.

*Goddard, S. (2009) *Mozipedia*, London: Ebury.

Goode, E. and Ben-Yehuda, N. (1994) *Moral Panics*, Oxford: Wiley-Blackwell.

*Goodman, D. (2006) *My Amazing Adventures with the Sex Pistols*, Liverpool: Bluecoat Press.

Goodyer, I. (2009) *Crisis Music*, Manchester: Manchester University Press.

Gould, R. (1991) 'Multiple Networks and Mobilisation in the Paris Commune, 1871', *American Sociological Review*, 56: 716–29.

Granovetter, M. (1973) 'The Strength of Weak Ties', *American Journal of Sociology*, 78: 1360–80.

Granovetter, M. (1978) 'Threshold Models of Collective Behaviour', *American Journal of Sociology*, 83(6): 1420–43.

Granovetter, M. (1982) 'The Strength of Weak Ties: A Network Theory Revisited', in Marsden, P. and Lin, N. (eds), *Social Structure and Analysis*, Beverley Hills, CA: Sage.

Hägerstrand, T. (1975) 'Space, Time and Human Conditions', in Karlqvist, A., Lundvist, L. and Snickars, F. (eds), *Dynamic Allocation of Urban Space*, Lexington, MA: Lexington Books, 3–14.

Halpern, D. (2004) *Social Capital*, Cambridge, UK: Polity.

*Haslam, D. (2000) *Manchester, England*, London: Fourth Estate.

Hebdige, D. (1988) *Subculture: The Meaning of Style*, London: Routledge.

Hedström, P. (1994) 'Contagious Collectivities', *American Journal of Sociology*, 99(5): 1157–79.

Hedström, P., Sandel, R. and Stern, C. (2000) 'Mesolevel Networks and the Diffusion of Social Movements', *American Journal of Sociology*, 106(1): 145–72.

Hesmondhalgh, D. (1998) 'Post-Punk's Attempt to Democratise the Music Industry', *Popular Music*, 16(3): 255–74.

Hesmondhalgh, D. (1999) 'Indie', *Cultural Studies*, 13(1): 34–61.

Hesmondhalgh, D. (2005) 'Subcultures, Scenes or Tribes?', *Journal of Youth Studies*, 8(1): 21–40.

*Hewitt, P. (2007) *Paul Weller*, London: Corgi.

Heylin, C. (1992) *From the Velvets to the Voidoids*, New York: Penguin.

Heylin, C. (2008) *Babylon's Burning*, London: Penguin.

Hield, F. (2010) 'English folk singing and the construction of community', Ph.D. Thesis, University of Sheffield.

Hield, F. and Crossley, N. (2014) 'Tastes, Ties and Social Space: Exploring Sheffield's Folk World', in Crossley, N., McAndrew, S. and Widdop, P. (eds), *Social Networks and Musical Worlds*, London: Routledge.

*Hook, P. (2009) *The Haçienda*, London: Pocket.

*Hook, P. (2012) *Unknown Pleasures*, London: Simon & Schuster.

*Howe, Z. (2009) *Typical Girls?* London: Omnibus.

Huron, D. (2007) *Sweet Anticipation*, Cambridge, MA: MIT Press.

Jeffries, M. (2011) *Thug Life*, Chicago, IL: University of Chicago Press.

Joas, H. (1996): *The Creativity of Action*, Cambridge, UK: Polity.

*Johnstone, R. (2006) *John Lydon*, Surrey, UK: Chrome Dreams.

Jones, S. (1988) *Black Culture, White Youth*, London: Macmillan.

Jonze, T. (2011) 'Dubstep', the *Guide* (*Guardian* supplement), 24/9/11, 4.

*Kent, N. (2007) *The Dark Stuff*, London: Faber and Faber.

*Kent, N. (2010) *Apathy for the Devil*, London: Faber and Faber.

Kim, H and Bearman, P. (1997) 'The Structure and Dynamics of Movement Participation', *American Sociological Review*, 62(1): 70–93.

*King, R. (2012) *How Soon Is Now?* London: Faber and Faber.

Kitts, J. (2000) 'Mobilizing in Black Boxes', *Mobilization*, 5(2): 241–58.

Korte, C. and Milgram, S. (1970) 'Acquaintance Networks Between Racial Groups', *Journal of Personality and Social Psychology*, 15(2): 101–8.

Krenske, L. and McKay, J. (2000) 'Hard and Heavy', *Gender, Place and Culture*, 7(3): 287–304.

Laing, D. (1985) *One Chord Wonders*, Buckinghamshire, UK: Open University Press.

*Larkin, C. (1992) *The Guinness Who's Who of Indie and New Wave Music*, London: Guinness.

Latour, B. (2005) *Reassembling the Social*, Oxford: Oxford University Press.

Lazarsfeld, P. and Merton, R. (1964) 'Friendship as Social Process', in Berger, M., Abel, T. and Page, C. (eds), *Freedom and Control in Modern Society*, New York: Octagon Books, 18–66.

Lazell, B. (1997) *Indie Hits, 1980–1989*, London: Cherry Red.

*Lee, C. P. (2002) *Shake, Rattle and Rain*, Devon, UK: Hardinge Simpole.

*Lee, C. P. (2007) *When We Were Thin*, Manchester, Hotun Press.

Leonard, M. (2007) *Gender in the Music Industry*, Aldershot, UK: Ashgate.

Lewis, D. (1969) *Convention*, Cambridge, MA: Harvard University Press.

Lewis. K., Kaufman, J., Gonzalez, M., Wimmer, A. and Christakis, N. (2008) 'Tastes, Ties and Time', *Social Networks*, 30: 330–42.

*Lilleker, M. (2005) *Beats Working for a Living*, Sheffield: Juma.

Lin, N. (2002) *Social Capital*, Cambridge, UK: Cambridge University Press.

Lizardo, O. (2006) 'How Cultural Tastes Shape Personal Networks', *American Sociological Review*, 71: 778–807.

Lizardo, O. (2011) 'Cultural Correlates of Ego-Net Closure', *Sociological Perspectives*, 54(3): 479–87.

Lomax, A. (1959) 'Folk Song Style', *American Anthropologist*, 61(6): 927–54.

Lopes, P. (1992) 'Innovation and Diversity in the Popular Music Industry, 1969 to 1990', *American Sociological Review*, 57(1): 56–71.

Lopes, P. (2002) *The Rise of A Jazz Art World*, Cambridge, UK: Cambridge University Press.

*Lydon, J. (2003) *Rotten*, London: Plexus.

McAdam, D. (1986) 'Recruitment to High Risk Activism', *American Journal of Sociology*, 92(1): 64–90.

McAdam, D. (1988) *Freedom Summer*, New York: Oxford University Press.

McAdam, D., McCarthy, D. and Zald, M. (1988) 'Social Movements', in Smelser, N. (ed.), *Handbook of Sociology*, London: Sage, 695–737.

McAdam, D. and Paulsen, R. (1993) 'Specifying the Relationship between Ties and Activism', *American Journal of Sociology*, 99: 640–67.

McAleer, D. (2009) *The Virgin Book of Top 40 Charts*, London: Virgin.

McGee, A. (2006) 'Foreword', in Johnstone, R. (ed.), *John Lydon*, Surrey, UK: Chrome Dreams.

McKay, G. (1996) *Senseless Acts of Beauty*, London: Verso.

McKay, G. (ed.) (1998) *DIY Culture*, London: Verso.

*Macleay, I. (2010) *Malcolm McLaren*, London: John Blake.

McNay, I. (1997) 'Independence Day', in Lazell, B. (ed.), *Indie Hits, 1980–1989*, London: Cherry Red.

McNeil, L. and McCain, G. (2007) *Please Kill Me*, London: Abacus.

McPherson, M., Smith-Lovin, L. and Cook, J. (2001) 'Birds of Feather: Homophily in Social Networks', *Annual Review of Sociology*, 27: 415–44.

McPherson, M. (2004) 'A Blau Space Primer', *Industrial and Corporate Change* 13(1): 263–80.

McRobbie, A. (1991) *Feminism and Youth Culture*, London: Macmillan.

McRobbie, A. (1994) *Postmodernism and Popular Culture*, London: Routledge.

McRobbie, A. and Garber, J. (1978) 'Girls and Subcultures', in Hall, S. and Jefferson, T. (eds), *Resistance through Rituals*, London: Routledge, 209–22.

Marcus, G. (1993) *In the Fascist Bathroom*, New York: Viking.

Marcus, G. (2001) *Lipstick Traces*, London: Faber and Faber.

Mark, N. (1998) 'Birds of a Feather Sing Together', *Social Forces*, 77(2): 453–85.

Mark, N. (2003) 'Culture and Competition: Homophily and Distancing Explanations for Cultural Niches', *American Sociological Review*, 68(3): 319–45.

*Marshall, B. (2006) *Berlin Bromley*, London: SAF.

Martin, P. (1995) *Sounds and Society*, Manchester: Manchester University Press.

Martin, P. (2005) 'The Jazz Community as an Art World', *Jazz Research Journal* 2, www.equinoxpub.com/journals/index.php/JAZZ

Martin, P. (2006a) *Music and the Sociological Gaze*, Manchester: Manchester University Press.

Martin, P. (2006b) Musicians Worlds, *Symbolic Interaction*, 29(1): 95–107.

Marwell, G. and Oliver, P. (1993) *The Critical Mass in Collective Action*, Cambridge, UK: Cambridge University Press.

Marwell, G., Oliver, P. and Prahl, R. (1988) 'Social Networks and Collective Action', *American Journal of Sociology*, 94: 502–34.

*Matlock, G. (1996) *I Was a Teenage Sex Pistol*, London: Virgin.

Mauss, M. (1979) *Sociology and Psychology*, London: Routledge & Kegan Paul.

Mead, G. H. (1967) *Mind, Self and Society*, Chicago, IL: Chicago University Press.

Melly, G. (2008) *Revolt into Style*, London: Faber and Faber.

Merleau-Ponty, M. (1962) *The Phenomenology of Perception*, London: Routledge.

*Merrick, J. (2001) *Shane MacGowan*, London: Omnibus.

Meyer, L. (1956) *Emotion and Meaning in Music*, Chicago, IL: University of Chicago Press.

Meyer, L. (1989) *Style and Music*, Chicago, IL: University of Chicago Press.

Meyer, L. (2000) *The Spheres of Music*, Chicago, IL: University of Chicago Press.

*Middles, M. (1985) *The Smiths*, London: Omnibus.

*Middles, M. (1993) *Red Mick*, London: Headline.

*Middles, M. (2006) *The Rise and Fall of the Stone Roses*, London: Omnibus.

*Middles, M. (2009) *Factory*, London: Virgin.

Middleton, R. (1990) *Studying Popular Music*, Buckinghamshire, UK: Open University Press.

Milgram, S. (1967) 'The Small World Problem', in Carter, G. (ed.), *Empirical Approaches to Sociology*, Boston, MA: Pearson, 111–18.

Mills, C. W. (1956) *The Power Elite*, Oxford: Oxford University Press.

Milroy, L. (1987) *Language and Social Networks*, Blackwell: Oxford.

Mische, A. (2003) 'Cross-Talk in Movements', in Diani, M. and McAdam, D. (eds), *Social Movements and Networks*, Oxford: Oxford University Press.

Mische, A. (2011) 'Relational Sociology, Culture and Agency', in Scott, J. and Carrington, P. (eds), *The Sage Handbook of Social Network Analysis*, London: Sage, 80–97.

*Mojo (2006) *Punk*, London: DK.

*Morley, P. (2000) *Nothing*, London: Faber and Faber.

*Morley, P. (2008) *Joy Division: Piece by Piece*, London: Plexus.

*Nice, J. (2010) *Shadowplayers*, London: Aurum.

*Nolan, D. (2006) *The Gig that Changed the World: I Swear I Was There*, Shropshire, UK: Independent Music Press.

*Nolan, D. (2007) *Bernard Sumner*, Shropshire, UK: Independent Music Press.

*Nolan, D. (2010) *Tony Wilson*, London: John Blake.

Office for National Statistics (1999) *Labour Market Trends*, London: ONS.

*Ogg, A. (2006) *No More Heroes*, London: Cherry Red.

Ogg, A. (2009) *Independence Days*, London: Cherry Red.

Oliver, P. and Marwell, G. (1988) 'The Paradox of Group Size in Collective Action', *American Sociological Review*, 53: 1–8.

Oliver, P., Marwell, G. and Teixeira, R. (1985) 'A Theory of Critical Mass 1', *American Journal of Sociology*, 91: 522–56.

*Ott, C. (2006) *Unknown Pleasures*, New York: Continuum.

*Parker, A. (2008) *Sid Vicious*, London: Orion.

*Parker, A. and O'Shea, M. (2011) *Young Flesh Required*, London: Soundcheck.

Passy, F. (2001) 'Socialisation, Connection and the Structure/Agency Gap', *Mobilization*, 6(2): 173–92.

Passy, F. (2003) 'Social Networks Matter. But How?', in Diani, M. and McAdam, D. (eds), *Social Movements and Networks*, Oxford: Oxford University Press, 21–46.

*Paytress, M. (2003) *Siouxsie and the Banshees*, Somerset, UK: Sanctuary.

*Perry, M. (2009) *Sniffin' Glue*, London: Omnibus.

Peterson, R. (1967) 'Market and Moral Censors of a Rising Art Form: Jazz', *Arts in Society*, 4: 253–64.

Peterson, R. (1990) 'Why 1955? Explaining the Advent of Rock Music', *Popular Music*, 9(1): 97–116.

Peterson, R. and Berger, D. (1975) 'Cycles in Symbol Production: the Case of Popular Music', *American Sociological Review*, 40(2): 158–73.

Plant, S. (1992) *The Most Radical Gesture*, London: Routledge.

*Reade, L. (2010) *Mr Manchester and the Factory Girl*, London: Plexus.

Reddington, H. (2012) *The Lost Women of Rock Music*, Sheffield: Equinox.

Reynolds, S. (1990) 'New Pop and Its Aftermath', in Frith, S. and Goodwin, A. (eds), *On Record*, London: Routledge, 466–71.

Reynolds, S. (2005) *Rip It up and Start Again*, London: Faber and Faber.

Reynolds, S. (2009) *Totally Wired*, London: Faber and Faber.

Reynolds, S. (2011) *Retromania*, London: Faber and Faber.

Riesman, D. (1950) 'Listening to Popular Music', *American Quarterly*, 2(4): 359–71.

*Robb, J. (1997) *The Stone Roses*, London: Ebury.

*Robb, J. (2006) *Punk Rock: An Oral History*, London: Ebury.

*Robb, J. (2009) *The North Will Rise Again*, London: Aurum.

*Rogan, J. (1993) *Morrissey & Marr*, London: Omnibus.

*Rombes, N. (2009) *A Cultural Dictionary of Punk*, New York: Continuum.

Rothenbuhler, E. and Dimmick, J. (1982) 'Popular Music: Concentration and Diversity in the Industry, 1974–1980', *Journal of Communication*, 32: 143–9.

*Salewicz, C. (2007) *Redemption Song*, London: HarperCollins.

Sandel, R. (1999) 'Organisational Life aboard a Moving Bandwagon', *Acta Sociologica*, 42(1): 3–15.

Sartre, J.-P. (1993) *The Emotions*, New York: Citadel.

Saunders, C. (2008) 'Using Social Network Analysis to Explore Social Movements: A Relational Approach', *Social Movement Studies*, 6(3): 227–43.

*Savage, J. (1991) *England's Dreaming*, London: Faber and Faber.

*Savage, J. (2009) *The England's Dreaming Tapes*, London: Faber and Faber.

Savage, J. (2011) 'We Have Lift off!', *Mojo* (September): 52–61.

Schelling, T. (1995) *Micromotives and Macrobehaviours*, New York: Norton.

Schutz, A. (1944) 'The Stranger', *American Journal of Sociology*, 49(6): 499–507.

Scott, J. (2000) *Social Network Analysis: A Handbook*, London: Sage.

Scott, J. (2011) 'Social Physics and Social Networks', in Scott, J. and Carrington, P. (eds), *The Sage Handbook of Social Network Analysis*, London: Sage, 55–66.

Shank, B. (1994) *Dissonant Identities*, Hanover, NH: Wesleyan University Press.

*Sharp, C. (2007) *Who Killed Martin Hannett?*, London: Aurum.

Shibutani, T. (1955) 'Reference Groups as Perspectives', *American Journal of Sociology*, 60(6): 562–9.

Shusterman, R. (2000) *Pragmatist Aesthetics*, New York: Rowman & Littlefield.

Shusterman, R. (2002) *Surface and Depth*, Ithaca, NY: Cornell University Press.

Simmel, G. (1902) 'The Number of Members as Determining the Form of the Group I & II', *American Journal of Sociology*, 8(1): 1–46 and 8(2): 158–96.

Simmel, G. (1906) 'The Sociology of Secrecy and Secret Societies', *American Journal of Sociology*, 11(4): 441–98.

Simmel, G. (1949) 'The Sociology of Sociability', *American Journal of Sociology*, 55(3): 254–61.

Simmel, G. (1955) *Conflict and the Web of Group Affiliations*, New York: Free Press.

Simmel, G. (1971) *On Individuality and Social Forms*, Chicago, IL: Chicago University Press.

*Simpson, D. (2008) *The Fallen*, Edinburgh: Canongate.

Small, C. (1998) *Musicking*, Hanover, NH: Wesleyan University Press.

Smelser, N. (1962) *Theory of Collective Behaviour*, London: Routledge & Kegan Paul.

*Smith, M. E. (2009) *Renegade*, Harmondsworth, UK: Penguin.

Smith, N. (2009) 'Beyond the Master Narrative of Youth', in Scott, D. (ed.), *The Ashgate Research Companion to Popular Musicology*, Aldershot, UK: Ashgate, 427–48.

Smith, N. (2012) 'Parenthood and the Transfer of Capital in the Northern Soul Scene', in Bennett, P. and Hodkinson, A. (eds), *Ageing and Youth Cultures*, London: Berg, 159–72.

Snow, D., Zurcher, L. and Ekland-Olson, S. (1980) 'Social Networks and Social Movements', *American Sociological Review*, 45(5): 787–801.

Snow, D., Zurcher, L. and Ekland-Olson, S. (1983) 'Further Thoughts on Social Networks and Movement Recruitment', *Sociology*, 17: 112–20.

*Southall, B. (2003) *A–Z of Record Labels*, London: Sanctuary.

Spencer, A. (2008) *DIY: The Rise of Lo-Fi Culture*, London: Marion Boyars.

Sperber, D. (1996) *Explaining Culture*, Oxford: Wiley.

*Stevenson, N. and Stevenson, R. (1999) *Vacant*, London: Thames & Hudson.

*Stevenson, R. (1980) *Sex Pistols File*, London: Omnibus.

Strachan, R. (2010) 'Liverpool's 1970s Bohemia', in Leonard, M. and Strachan, R. (eds), *The Beat Goes on*, Liverpool: Liverpool University Press.

Strauss, E. (1973) 'A Social World Perspective', *Studies in Symbolic Interaction*, 1: 119–28.

Straw, W. (1991) 'System of Articulation, Logics of Change', *Cultural Studies*, 53: 368–88.

Street, J. (2012) *Music and Politics*, Cambridge, UK: Polity.

*Strummer, J., Jones, M., Simonon, P. and Headon, T. (2010) *The Clash*, London: Atlantic.

Sudnow, D. (1993) *Ways of the Hand*, Cambridge, MA: MIT Press.

Sylvain, S. (2010) 'Obituary for Malcolm McLaren', *Quietus*, http://thequietus.com/articles/04059–malcolm-mclaren-obituary-by-new-york-dolls-sylvain-sylvain (last accessed 05/12/13).

Tarde, G. (2000) *Social Laws*, New York: Batoche Books.

Taylor, N. (2010) *Document and Eyewitness*, London: Orion.

*Thompson, D. (2009) *London's Burning*, Chicago, IL: Chicago Review Press.

Thornton, S. (1994) 'Moral Panic, the Media and British Rave Culture', in Ross, A. and Rose, T. (eds), *Microphone Fiends*, New York: Routledge, 176–92.

Thornton, S. (1995) *Club Cultures*, Cambridge, UK: Polity.

Tilly, C. (1978) *From Mobilisation to Revolution*, Reading, MA: Addison-Wesley.

Tilly, C. (2006) *Identities, Boundaries and Social Ties*, New York: Paradigm.

Travers, J. and Milgram, S. (1969) 'An Experimental Study of the Small World Problem', *Sociometry*, 32: 325–43.

UK Music (2013) 'Wish You Were Here: Music Tourism's Contribution to the UK Economy', www.ukmusic.org/assets/media/MUSICTOURISM-REPORT-WEBsite%20version.pdf (last accessed 06/12/13).

*Vermorel, F. and Vermorel, J. (1987) *Sex Pistols*, London: Omnibus.

*Waller, J. and Humphries, M. (1987) *Orchestral Manoeuvres in the Dark*, London: Sidgwick & Jackson.

Wasserman, S. and Faust, K. (1994) *Social Network Analysis*, Cambridge, UK: Cambridge University Press.

Watts, D. (1999) *Small Worlds*, New Jersey, NJ: Princeton University Press.

Watts, D. (2004) *Six Degrees*, London: Vintage.

White, H. (2008) 'Notes on the Constituents of Social Structure', *Sociologica* 1, www.sociologica.mulino.it/journal/article/index/Article/Journal:ARTICLE:200/Item/Journal:ARTICLE:200 (last accessed 06/12/13).

Williams, R. (1970) *Communications*, Harmondsworth, UK: Penguin.

Willis, P. (1978) *Profane Culture*, London: Routledge & Kegan Paul.

Willis, P. (1990) *Common Culture*, Boulder, CO: Westview.

Willis, P. (2000) *The Ethnographic Imagination*, Cambridge, UK: Polity.

*Wilson, T. (2002) 24 *Hour Party People* (FAC 424): Basingstoke, UK: Channel 4 Books.

Wittgenstein, L. (1953) *Philosophical Investigations*, Oxford: Blackwell.

*Wobble, J. (2009) *Memoirs of a Geezer*, London: Serpent's Tail.

Young, R. (2007) *Rough Trade*, London: Black Dog.

Websites

Hundreds of websites were consulted when compiling the network data sets analysed in this book and it is not clear that listing their URL addresses here would serve much purpose. My methodology when conducting these searches was to start with a series of key words (which very often included names of bands I knew to have been involved in a particular music world) and then to snowball from the sites found. Specifically I sought to follow up leads about other bands or individuals mentioned, whether or not there was a link on the source website.

Videography and discography

Videography

(DVDs and video sources used as sources of network data)

Büld, W. (1978) *Punk in London*, Salvation Films
Corbijn, A. (2008) *Control*, Momentum
Factory (2007) 'Manchester from Joy Division to Happy Mondays', BBC4 Broadcast 21 September
Letts, D. (2000) *Westway to the World*, 3DD
Letts, D. (2008) *The Punk Rock Movie*, Freemantle Media
Nice, J. (2006) *Shadowplayers*, LTMDVD
Rock Family Trees (1998) *And God Created Manchester*, BBC TV Broadcast 9 October
Savage, J. (2007) *Joy Division*, Hudson
Sex Pistols (2005) *Live at the Longhorn*, Mawa Film
Temple, J. (2003) *The Filth and the Fury*, Film4 Video
Temple, J. (2007) *The Future Is Unwritten*, Film4
White, M. (1980) *Rude Boy*, Salvation Films
Winterbottom, M. (2002) *Twenty-Four Hour Party People*, Revolution Films
Wood, E. (2005) *Made in Sheffield*, Slackjaw Film

Discography

Singles and EPs
Bauhaus (1979) 'Bela Lugosi's Dead', Small Wonder
Buzzcocks (1977) 'Spiral Scratch', New Hormones
Buzzcocks (1977) 'Orgasm Addict', United Artists
Cabaret Voltaire (1979) 'Nag, Nag, Nag', Rough Trade
Chelsea (1977) 'Right to Work', Step Forward
The Clash (1977) 'White Riot', CBS
The Damned (1976) 'New Rose', Stiff
The Desperate Bicycles (1977) 'Smokescreen/Handlebars', Refill

The Desperate Bicycles (1978) 'The Medium Was Tedium', Refill
Joy Division (1978) 'An Ideal for Living', Enigma
Joy Division (1978) 'An Ideal for Living' (12-inch), Anonymous
Joy Division (1979) 'Transmission', Factory
Joy Division (1979) 'Love Will Tear Us Apart', Factory
Joy Division (1980) 'Atmosphere', Factory
Little Richard (1956) 'Rip It Up', Speciality
Orchestral Manoeuvres in the Dark (1979) 'Electricity', Factory
The Ruts (1979) 'Babylon's Burning', Virgin
Scritti Politti (1978) 'Skank Bloc Bologna', St Pancras
Sex Pistols (1976) 'Anarchy in the UK', EMI
Sex Pistols (1977) 'God Save the Queen', Virgin
Sex Pistols (1977) 'Pretty Vacant', Virgin
Various (1978) 'A Factory Sample', Factory
Various (1979) '1980: The First Fifteen Minutes', Neutron

LPs

The Clash (1977) *The Clash*, CBS
Durutti Column (1980) *The Return of the Durutti Column*, Factory
Iggy and the Stooges (1972) *Raw Power*, Columbia
Joy Division (1979) *Unknown Pleasures*, Factory
Joy Division (1980) *Closer*, Factor
King Crimson (1970) *In the Wake of Poseidon*, Islan
The Ramones (1976) *The Ramones*, Sire
The Slits (1979) *Cut*, Island
Patti Smith (1975) *Horses*, Arista
Various (1973) *Nuggets*, Elektra
Various (1978) *Short Circuit: Live at the Electric Circus*, Virgin
Various (1979) *Street to Street – A Liverpool Album*, Open Eye Records
Various (1980) *A Bouquet of Steel*, Aardvark
Various (1982) *To the Shores of Lake Placid*, Zoo
Yes (1973) *Tales of Topographical Oceans*, Atlantic

Album tracks

Echo and the Bunnymen (1982) 'Read It in Books', on *To the Shores of Lake Placid*, Zoo
Richard Hell and the Voidoids (1977) 'Blank Generation', on *Blank Generation*, Sire
Sex Pistols (1977) 'EMI', on *Never Mind the Bollocks*, Virgin
Sex Pistols (1979) 'God Save the Queen (Symphony)', on *The Great Rock 'n' Roll Swindle*, Virgin
The Teardrop Explodes (1980) 'Books', on *Kilimanjaro*, Fontana
Velvet Underground (1968) 'Sister Ray', on *White Light/White Heat*, Verve

Index